Florence Lawrence, the Biograph Girl

FLORENCE LAWRENCE, THE BIOGRAPH GIRL

America's First Movie Star

by
KELLY R. BROWN

McFarland & Company, Inc., Publishers
Jefferson, North Carolina, and London

The present work is a reprint of the library bound edition of Florence Lawrence, the Biograph Girl: America's First Movie Star, *first published in 1999 by McFarland.*

LIBRARY OF CONGRESS CATALOGUING-IN-PUBLICATION DATA

Brown, Kelly R., 1967–
    Florence Lawrence, the Biograph girl : America's first movie star / by Kelly R. Brown.
      p.   cm.
    Filmography: p.
    Includes bibliographical references and index.

    ISBN-13: 978-0-7864-3089-5
    (softcover : 50# alkaline paper) ∞

    1. Lawrence, Florence, 1890–1938. 2. Motion picture actors and actresses—United States—Biography. I. Title.
PN2287.L28944B76 2007
791.43'028'092—dc21
[b]   99-19661

British Library cataloguing data are available

©1999 Kelly R. Brown. All rights reserved

No part of this book may be reproduced or transmitted in any form or by any means, electronic or mechanical, including photocopying or recording, or by any information storage and retrieval system, without permission in writing from the publisher.

On the cover : Florence Lawrence during her "Biograph" years, ca. 1908–1910 (photograph by Moody of New York; provided courtesy of the Wisconsin Center for Film and Theater Research)

Manufactured in the United States of America

McFarland & Company, Inc., Publishers
  Box 611, Jefferson, North Carolina 28640
    www.mcfarlandpub.com

To my two peppermint patties

ACKNOWLEDGMENTS

I have so much to be thankful for. To God be the glory. "He who has ears to hear, let him hear."

Eternal gratitude goes to my family for putting up with me while I was writing this book. Mommy is done with the computer for a while.

Thanks to the staff at the Iredell County Public Library. Margie Wessels will probably be bored now, without my endless requests for obscure books on interlibrary loan.

Thanks to my fellow film fanatics: Sally Dumaux, Joe Eckhardt, Philip Leibfried, Gene Vazzana, Bruce Long, John Cocchi, Tony Slide, Bill Mann, Lois Johe, William Drew, Charles Musser, Rick Worland, Dick Braff and especially Annette D'Agostino, who made the trip. Appreciation is also expressed to the Academy of Motion Picture Arts and Sciences for assistance.

Thanks to the various libraries and museums I have worked with: University of North Carolina at Chapel Hill, Hamilton Public Library in Ontario, Canada (Margaret Houghton), Natural History Museum of Los Angeles County (John Cahoon at the Seaver Center), Wisconsin Center for Film and Theater Research in Madison, Neversink Valley Area Museum in Cuddebackville, New York (Donna Steffens), Museum of Modern Art, Appalachian State University, Arizona State University, Buffalo Public Library (Cynthia VanNess), Los Angeles Public Library, San Francisco Public Library, Toronto Public Library, Fort Lee Public Library (Rita Altomara), St. Louis Public Library and Philadelphia Free Public Library. Thanks also to local historians including Edmund Moderacki of River Vale, New Jersey, and Charles Shallcross of Elizabeth, New Jersey.

And finally, thanks to all the women who proudly posed for those early flickers. Your names may be lost, but your spirit lives on.

Contents

Acknowledgments	vii
Preface	xi
Prologue	xiii
1—Child of Canada	1
2—Moving and Shaking	13
3—A New Family	23
4—Laemmle's Imp	39
5—St. Louis	47
6—Moving On	59
7—Independence	73
8—Among the Roses	85
9—Comeback Again	97
10—And Again	113
11—The Quiet Years	127
12—Her Last Part	139
13—Florence Who?	151
Filmography	159
Notes	181
Bibliography	199
Index	203

PREFACE

"Why write a biography of Florence Lawrence?" This is a question I have heard dozens of times since I began seriously working on this project in 1993. The query has come not just from my indulgent family and bemused friends, but even from members of the film community. I know I certainly asked myself that question more than once.

So why write a biography of a woman whose life, with its dizzying ups and downs, was ultimately tragic, whose works have been lost and largely forgotten, whose existence seems barely remembered by the industry that made her famous?

Quite simply, because Florence Lawrence's story begs to be told.

I first heard of Florence Lawrence years ago when I received as a gift the oversized and simplified view of film study called *The World's Great Movie Stars and Their Films*. The short paragraph that summed up Florence's life (and I now realize how lucky she is even to have been included!) said that she was important to film history, but that her story was really known only to film scholars. The name stuck with me—Florence Lawrence; how could it not? Armed with that scant knowledge, I kept my eyes open for more about Florence, who despite her ill luck had been instrumental in the birth of the movie star system. Surely someone that important could not be that enigmatic.

It turned out that her story was even less known than I had been led to believe. Movie scholars knew only the barest facts of her life.

In college, I discovered Daniel Blum's *Pictorial History of the Silent Screen*. Within its pages, Florence was alive and beautiful and active, as were hundreds of other even more forgotten players. In college I also discovered the silent short film. Perhaps this medium appealed to my short attention span, or perhaps to my broad sense of humor; at any rate, I got past the initial prejudice against flapping arms, moon-faced pining and theatrical posturing to see the talent and the stories. Suddenly, the "D.W. Griffith" stamp from my childhood stamp collection meant something, and gradually other pieces began falling into place. Florence's papers were at a museum out in California. Hundreds of photos were in Wisconsin. Press clippings were scattered at libraries all over the country. Typing "Florence Lawrence" onto an Internet search engine brought up references I had never dreamed of. Film scholars were offering opinions from all over the world. Before I knew it I actually had a book in the making.

Writing Florence's story has been wonderful, but finishing it has been bittersweet. I learned a great deal about Florence, but I couldn't find out much about the people around her. Her first husband, Harry Solter, a prolific film pioneer, languishes in even greater obscurity than Florence. Her second husband was a war hero whose records were lost in a fire. One of her brothers was a policeman in San Francisco. Of her other brother no trace appears to remain. Who were all of these people and where did they go? To be lost forever in history seems such a terrible destiny.

So I have written out Florence's story, in the hope that she will now be remembered as she deserved to be.

Kelly Brown
16 December 1998

PROLOGUE

The motion of the train was hypnotic. The gentle swaying, the rhythmic clacking of the wheels, the squeaky crush of the velvet seats.

Miss Florence Lawrence, the film actress formerly known as the Biograph Girl, now known as the Imp Girl (for her new employer, the Independent Motion Picture Company), felt the motion of the train around her but paid it no attention. She had been on the rails for several days, sleeping in a Pullman, nervously wondering what might happen in St. Louis, her destination. The whole last month of her life had been so unsettling. Newspapers had reported that she was dead. Telegrams from the theaters that showed her films poured in from around the country, demanding to know the truth. Her boss, Mr. Laemmle, was trying to prove she was alive and well in the flashiest way he could imagine: a personal appearance. She—little Floie to her brothers, Queenie to her mother, Mike to her husband—was about to make a personal appearance. Florence couldn't imagine Billie Burke or Maude Adams doing this.

The Union Station stop in St. Louis was announced. Florence unconsciously smoothed out the skirt of the lovely navy travel dress, adjusted her smart little hat and buttoned her blue cloak with its big black buttons. As she stood, she fingered the large buttons carefully, not dreaming for an instant that they wouldn't be there in ten minutes. She smiled nervously at Harry Solter, her husband and director, now standing beside her. He smiled back, and she knew he at least believed in her. He wasn't the easiest person to understand or live with, but he had a strong and steady arm to lean upon when she needed it. And she needed it now.

The train groaned to a halt. A man boarded her car almost instantly, and Florence became aware of voices outside the train. Parting the curtains only slightly, she saw a huge throng of people pouring through the gatekeeper's post and onto the platform. All held little white tickets in their hands. She let the curtain fall closed as she sat back in amazement. She'd never seen so many people running for a train before in her life, not even in New York.

She was quickly introduced to Mr. Talbot, who with Mr. Laemmle had arranged this trip. "Missourians must be anxious about missing their trains," she said to make small talk, gesturing toward the window. Many voices could now be heard even over the hissing and churning of the unloading train.

"Oh, no, Miss Lawrence," Mr. Talbot said after a moment's hesitation and a startled glance at Harry. "They're here to see you."

An awkward silence filled the compartment, which suddenly seemed terribly cramped. "Me?" Florence heard herself say with a squeak in her voice. She clutched Harry's arm tightly. Mr. Talbot and Mr. Laemmle chuckled in low tones, almost to themselves.

"You've done a good job here, Talbot," Mr. Laemmle said, reaching out to shake the St. Louis man's hand. "Riled them up but good. Come on, Solter, bring her out."

Harry only hesitated a split second before turning to Florence. "Come on, my dear," he said comfortingly. "It's just another role, like at the theater. Those people are just an audience." He led her to the door of the train and opened it slightly. The crowd noise increased.

"Just an audience," Florence murmured to herself. "Just another role." She closed her eyes, then pushed the door open.

Chapter One

CHILD OF CANADA

> *We who play, who entertain for a few years, what can we leave that will last?*
> —Ethel Barrymore

To say that Florence Lawrence made movies would be correct only if two definitions of the verb "to make" would be understood in the same sentence simultaneously. Florence Lawrence did indeed make movies—well over 250 of them, many of them short "one-reelers" that challenged writers, directors and pantomime artists-turned-actors to an extreme. And Florence Lawrence also made movies—she helped define the parameters and styles of film art that are accepted today. She was a pioneer in a medium that had to fight to be accepted as an art form from the beginning. Her love for her profession was evident in all phases of her life—films gave her a voice, a freedom and a goal. Then just as film had given her all she could want, film took everything away from her, making her a victim of the industry that barely knew it was one.

The idea of moving pictures was born even before Florence was. Eadweard Muybridge devised a way to shoot consecutive photographs of a horse running in 1878. Etienne Marey developed a camera that shot photos like a gun, up to 100 consecutively at a time, in 1882. George Eastman created exposable film in paper rolls in 1885. Florence was born the next year, three years before Eastman patented commercial celluloid roll film. Then America's residing genius, Thomas Edison, stepped into the moving picture arena by introducing the Kinetoscope in 1889. Five years later, Edison opened an arcade in New York City with ten of his new "peep show" machines installed. The short films showed the most common of subjects—including Fred Ott's sneeze—within a small black box where rolls of film moved past a light. Then in 1895, the Brothers Lumière created the Cinematograph, a combination projector-camera, and first exhibited their films in Paris that December. Within a few months, Edison countered with the Vitascope, invented by Thomas Arnat and Francis Jenkins; mere months after that, American Mutoscope and Biograph rolled film with its Biograph Projector.

Moving pictures fit slowly into American entertainment. The Vitascope was initially a feature at the end of vaudeville programs, which could be in stationary halls or traveling shows. Arcades lined the Kinetoscope viewers up along their walls, eventually setting aside rooms with a sheet hanging on one wall to allow for projected images. Ordinary men working for common companies suddenly discovered that they could make moving pictures for individual profit.[1] All these things happened before the turn of the century, when a child actress from Canada temporarily retired from the stage to work on getting an education in America.

Florence's beginnings were not unlike many of the other pioneering silent film actors and actresses whose names soon overshadowed hers. Like Mary Pickford and Mack Sennett, she was born in Canada. Like Mary and Lillian Gish, she was on the road as a stage actress when she could barely speak. Florence had a domineering, stage-oriented mother; oddly enough, that appealed to her early director, D.W. Griffith.

Florence Annie Bridgwood was born in Hamilton, Ontario, Canada, on January 2, 1886, the seventh child to her father and the third child to her mother. Her parents, George Bridgwood, a carriage-builder by trade, and Charlotte "Lotta" Dunn Bridgwood, a young actress, made an unusual married couple. George had been married previously to Ellen Dalton, who had borne him four children before she died of breast cancer in 1878. These Bridgwood children—John, James, William and Charlotte Louise—were all older than their new stepmother whom their 56-year-old father had married on December 13, 1880. Lotta, then 19, bore him three more children, George Alexander Jr., Walter Norman and Florence.

This "second family" of George Sr.'s did not seem to know their father very well. The first four children did not acknowledge this second marriage, not bothering to provide the funeral home with his widow's name when their father died. Within four years of Florence's birth, her father and mother were living apart; according to the 1891 Canadian Census, his official residence was the rear of his carriage-building shop on working-class Jackson Street in Hamilton. Lotta probably didn't even notice; she was on the road touring with Lawrence Dramatic Company in vaudeville-type short productions. Lotta took the last name as her own, as did her oldest son George and daughter Florence. Only Norman retained his original name of Bridgwood, although neither of the brothers were performers past their earliest childhoods.

Hamilton itself was an active town, the railroad entering life there in the 1850s and bringing with it manufacturing industries that culminated in big steel mills before 1900. Because most of Hamilton's settlers and immigrants were from the British Isles, many traditional cultural norms and customs

A beautiful photograph of Florence Lawrence taken by Moody of New York, perhaps as early as 1910.

became entrenched, theater most prominently. The city boasted many large theaters in the latter part of the nineteenth century, and Hamilton hosted almost every notable company that toured Canada.

Florence was not the only renowned player to come from Hamilton. Julia Arthur, born Ida Lewis in Hamilton in 1869, had a very successful stage career, including Broadway. She also appeared in several Vitagraph films in the late 1910s, portraying Italy in 1918's *The Common Cause* and Edith Cavell in *The Cavell Case*. In addition, Florence's future Biograph co-worker, Frank Powell, also was from Hamilton.

Acting proficiency may have been in the water. Hamilton–reared Lotta Lawrence herself was a talented performer, prompting Monte Katterjohn, Florence's 1914 co-writer for *Photoplay* magazine, to explain, "The mother of Florence Lawrence was one of the best actresses of her day, and though distinctly inclined to do comedy, she did some of her best work as a portrayer of serious roles. She was most versatile, and as leading lady of her own production company which produced all sorts of plays, comedy, drama, melodrama and tragedy, she has played no less than five hundred different roles."[2] Florence herself quickly learned to relish the attention she received onstage. At age three, when she began to appear in song and dance routines with her mother, "the audience would see the child come on and think it an error, until she began to join her mother and began to mimic her steps, and then a storm of cheers and applause would follow."[3] Her favorite solo performances were "Down in the Shady Dell" and "Come Help Me Tie My Shoe String." Florence also was quite an elaborate tune whistler, a habit she carried throughout her life.

Florence never had much choice about the career path chosen for her, and fortunately she did not mind. She was born to perform, as proven when she imitated the other actors and actresses in her mother's company after she had watched them onstage. "It was a hard matter to keep her in her mother's dressing room," reported Katterjohn. "She learned to wink at her audience the very first time she ever appeared on the stage alone."[4] Florence also developed a bad habit of simply appearing onstage during productions, forcing the performing actors to ignore her or include her in the action.

When she was old enough to begin memorizing lines, her mother added her on the billing. Florence particularly remembered playing "Little Lord Fauntleroy" around a hundred times. The depressing topics that the Lawrence Dramatic Company was well known for performing distressed Florence to the point where she cried herself to sleep at night. "She told her mother that she didn't think they ought to make people cry, because people didn't feel good when they cried," causing Lotta to drop "East Lynne" and "Dora Thorne" from their repertoire.[5]

The touring life was not desirable from any standpoint. Mary Pickford, herself a child stage performer, called it the "endless odyssey of the road," with bad hotels and red-eye train rides from one little town to another.[6] Florence confessed on her 1910 publicity trip to St. Louis that it was not her first visit to that city, but that she did not recall really having been there before either. "I was but four years old and it was fourteen years ago that I appeared here with Daniel Sully in a play the name of which I cannot recall,"[7] she told a reporter apologetically. She shouldn't have been; at least she had been legitimately employed for tour after tour. Fortunately, Florence chose to keep only the good memories of life on the road, fondly talking about traveling across the western United States, "picnicking along the roadside, happy in the freedom of the hills and well-filled pockets."[8] Other actors and actresses of the era were not so lucky as to find work regularly, struggling for every role, every tour. Linda Arvidson, soon to be Florence's confidant and fellow player at Biograph, remembered pounding the pavement for roles promised to last for weeks, only to close within days. Lillian Gish tried to keep the good memories of being on the road when her family was together, but was miserable when they were apart, something Florence never had to deal with. "I learned early to be self-sufficient and flexible," Lillian recalled. "Our lives were divided between the theatre and trains."[9]

But up until 1910, there was little choice for those who had selected acting as a profession. Either an actor was lucky and intelligent enough to land a role in a stationary show, such as on Broadway or in Boston or a smaller, local, dead-end stock company, and stay there without touring for a season, or an actor landed a role which took him or her from theater to theater around the country. Often the choice was blunted still by doing both; Mary Pickford had a very sound role in David Belasco's *The Warrens of Virginia*, which was considered a Broadway show, but it still toured from Boston to Washington, D.C., before and after its run in New York.

When Florence was ten, she had at least five full-time touring seasons behind her. Several factors changed Florence's life around this time. One was that her father died an accidental death from coal gas poisoning on February 18, 1898, in his home. Another was that her mother moved her family across the Niagara River from Ontario to Buffalo, New York, to live with her mother, Ann Dunn. A third major factor was that Lotta decided to take her children off the road to enroll them in school.

Florence's father had played little or no role in her growing up; subsequently she does not mention him in any interviews or even correspondence. His death merely opened more doors for Lotta, freeing her from any ties to Hamilton. From the earliest memories Florence had, her mother had been the one there for her. The bond they formed after so many years touring and living together was close and practically telepathic. Her parent's loosely-formed marriage did not help Florence's attitude toward love and marriage in her own life. She had seen her mother "acting" as a wife most of the time; was that just another role?

The connection between Florence and her mother was only tightened by living with her maternal grandmother. Ann Dunn was a solidly Irish widow who had emigrated with three children to Canada after the great potato famine, soon moving to the United States. She was renting a two-story house in a pleasant neighborhood of Buffalo and took in her daughter and grandchildren with ease. Florence and Norman were sent off to school and George went to work.

According to her 1914 autobiography, she began attending school in Buffalo after her mother moved there. Other interviews state that she attended the Loretto Academy in Toronto. Either way, she is difficult to find in either system. The Buffalo School System does not have Florence Bridgwood or Florence Lawrence listed as a pupil. The Loretto Academy was unable to find a transcript for either name.

Florence's family worried that Florence, used to her own way on the road, would not like school very much. Surprisingly, Florence adjusted well to the more stable environment, working diligently on homework every afternoon and befriending classmate and teacher alike. Katterjohn reported that Florence "liked to throw paper wads, whisper, make faces behind the teacher's back, and perpetrate all the other innocent misdemeanors of school rooms."[10] She took large parts in the school productions, reciting traditional poems such as "Curfew Shall Not Ring Tonight" and singing holiday songs. She claimed to have been a "gang" leader: "I had all the boys in my crowd scared to death because I was the champion rough-and-tumble fighter of the neighborhood," she bragged years later.[11] She also played baseball until she broke her nose and thumb, then became a cheerleader. She most unashamedly called herself a "tomboy," favoring horse-riding and sports to the usual dolls and tea parties expected of a proper Edwardian girl. She did slow down long enough to learn how to play a cornet to perfection and to study violin.

Her relationship with her brothers does not seem to have been anything outside the ordinary. Her mother often said that the two boys were supposed to look after Flo, but that "she never needed anyone to look out for her."[12] Brother George moved to San Francisco sometime before 1910 and was only in loose contact with his family after that. "I am just hungry to see you; it is quite a number of years since we have saw each other and would do us both good to meet again,"[13] he wrote his mother in 1911, with more sincerity than grammar. His letters to Lotta and Florence were long descriptions of small things, unconsciously showing his lack of self-esteem, schooling and business understanding. "Last Saturday, I handled something like forty five hundred dollars not counting the checks I had, So I am trusted pretty well don't you think," he bragged in the same letter.[14] He eventually worked for a banking equipment company and as a patrol officer with the San Francisco Police Department. He and Florence were no doubt in closer contact during the 1920s and 1930s when she lived in California, though little correspondence between the two of them remains.

Florence's relationship with Norman was different still. Norman seems to have been rather shy, emotionally and intelligently eclipsed by his overbearing mother and outgoing sister. His surviving letters to Florence are also badly written, with creative spelling and grammar. He remained in Buffalo, doing various kinds of odd jobs throughout the years, never finding a solid niche for anything in particular. He did ask Florence for money quite often, usually to pay a specific bill. Florence just seemed to tolerate him to the point of ignoring him, but then usually came through at the last minute. She sent her brother a tie pin for Christmas 1910, for example, which he thanked her for in a postscript. Letters within the family usually ended with many Xs to suggest kisses, even if they were angry throughout the letter otherwise. Florence wrote a ventingly forceful letter to her mother in 1912, only to end it, "Well I'll ring off, to write more will only prolong the agony Flo XXX."[15] Nicknames and diminutives were frequently used, sometimes to soften the impact of a letter. "Floie" and "Queenie" were often used for Florence, Lotta was "Mardie" and Norman was "Normie."

Florence said that she graduated from School No. 10 on Delaware Street, probably sometime between 1903 and 1905, but records show this school was a grammar school rather than a high school. If she indeed had attended there, she may have "finished" her education at the Loretto Academy in Toronto. In 1906 she was 20 years old and longing for the career of her childhood. She joined her mother on tour and finished out the year on the road. Sometime in the middle of the decade, Lotta disbanded the Lawrence Dramatic Company. Her timing is puzzling, for suddenly she had a well-trained ingenue at her disposal. Perhaps the stage just wasn't big enough for the two of them in their small organization.

The year 1906 found Lotta and Florence in New York City without employment. Florence had intended to work as an artist's model or perhaps pose for some of the newfangled Mutoscope photographs. In the New York theatrical circles, the American Mutoscope and Biograph Company let it be known that they were seeking actors and actresses for five-minute plays to be made into Mutoscope novelties. Florence was discouraged to even apply by a girlfriend who had not found work with the nickelodeon slot machines. Mutoscopes took prints of the films made and placed them on cards that were then ticked off in consecutive order by means of a huge wheel and crank. Patrons paid their nickel to peer into these black boxes, turn the crank and see a short action sequence, similar in impact to the Kinetoscope.

Florence remembered seeing her first moving picture in New York around that time. Several that stood out in her mind were *Rip Van Winkle* with stage actor Joseph Jefferson, and *Life of an American Firefighter* and *Moonshiners*, which Florence thought to be the first dramatic picture produced in the United States. She didn't recall seeing *The Great Train Robbery* (1903), but she did remember seeing other short films of the everyday happenings, such as "a bootblack shining a pair of shoes, a horse eating hay, or a man kissing his wife," she said. "I do not mean that all the moving pictures of eight years ago [1906] were of this sort, but that bulk of those I had witnessed were."[16]

Florence had no serious thoughts of entering the film business, even though there was a certain vogue among stage actors and actresses to disdain the new medium yet watch its activities with one eye. Films were providing struggling—and not-so-struggling—actors and actresses with one more way to express their art and pad their wallets. The work required no more than a few hours, with little commitment and even less publicity. The pay, at a couple of dollars a day, was usually enough to pay a week's rent and buy a few meals. Terry Ramsaye pointed out that Edison's second New York location in the Bronx was "far enough away from Broadway that abashed actors need not fear they would be discovered in the artistic felony of working in pictures."[17]

And Florence was also beginning to wonder about how her "legitimate" theatrical profession would compare with the play-acting she had done during childhood. Less than four years later, she looked back to this pivotal point in her career: "I started to resume my work in the serious drama. But I found the work most uncongenial. Managers were so difficult to approach, and then they exacted so much and gave so little in return. I had always been with my mother and in the years that I had been off the stage gaining my education I found things had changed greatly and that managers had lost that high regard for women who were struggling to make a success that they had shown when I was with Mother."[18] In a feature story written several years later, writer Gladys Roosevelt implied Florence was too stressed to return to her work on the stage. "So heavy and so arduous were those claims [of the stage], and so great a strain upon her sensitive nature, that a nervous breakdown was imminent."[19]

Florence's professional acumen was for once on target. The theater was in a period of upheaval, brought on by psychological changes in the way man saw himself post–industrial revolution, and by the mere fact that American playwrights were not creating the plays similar to the great productions of the Victorian era. "The decade between 1905 and 1915 brought a decided shift among commercial managers to the American play," John Anderson wrote in his book *The American Theatre*. "At this point the theatre was feeling pressure from many quarters, both artistic and commercial ... 'the road' was steadily shrinking. According to figures compiled by *The Dramatic Mirror*, the number of plays on tour declined from an average of about 308 between the years 1900 and 1904 to 68 between the years 1925 and 1927. This was due ... partly to the mismanagement of the producers, and their mistreatment of both the actor and the public, and partly to the increase in railroad rates, but most of all because of the cheaper and more popular competition of the movies."[20] James Cleaver agreed, pointing out that plays produced in the early years of the century were not chosen from the actor's standpoint, but "for their entertainment and commercial value.... The theatre was indeed Big Business now."[21] The fact that Florence recognized she was becoming too small a fish in the big pond showed a pattern that she established in her film career. She was much better, artistically and mentally, when she was a big fish in the small pond. Motion pictures were then "the small pond," and continued to be for several years.

At the end of 1906, Florence and Lotta heard that the Edison Studios were seeking actors and actresses for a big historical photoplay, scheduled to be 1,000 feet in length. With more bravery than sense, they set out from their flat on 38th Street to the Edison Studios at 41 East 21st Street. Outside the studio, they found themselves in a crowd of 20 to 30 people also seeking work. Edwin Porter and Wallace McCutcheon met them with a descriptive list of the characters needed, for example, "One character man who can make up to look like Daniel Boone ... One middle aged woman to play Mrs. Daniel Boone ... Two young girls about sixteen years old to play Daniel Boone's daughters ... Six men who can make up as Indians."[22]

Porter was then chief producer and manager of the Edison Studio, and McCutcheon directed the films under Porter's supervision. Appropriately, America's first movie star was introduced to the craft by America's first film company. After Thomas Edison patented his Kinetograph camera in 1893, he stayed interested in his new toy for only a few years, then turned over the production of films for entertainment to Porter, among others. His patents' rights, enforced with a vengeance during these early years, almost brought an end to the industry before it even started. Edison was in court with both Siegmund Lubin and American Mutoscope in the first decade of the new century, trying to prevent them from using a camera, or parts of a camera, which resembled his invention for making motion pictures. However, other cameras from Europe, such as the Cinematograph and the Phantascope, had appeared on the scene quietly, and a competitive, thriving industry was born.

Florence had no notion of the problems going on behind the camera at Edison's studio. She was nervously approaching the "great clumsy" moving picture camera for the first time, having won the role of one of Boone's daughters. Her mother was assigned to play Mrs. Boone, and others in the cast were Susanna Willis and Mr. and Mrs. William Carver. The scenario was written to be almost completely an outdoor drama; the exteriors were filmed in the Bronx Park in New York City and the few interiors were done on the single-set roof of the Edison Studio. The newly hired actors were dismissed, only to report to work in zero-degree weather several days later. Florence remembered huddling around a bonfire, waiting for the right amount of sunlight. Her stamina was further tested when given a more spirited horse to ride than she was used to. "As a child I was fond of horses and had always prided myself on being able to handle them, but the horse hired by Mr. Porter was evidently a wilder breed that the ones I knew ... I was not thrown once, however," she added proudly.[23] Considering the horse may have come from a wild west show then playing at the Hippodrome, where many of the extras had been hired from,[24] Florence may have been lucky to have stayed on the horse. The *Daniel Boone* players worked around the schedule of these freshly-hired extras' schedules, pushing production time to an unbelievable three weeks. When finally completed, the drama had over 20 scenes, including the obligatory "tableau" summary at the end.

Florence vividly remembered seeing herself on screen, sometime in March or April 1907, for the first time. She was horrified. "In one scene I was shown crossing a log over a stream, and wearing shoes with high heels. Just think of the situation! Daniel Boone's daughter wearing high-heeled shoes! Why, in those days girls were fortunate indeed if they possessed a pair of moccasins," she said in 1914, recalling her "indignant" reactions.[25] Despite Florence's perceived personal failings, Edison's *Daniel Boone, or Pioneer Days in America*, was a well-received film. The advertising proclaimed, "Perfection Itself, Adjectives Unnecessary."[26] Its coverage in *Moving Picture World* was nothing more than a summary of the scenes, and no names are mentioned. Even the Edison name was very discreet. Florence sniffed later, "The public did not demand perfection in those days."[27]

The self-seen inadequacy of her portrayal, if not her entire performance, goaded Florence into becoming better at motion picture acting, and her own gauntlet was laid down. She became increasingly fascinated by films, going from show to show to observe each of the different companies. She studied the motions and appearances of the players, particularly the actresses who appeared in the French Pathé Frerès films. Florence made her most crucial step toward leaving the stage by announcing to her mother that she intended to seek work as a moving picture actress.

Lotta had not liked the work at all during that frigid January. All good actresses were supposed to feel that moving picture acting was beneath the theater-bred player; Lotta was no exception. Nothing could replace walking across the boards under the lights in front of a live audience. She did the first thing she could think of to discourage her daughter: laugh. When Florence persisted in her idea, Lotta became alarmed. Their family honor was at stake. She begged Florence to reconsider.

Florence apparently listened to her mother, or at least decided to give the stage one last try. In the middle of 1907, Lotta and Florence both landed roles in the Melvin B. Raymond Musical Travesty Company production *The Seminary Girl*. To their disappointment, they learned they had to wait six weeks before rehearsals started. Florence began making the rounds of the film manufacturing companies and somehow convinced J. Stuart Blackton and Albert Smith at the Vitagraph Company that she was born to play the role of Moya, the female romantic lead of a film adaptation of Dion Boucicault's *The Shaughraun*, by using her "broadest Irish brogue."

"Show us how an Irish girl would look and act," Blackton ordered, after Smith had told her that she was too young. Nerves quaking, Florence went about setting her stage: "After doing two or three little bits of business, I stepped over to a corner of the room, smoothed my hair and walked out to them again, with my most dignified air, and awaited their decision." With a glance and a word at one another, Blackton and Smith awarded her the part.

Florence thoroughly enjoyed working at the Vitagraph, particularly on

A common publicity photograph, distributed sometimes as a postcard by both Biograph and Lubin. The facsimile signature may or may not have been written originally by Florence. Florence usually used capital E in place of lower-case E when signing her name.

this production. She shared the lead with Scotchman William Shea, another stage veteran, who portrayed Conn. She did not realize at the time what an impression he made on her, but even years later she was full of praise of him. "William Shea, in real life, is as good-natured, jolly and friendly as he is on the screen.... He is to be complimented." Another thing she favorably remembered was that he stayed with Vitagraph throughout his career: "He has been content to work for his original employers, never letting changes in the industry effect him whatsoever."[28] Staying power evidently impressed her.

Although she loved her new work, Florence left the film business for the stage one last time. *The Seminary Girl* was due to start for a fall tour. Florence was well aware of what was at stake. The moving picture industry was at best a fleeting occupation in 1907; the theater had been around forever and was solid employment. With a heavy heart and maybe not as much enthusiasm as her mother would have liked, Florence began work with Lotta in Melvin Raymond's Company.

Lotta portrayed Miss Penelope Wilkins, and Florence had the lead role as Mary Dwyer. Florence was able to show off her singing abilities in this production with at least four songs, including "My Chocolate Cream" and "Nobody Ever Said Boo," plus one duet ("I Don't Know") with leading man Ben Mulvey. The company performed the popular play in medium-sized arenas in receptive theater and vaudeville towns such as Louisville, Kentucky, and Joliet, Illinois. The *Washington Democrat* heralded the attendance at the play as "the bumper crowd of the season," and called Florence's work "good." Florence and Mulvey were also credited with several encores following the performance.[29]

And that was the end. The show closed as expected in early 1908, and Florence made the rounds of the moving picture company offices rather than Broadway.

Chapter Two

MOVING AND SHAKING

> *The Vitagraph Corporation really was a great big happy family.*
> —James Morrison

Florence had already learned that breaking into the moving picture business as a full-time profession would be as difficult as getting any other acting job in the real world in 1908. "I suppose I considered myself a superior actress—who doesn't at that age—but I was soon convinced that my services were not in demand."[1] Florence did not have to worry much longer. When *The Seminary Girl* ended, she went again to the Vitagraph Company, and Smith soon selected her to play the lead in a Civil War story, *The Despatch Bearer*. This 725-foot film was released in November 1907, about three months before *The Shaughraun*, so either Florence's tour was rather short or she misremembered when she made this film in her 1914 writings.

Florence portrayed a young woman who carried valuable papers across the lines for Union forces when her beau was injured. The necessary chase scene called for Florence to ride on horseback through a thicket of trees, closely pursued by Confederate soldiers. J. Stuart Blackton vividly remembered that Florence came close to a serious accident during the filming of these scenes. "Miss Lawrence made one or two rides through the winding path among the trees.... One of the runs was not fast enough, and had to be done over. As Miss Lawrence came dashing toward the camera at break-neck speed, her horse suddenly swerved and ran so close to one of the tree trunks that it seemed to all of us that her brains must certainly be dashed out." Florence missed the tree by inches.[2] Florence averred, "I don't think meaner or wilder horses were ever engaged for picture work than those Mr. Smith hired for me to ride." (She must have already forgotten the ones hired by the Edison Company for *Daniel Boone*.) The Vitagraph Company went through three different mounts before they finally completed Florence's scenes. "To this day," Florence passionately declared six years later, "I am certain that my life was in danger throughout the production of this picture."[3]

The Vitagraph Company was experiencing a great surge of growth during this time. The building they were now occupying at East 15th Street and Locust Avenue in the Flatbush section of Brooklyn was still practically under construction when they began making films. Vitagraph President William Rock had put up the money—$25,000—for the studio, which was state-of-the-art in that era. The concrete block building had a generator that operated the lights, heat and power. The indoor stage had a bank of Cooper Hewitt lights. An article in *Views and Film Index* described the modern interior: "The entire roof and upper part of the building is covered with a specially designed prismatic glass. This construction of glass diffuses and intensifies the rays of light so that shadows are not perceptible."[4]

Florence did not have much to say about President Rock, but she was full of appreciation for Smith and Blackton, treasurer and secretary of the company respectively. "These two always worked together on the early Vitagraph pictures, serving in the capacity of director, camera-man and property man," she said. "They have achieved their wonderful success only through the hardest kind of work, always studying, experimenting, and trying to improve their output.... Above all, they were unfailingly kind and generous, always ready with an encouraging word for anyone who needed it."[5] Blackton and Smith had worked very hard to make the best of the ten-year-old company. *Moving Picture World* commented in 1908 that the firm "had been in the hit line from the very start,"[6] when they were making films on the rooftop of their old Nassau Street building. Film historian Anthony Slide has pointed out that the Vitagraph Company was the "most important" film manufacturer in its time: "It was the first to build up a stable of stars, the first to experiment successfully with animated and trick film, the first to film the classics from Shakespeare and Dickens, and the first to use the motion picture for propaganda purposes."[7] The Vitagraph Company suffered a substantial loss of film history in 1911 when a fire destroyed over 1,000 reels of old films,[8] but many exhibitor copies still were circulating at that time, even prints of the oldest of their titles (from 1898). These have found their way into permanent archives such as the Eastman House in Rochester and the Library of Congress in Washington, making Vitagraph films some of the best preserved of the early studios' works.

Vitagraph began producing films that had more literary quality than other manufacturing firms before 1910, resulting in an impressive roster of titles and lofty attempts to place Shakespeare and other classics into a single reel. *Oliver Twist* (July 1907), *Francesca da Rimini, or The Two Brothers* (February 1908), *Macbeth, Shakespeare's Sublime Tragedy* (April 1908), and *Romeo and Juliet, a Romantic Story of the Ancient Feud Between the Italian Houses of Montague and Capulet* (June 1908) were all released by Vitagraph. The last title is one that is a source of controversy as far as Florence's role in it; she was working for Vitagraph during the time that it was produced and released, but so was Florence Turner, another pioneering silent film actress of considerable talents.

Who played Juliet? The still photographs from the 1908 photoplay do not reveal with any certainty who the actress was beneath the long blonde wig. Florence stated in her 1914 memoirs that it was Florence Turner who played half of the star-crossed lovers with Paul Panzer as the other half. But again her memory was tricking her, for she remembered that she saw the production of the film on the first day she was there.[9] This could not have been, for *Romeo and Juliet* was released a full seven months after *The Despatch Bearer*. Very likely Vitagraph was filming another dramatic love story, such as *Francesca da Rimini*, and Florence did not know what was being filmed. The error did not go unchecked for long. Not two years later, Florence Lawrence claimed the honor of being America's first screen Juliet for herself, a title that followed her throughout her career and into her meager path of film history. Very few modern filmographies omit Florence Lawrence in *Romeo and Juliet*. The 1980 *Films in Review* listing denies it to her based solely on the 1914 interview, but lists compiled by the *American Film Institute Catalogue,* National Archives, Daniel Blum, Ephraim Katz, Lauritzen and Lundquist and many others do give her unconditional credit, as does Albert Smith in his autobiography and J. Stuart Blackton in a reminiscent article in *Photoplay*. Robert Ball tried to sift through the conflicting stories in his book *Shakespeare on Silent Film,* giving Florence Lawrence's story and naming the few times Florence Turner listed *Romeo and Juliet* in her own credits. He also has proof from an interview with Paul Panzer himself, who remembered Florence Lawrence was his Juliet.[10] Of course, Florence Lawrence or Florence Turner may have enacted a role other than Juliet in the photoplay, but Ball, Blum and Smith do not even give that possibility credence, identifying Florence Lawrence solely as Juliet.

Her other credits at Vitagraph are almost as unclear. She remembered making *The Athletic Girls of America* (or *The Athletic American Girls*), which was released in August 1907, months before *The Despatch Bearer*. The athletic film was memorable for Florence because she punched out one of her co-stars during a sparring match. "During the actual taking of the scene I became a little angry when the athletic girl 'biffed' me a little harder than I thought she ought. My ire rose and I went for blood, landing blows left and right, and I sent Miss Athletic Girl to the floor in a jiffy."[11] Buffalo's little terror had moved on to bigger targets.

Other credits were less memorable. She probably appeared in *Julius Caesar* and *Francesca da Rimini*, but these are hard-to-find films and confirmation is difficult. Even the scarce stills or frame enlargements are hard to identify. Other titles that appear in contemporary and modern filmographies are *Love Laughs at Locksmiths, an Eighteenth Century Romance*; *The Viking's Daughter, the Story of the Ancient Norsemen*; and *Lady Jane's Flight*. Robert Ball spotted her and Florence Turner in a banquet scene still from *Macbeth*. She may have been film's first Cleopatra or she may have played the Egyptian's maid in *Antony and Cleopatra* (Ball credits Betty Kent as Cleopatra, but Slide does not mention an actress with that name in *The Big V*), and she may have been Salome doing the dance of the seven veils in *Salome*. Florence may not have been clear on her roles at Vitagraph, but nevertheless was proud of her work. "I do not think I am vain to say that I made good with the Vitagraph people, for they did not discharge me, but kept me long after *The Despatch Bearer* was finished. I appeared in a dozen or more pictures."[12] In extremely rare commentary for its time, *Moving Picture World* commended the work of the Vitagraph Company for its skillful interpretation of *Antony and Cleopatra*, in which Florence may or may not have appeared. "The Vitagraph Company can take pride in the production. The elaborate stage effects and superb costumes, together with the magnificent manner in which the parts were played, is a credit to the company."[13] Smith and Blackton's work was certainly being noticed.

Smith and Blackton let others direct by the middle of 1908, namely their studio manager William V. Ranous and stage actor Charles Kent. Ranous became an important mentor to Florence as he directed several of Vitagraph's larger photoplays in 1908. He once turned her away from the projection room when she tried to watch herself before the film was released. "How in the world do you think I can ever improve my work if I never see how I act?" she asked him after he had told her that Blackton, Smith and Rock were the only ones allowed in the projecting room. "For a second Mr. Ranous seemed to be considering my request, which was certainly reasonable, but he said, 'My dear little girl, don't worry. Mr. Blackton or Mr. Smith will tell you all you need to know about your work. If you don't improve, they will tell you.'" Florence sadly concluded, "It was useless to argue further."[14]

Charles Kent, a veteran stage actor, joined the Vitagraph fold in 1908, acting and directing. He fondly called Florence "that new little girl," commenting on her lovely golden hair. Florence, greatly impressed with his extensive theatrical career, thought that he was one of the first important stage stars to leave it for moving pictures.[15] Robert Ball said Kent had been onstage since 1875 and had turned to film work only after losing his stage voice.[16] Kent is generally accepted as the director of *Antony and Cleopatra*, and is also credited with directing a handful of other pictures until 1913 and appearing as an actor in hundreds until his death in 1923.

One more important person walked through the doors at the Vitagraph studio and into Florence's life. Harry Lewis Solter was another down-on-his-luck actor who needed to make the rent and sought out a day's work as an extra in moving pictures. Florence remembered that Blackton seized Harry immediately to play in a role that Blackton himself was doing the stunt driving for. "Mr. Blackton looked across at the newcomer, then rushed toward him, jerked his hat off his head and looked at him, full face, side face, compared their respective heights, then said, 'You'll do,' and instructed the surprised actor to make up so as to look as nearly as possible like him." Harry did all the work in the play except the driving of an automobile—Florence said that at that time the "combination of actor and chauffeur was very scarce"—when Blackton did the driving. Thus Harry was given a quick introduction to the moving picture world, where he stayed for the rest of his life.

Harry Solter, one of ten children from an old Baltimore, Maryland, family, crisscrossed the country as an actor in various tours before being stranded in San Francisco when the company ran out of money. There he became acquainted with David Wark "Lawrence" Griffith, who was just as theater-worn and broke. Linda Arvidson remembered that Griffith had been promised leading roles with a company back East, and Harry recalled that the two of them came back to New York with nothing in their pockets, searching for work. "We seemed to fare worse on Broadway than when out in 'Frisco," Harry said. "We decided we could do best by looking for work alone. Each was pledged, if he got a job and a possible chance for another, immediately to cinch it." At this point Harry ventured into the Vitagraph studios, and claims to have encouraged Griffith to try the other picture companies, especially Kalem and Biograph.[17] If Harry was the "Gloomy Gus" Salter that Griffith remembered in his autobiography, then Harry was the one who did push him toward films. Griffith checked for work at both of the companies Harry suggested, but wound up working at Edison to make *Rescued from an Eagle's Nest*, before being hired as a permanent extra at Biograph.[18]

At Vitagraph, Harry and Florence became friends almost immediately. Each saw the other in their backgrounds, a tie that held them together while at Vitagraph. Harry saw Florence's potential as an actress and admired it, as much as he admired the young lady. He wisely and quickly became friends with Lotta as well. By the end of May 1908, Harry was writing love letters to Florence (some addressed both to Lotta and Florence, if she had shunned him for some reason). Harry realized how much Florence depended upon her mother's advice and support. He also noticed the things that irritated her, particularly her own active self-criticism when it came to her work. Finally he recognized that they were equally determined in their career paths. Florence herself had agreed, referring to herself and Harry (and others at Vitagraph) as "ambitious beings, each harboring the belief that he or she was destined to become famous." Florence ironically added, "How? We did not know."[19]

Florence was not without serious suitors from the time she was 18 years old. Several had even gone so far as to ask Lotta for permission to marry her. "I have spoken to your mother all about what I spoke to you about and she says that if you care anything for me Dear and you think that I should make you happy she will not come between us as she says your happiness is all that she cares about," rambled a letter from a fellow Canadian, Will Fleming, in

1904.[20] He vanished out of Florence's life only to be replaced by an unknown Tom, whose well-penned love letters extended until she met Harry. To Florence, however, Harry was different. After him, the only love letters she kept were the "mash" notes from fans.

Their friendship obviously did not end when Harry left Vitagraph in early 1908. He had gone to Biograph, where Griffith soon found him a position as an extra. In early 1908, Harry appeared with Griffith and Linda Arvidson, whom he no doubt knew, in Biograph productions, such as *When Knights Were Bold* and *'Ostler Joe*. Harry stayed with him when Griffith was offered the directorial duties at the time Wallace McCutcheon became ill. After being assured that he would keep his acting job even if the photoplay failed, Griffith confidently took the new position. Gene Gauntier takes credit in her memoirs for being the one to suggest to Biograph management that Griffith be allowed to direct.[21] Linda Arvidson thought cameraman Arthur Marvin was the one to suggest Griffith's name as a potential director.[22] Cameraman Billy Bitzer said it was writer Joe Dougherty.[23] Regardless, Griffith's first film for Biograph was *The Adventures of Dollie*, released July 14, 1908. Griffith's work at Biograph brought the company back up to its once-high standards of quality. He also changed the face of moving pictures, from the targetless scramble of scenes pre–1908 to the smooth cinematic art form we can recognize today. Griffith tried to explain the humble beginnings of his success in 1916: "Of course it hurts my sense of modesty to admit the fact, but it is true that in a few months Biograph pictures were considered far away the best."[24]

Harry floated into the ambiguous position of "assistant director." (In those days the definition of "director"—also then called "producer"—was still up in the air.) Harry said later that he "was a sort of studio jack-of-all-trades, being actor, assistant to the director, and general utility man."[25] Whatever Griffith wanted, Harry found for him. When Biograph's leading actress Marion Leonard left for a stage tour in the middle of 1908, Griffith knew he needed to find a regular leading lady to add another feminine face into the loosely formed roster. He also knew that Western films were doing well at the box office, so he set Harry to find a talented woman who would be a fresh face, with the ability to do stunts and tricks on a horse. His personal pick was Vitagraph's Florence Turner. Harry agreed and set off for the Vitagraph studios to see if Turner could be lured over to Biograph. Instead, Harry ran into Florence Lawrence, probably not by accident, and offered her the position.

Linda Arvidson remembered things differently, of course, claiming that Griffith "stole little Florrie, he did," after seeing her excellent work in *The Despatch Bearer*. "One could easily see that besides having the ability Florence Lawrence had had excellent direction," she added, recalling Griffith's praise of William Ranous.[26] Florence was offered $25 a week, $10 a week over her salary at Vitagraph. She would not be expected to make the costumes or painted backdrops as she had at Vitagraph. Florence accepted with joy.

The little world of moving picture creating and manufacturing was changing every year. The population was gradually getting used to them as a new entertainment source. In her excellent reference *The Transformation of Cinema*, Eileen Bowser pulls together figures from several sources for the numbers of nickelodeon theaters in the United States during 1907 and 1908. "*Variety*'s conservative estimate was 2,500 nickelodeons for the entire country at the beginning of 1907. In May 1907 Moving Picture World said there were 2,500 to 3,000, and in November, the figure cited by [Joseph Medill] Patterson [in a 1907 *Saturday Evening Post* article] was 'between four and five thousand.' By July 1908 an approximate figure of 8,000 was given by an Oakland, California, newspaper."[27] Gene Brown gives 9,000 as the number of theaters at the beginning of 1909.[28] A 1906 *The Billboard* editorial claimed that "in every town of sufficient size to support it there exists a theatre where moving picture shows are given exclusively." A month later, an article in *Billboard* said that nickelodeons were "the jack-rabbits of the business of public entertaining," noticing how a theater was now on every major city block and in every middle-sized American town, ponderously commenting, "No one can tell what the total will eventually be."[29]

One magical sociological question from this era is to ask just who attended moving picture shows. While it could be easy to assume that no upper or upper-middle income families went to film shows regularly, it is also erroneous to assume that they *never* attended a show. Some theaters in New York City, for example, were set into shopping districts where a broad cross section of people could pay their nickel, sit down and relax. Robert Allen used business directories to pinpoint the location of New York theaters within their neighborhoods as a whole, shedding some light on who might have frequented them. Moving picture theaters were crowded next to the established, cheaper entertainment complexes, such as New York's Bowery and Union Square, competing directly with shooting galleries, vaudeville halls and dime museums. The residential areas around these areas—the Lower East Side—were teeming with Jewish immigrants. Allen points out that only 42 of Manhattan's 123 theaters were located in the Lower East Side. Other concentrations of immigrants, such as Little Italy and Yorkville, had high theater-to-population numbers.[30] Garth Jowett looked at the theatergoer in terms of who had time and inclination, rather than proximity to a theater. He identified three "new" audiences that came around to moving pictures as the industry grew. First were those previously restrained by religious theater restrictions. These people were seeking a new entertainment and were encouraged by the morality of many of the early films. Second were working-class fans of the legitimate stage, especially melodramas. This group of people had money to spend on leisure activities anyway, and the moving picture provided new stories, more often. Third were the inner-city workers, including the immigrants who used films as an educational experience, learning history, manners and problems of American life.³¹ Even when film show prices were raised from the carfare nickel to the weeding-out quarter, moving pictures were still one of the best entertainment values that a $12-a-week worker could afford. Historians have also been faced with base prejudice in studying this aspect of film. One unbelievable statement from a 1907 article states that "as might be expected, the Latin races patronize the shows more consistently than Jews, Irish or Americans." This dated stereotyping also included sailors as "devotees," but also correctly added that children nationwide made up one-third of every audience.³²

Opening a nickelodeon was not as difficult as one might imagine. The Sears and Roebuck catalogue for 1908 offered not only the "Motiograph" moving picture machine, but a special 160-page catalogue that offered everything from song slides to stereopticons. There is no mention of the Edison stranglehold on film sources in the advertising, but the copy does boast that "the moving picture business has grown to immense proportions, developing into a world wide enterprise, involving an invested capital of millions of dollars." Nickelodeons were of course the main feature, but machines could be purchased by "churches, lodges and schools."³³ In 1907, *Moving Picture World* gave an almost tongue-in-cheek recipe for opening a nickelodeon: "Here are the ingredients of a 5-cent theatre: One storeroom, seating from 200 to 500 persons. One phonograph with extra large horn. One young woman cashier. One electric sign. One cinematograph, with operator. One canvas on which to throw the pictures. One piano. One barker. One manager. As many chairs as the store will hold. A few brains and a little tact. Mix salt and pepper to taste."³⁴

More than condiments were needed at this point. Linda Arvidson wrote in 1916 that the faith of the players initially wavered, especially when it came to the actual theaters. "The motion picture public of to-day didn't go to a 'movie' show eight years ago," she said. "One could hardly criticise them for not going, for it took courage to sit through a show in the dirty, dark little stores that hung up a sheet on one end and turned on the projecting machine from the other."³⁵

Since everything about the moving pictures was generally regarded as trashy, good performers were simply not going to flock to the studio doors awaiting work. In fact, many of the early players were not even actors. "Some of them were drifters who could handle props or pack film or sweep floors; most of them were young and strong, although sometimes lazy and lacking in professional experience," Billy Bitzer wrote in his memoirs. "Others were servant girls or waitresses from the neighborhood, who could easily be seduced into appearing before the camera." To get a real actor was considered "lucky."³⁶ Florence saw the same thing in those around her. "We came from here, there and everywhere, and from all walks of life. Some of us had had stage experience and some had not." But Florence knew not to judge fellow players just on their backgrounds. "Generally speaking, the actors and actresses employed in those days were far below to-day's standard, and still a few of them are superior to many of the present day players."[37]

Even by the middle of the next decade, the anonymous stars of 1907 and 1908 were largely gone. For example, Kathlyn Williams and Paul Panzer worked for several of the old companies, Biograph and Vitagraph, before blossoming into real personalities when the star system was finally firmly established. Hobart Bosworth also made films in the early days before he learned that his real talents were on the other side of the camera. By and large, however, the actors in these early films were destined to limited film careers — Florence included. Florence was a talented and dedicated actress who could follow the trends in the industry, making any change needed to fit her range. Others such as Williams and Panzer were as good and as talented as Florence, and both settled into film careers suited to their capabilities. Williams retired from the screen in the 1920s after a successful run in serials and producing her own films in the 1910s. Panzer kept making movies, highlighted as the villain in *The Perils of Pauline* (1914), although later on he was often in small roles. (He died in 1958.) So many other players who had plenty of work before 1910 were just lost by the turn of the decade.

But Florence wanted more than just the happenstance grind of filmmaking that she was becoming accustomed to. She now saw glimpses of what could be in moving pictures, as stories became more complex and lengthy and production costs began to grow. She saw her demand as an actress rising, as different companies were already bargaining for her talents. She had found a man who could see as rosy a vision of where her future successes would lie; a man who could be her partner in life as well. Florence left the cinder-block building of Vitagraph studios in Brooklyn and headed for the old brownstone in the Bronx without looking back.

Chapter Three

A NEW FAMILY

> *It is a living, silently speaking profession, very probably an Art, with a promise of immortal life because Griffith gave it a soul.*
> —Henry Stephen Gordon, 1916

When Florence joined the Biograph Company, she already had a sense of the changes in the industry—her salary alone told her that—but she could not have had any idea of what history she was making when she entered Biograph's brownstone at 11 East 14th Street. No one did. The players who worked there have, over the years, tried to capture the sense of magic and mystery that took place within the ballroom that had once played host to society dances and dinners. The magic did not last long. In 1925, Linda Arvidson poked around the house, still parceled and leased to tenants, and was denied permission by then-resident sculptor Stirling Calder to enter the old studio. Even then, a scant 20 years later, movies had grown up and moved away from Manhattan, away from New York City, away from the East Coast.

Mabel Normand, who arrived shortly after Florence had departed Biograph, summed up the sentimental feelings of the studio well. "Those old Biograph days! Will they ever be equaled, I wonder, for their effect on the industry and for the atmosphere that surrounded the little group? I doubt it.... We didn't realize we were making movie history."[1] Lillian Gish remembered the life that the players breathed into the old building. "When we worked there, the house was alive with movement; filled with people with strange painted faces, wearing odd costumes.... They brought to their work an excitement and spontaneity that did not exist anywhere else and has regrettably long since disappeared from most movies."[2] Mary Pickford hated the actual studio, but found the working conditions to be wonderful. "I have since come to know that if people are to associate in work twelve and fourteen hours a day, a whole-hearted familiarity and intimacy are a necessary letdown.... As I had never been associated with other young persons, I had to undergo a great deal of teasing."³ Linda Arvidson wrote in 1916, "I feel constrained to use the trite old saying, 'Those were the good old days!' And I think that the little band of pioneer actors and actresses who began working together so earnestly and so sincerely and withal so humbly, at the old Biograph studio eight years ago, will all agree with me in that they were."⁴

Of course most of the players recognized that the magic centered on their director, Griffith. Their admiration and devotion to him has developed into something that seems quite sacred, very reverent. Lillian Gish's biography is simply entitled *The Movies, Mr. Griffith, and Me*, because he had shown her that "it was more fun to work than to play."⁵ The first time Lillian met Griffith, he had fired a gun into the air in order to get her and sister Dorothy to show the right degree of fright during their screen test. She thought him to be a madman.⁶ Gene Gauntier, the Kalem Girl, who spent the spring of 1908 with the Biograph Company, remembered Griffith as being revolutionary and shocking. "I was uncomfortable in his presence, never knowing what he would say next. His intellect fairly blazed."⁷ Mabel Normand, however, loved his voice; "It had a timbre and a gentleness that encouraged me."⁸ Griffith himself was quick to deflect all the praise from himself: "I did not 'teach' the players with whom my name has been linked. We developed together, we found ourselves in a new art and as we discovered the possibilities of that art we learned together."⁹

Florence Lawrence, too, was enchanted by the Biograph Company and its resident wizard: "The story of Director Griffith is as necessary to my account of Biograph days as is flour to the making of biscuits. That is, my story cannot be told coherently without considerable mention of David W. Griffith. As for biscuits, I doubt very much if they would be coherent without the use of flour. Frankly there would not be any biscuits."¹⁰ Some critics called Florence's Biograph work her best. Her screen acting skills were refined and toned to an exceptional degree during her tutelage with Griffith. But just as it taught her well, it also limited her. The vogue of moving pictures was changing constantly during these very early days of the industry. Styles were created, then improved upon. Accepted gestures for a certain emotion one day were passé the next. Florence's stage training proved invaluable during this year at Biograph; it gave her a stable base on which to build her new craft. Griffith added onto her range in the style that was expected and accepted at that time. She continued to adapt for a few years, or until the industry had changed too much for her to keep up with.

Florence clearly remembered walking into the Biograph offices that first day, when Harry had been told to bring back Florence Turner and instead showed up with Florence Lawrence. She was a bit miffed and slightly insulted when Griffith seemed to negotiate with Harry rather than with her. "If he intended giving me work, I was the person to be told and not Mr. Solter."[11] Griffith no doubt knew of Harry's interest in the fair-haired actress—as must have Florence herself by this time. She was told to dress immediately in Western style clothes—"knee-length skirt, leggings, blouse waist with sleeves rolled above my elbows, pistol holster swung about my waist, a water pouch slung carelessly over my shoulder, and a big sombrero on my head"[12]—for a part in what she remembered was *The Outlaw and the Girl*. She loved riding horses, and spent all the exterior scenes riding: "I think it was my riding in that picture that made me a permanent fixture around the Biograph studio."[13]

Linda Arvidson remembered that Florence was given a "grand rush" when she joined Biograph. (She also remembers that Griffith and Harry called on Florence and Lotta at their boardinghouse rather than Florence's version of her hiring.) Linda also thought that Florence was "an awfully good sport about doing stunts," repeating the story that Blackton told about Florence almost hitting a tree while on horseback (except that Linda remembered the stationary object being the camera).[14]

Florence, Linda and Marion Leonard alternated playing the leads of films for some time. But they also took turns in the background as extras. Before *The Girl and the Outlaw* was released on September 8, 1908, Florence pops up in several other split-reel stories, such as a member of the wacky wedding party in *Balked at the Altar* and a maid in *The Bandit's Waterloo*. Her first real leads came in *Betrayed by a Handprint*, portraying Myrtle Vane, a society kleptomaniac, and *Behind the Scenes*, as Mrs. Bailey, a struggling actress and mother, both released in September. "Throughout my year at the Biograph Studio I worked along this plan—a Western picture, a society drama or comedy, and then a frontier or Indian picture.... Nowadays [1914] if a director should ask his leading lady to do as much she certainly would have something to say."[15]

Somehow in this mad rush of work, Florence and Harry found time to be married. On August 30, 1908, they slipped across the river to Elizabeth, New Jersey, well south of Fort Lee, to be married. Rev. Brockholst Morgan, the assistant rector at Elizabeth's St. John's Episcopal Church, married them at the elegant house where he lived at 607 Westminster Avenue.[16] The witnesses appear to be local acquaintances rather than film associates. Harry was 34 and Florence 22. The marriage was kept a secret at the studio, as was the one between Linda Arvidson and D.W. Griffith. This may not have been as difficult as it seems now. Many of these players were still not used to working with the same people every day and friendships were not struck up casually. Plus, several of the players were either shy or dominated by another, such as a mother or a spouse. Others were simply closemouthed. Griffith biographer Richard Schickel said that no one remembered having intimate conversations with Griffith in their memoirs.

Still, funny situations must have occurred. Linda Arvidson remembered that Harry was the only person in whom her husband had entrusted the secret

Biograph director David Wark Griffith, from around 1910. Florence liked Griffith, and the Solters and the Griffiths seemed to be friendly outside the studio as well. "There can be no doubt that he is a very able artist," Florence said of him in 1914.

of their marriage, and evidently Griffith knew of the recent Solter union. "A fellow-feeling probably had made David a bit confidential—an unusual thing for him." (Linda said that Wilfred Lucas and Paul Scardon, who had known them before their marriage, also were in on the secret.) Linda also recalled a time when the Solters and the Griffiths were out on a boat ride. "We were quietly enjoying the ride, not a word being spoken, when Harry Salter [sic], pointing to a hole in the heel of David's stocking, at the same time turned to me and with a knowing smile said, 'Miss Arvidson, look!'"[17]

Besides the Griffiths and the Solters, several other romances were lurking within the Biograph. Mary Pickford, a 1909 arrival, was ardently and successfully wooed by Owen Moore, and James Kirkwood began romancing Gertrude Robinson. Anita Hendrie and David Miles, and Marion Leonard and E.V. Stanner Taylor were already married. Several years later, Griffith looked back and shrugged. "I could tell countless love affairs that developed into matrimony in those early days, but everyone had to work so hard, and so long, that it is difficult to understand how time was found for sentimental incidents."[18] Several of these marriages ended in divorce, including Griffith's own, so these words were prophetic and revealing.

The mail addressed to the unnamed players in the moving pictures began arriving in late 1908. Florence kept a great deal of her fan mail, using it to bolster her self-esteem whenever it flagged. One letter from December 1908 begged the Biograph Company to give him the name of the actress who had appeared in *After Many Years* and *The Reckoning*. "My reason for asking the above information was the outcome of a wager that I did not have courage to form an acquaintance [sic] with this young lady.... P.S. Please consider this a confidential matter." Florence's mail began pouring in from everywhere Biograph films were shown. She recalled receiving cards and letters from all over the United States, Canada, France, England, Germany, Australia and Russia, "letters from boys and girls who were stage-struck for moving picture show acting, who wanted to know what school of dramatic art she would advise; notes from dazzled youth and moneyed bachelors and fickle married men and merry widowers, pledging everlasting love and devotion; a surprising number of autograph hunters, even offers of marriage from men who claim enough combined wealth to pay the national debt."[19]

The work was hard, the hours were long. Characters were improvised on the whim of Griffith, who often created the story lines as he went along (unless an idea was "borrowed" from another source). Griffith often physically showed his actors what he wanted from them; Florence could keep up with him. Both Griffith and Florence, being students of the old stage, were well versed in the "histrionic" traditions of acting—that is, providing broad, exaggerated movements to suggest a certain emotion. Histrionic acting was a carefully described routine; books were written for amateurs to master the art. A majority of the early silent films are remembered for what is seen today as "overacting." Florence herself considered "bad acting" to be when the actor looked at the camera.[20] Gradually, the restraint of these emotional flags began creeping into film usage. Currently this is called "verisimilar" actions (propounded by Roberta Pearson), the less obvious motions that just as clearly indicated sentiment in a way better suited to film as a medium. Pearson, in her book *Eloquent Gestures*, uses Griffith's Biograph years as an excellent example of how the histrionic meets the verisimilar, the combining collision, and the tentative end results. Pearson points out that while mostly histrionic actions were used in 1908 and more verisimilar in 1912, bright examples of the opposite show through. In *One Touch of Nature* (released January 1, 1909), Florence holds a doll, showing her grief at her child's death through the automatic care she gives the doll: "The use of the prop seeming to inhibit histrionic gestures."[21] This example is an exception, of course; critics then and now recognize that Florence possessed a "mastery" of histrionics unparalleled by period actresses.

The Biograph studio must have been nothing short of chaos most of the time. Players practicing around the edges, people adjusting and elaborating on costumes, the clacking grind of the camera, Griffith shouting or pleading directions, the ever-present buzz of the lights, music floating about to help put the players in the right mood, and the business of the studio being transacted around all of this. Gene Gauntier remembered the Biograph studio being "bedlam," especially after the calm and order of the Kalem studios.[22]

Florence never knew who she was going to be from one day to the next when she showed up at the studio. She certainly portrayed a wide range of characters just within the first few months of her work there. By the end of the year, she had been acting in one or two releases every week (a release was usually one reel), most often playing the lead after Marion Leonard returned to the stage for a short tour. Within those dozen weeks, Florence had enacted a Japanese princess, several heartbroken society women, a grieved mother, a Greek slave, a Jewish woman, the ubiquitous tomboy, Shakespeare's Kate, an underpaid worker and a new character called Mrs. Jones, among a score of others.

After a year or so of moving picture work with almost no feedback, Florence and others must have been gratified that trade journal *Moving Picture World* finally started reviewing the films in October 1908, rather than merely summarizing the action from the publicity releases. Under the heading "Comments on Film Subjects," films were briefly reviewed with story summary limited to naming the genre of the film, if that.[23] Linda Arvidson most vividly remembered when films began to be reviewed in the *New York Times* exactly a year later and that Frank Woods at the *New York Dramatic Mirror* began reviewing films in June 1908 as "The Spectator."[24] *Moving Picture World*'s reviews were at best ragged for the first several years. Reviewing filmwork, being an art form all of its own, was finding its own voice during this period. When films were not taken seriously, reviews were not taken seriously. One week the harried reviewer watched Biograph's *Taming of the Shrew* and didn't know what to make of it: "A rather confused film, presented on an overcrowded stage." The next week, either he or another reviewer watched it and bubbled over with enthusiasm. "Too much praise cannot be bestowed on this picture. To tell the story of the taming of the shrew in moving pictures is a task that the cleverest of film makers might shrink without discredit.... As the subject is here presented it would please an audience of Shakespeare scholars and at the same time delight the humblest intelligence."[25]

Florence and Harry both were singled out in the second review, even though unnamed. "After seeing the play my first duty is to speak in unreserved praise of the lady who took the part of the shrew, and the gentleman who portrayed Petruchio [Arthur Johnson]. There is not a false move anywhere." Harry's credit ran into the writing department, where he and Griffith had collaborated: "A word of acknowledgement is also due to the adapter, who has done his work well."[26] Billy Bitzer tried to give Harry credit for playing Petruchio in his annotations on the Museum of Modern Art's copies of the Biograph Bulletins (eventually reprinted, notes and all, with an introduction by Eileen Bowser), an error that was picked up by several subsequent writers. Robert Ball points out that the actor was too tall to be Solter.

When all the dust had settled over the Shakespearean triumph, Griffith himself must have seriously watched the film. One modern writer commented, "This was Griffith's first Shakespearean film and, after viewing it, we can see why it was also his last."[27] Ball, in making a serious study of Shakespeare as condensed into a single reel, felt that the *Moving Picture World* commentary was "hardly acute and certainly over-enthusiastic," but adds that Florence Lawrence and Arthur Johnson acted with "pleasant zest."[28]

The year 1909 opened with a new whirl of roles and one reprised role—Mrs. Jones. The "Jonesy" comedies have long been credited as one of the first "series" of films that the public noticed. Older, portly John Cumpson portrayed the bewildered Mr. Jones (Mr. Bibbs in only the first film) and Florence was his pretty young wife, Emma. The stories were pure slapstick comedy, straight from vaudeville, where usually a misunderstanding escalated into the kind of comic violence which audiences loved. Florence enjoyed working with Cumpson. "Mr. Cumpson was the most serious comedian I have ever known. Nothing was ever funny to him, and he never tried to be funny," she said. "When all the rest of the company would laugh at something he had said or did, he would become indignant, thinking we were making fun of him."[29]

After the dramatic roles that she had been so successfully portraying, the recurring character of Mrs. Jones must have been a refreshing change. Emma Jones was a wealthy society-type lady with a broad sense of humor, and she took a devilish delight in confounding her husband. She also seemed to enjoys the scrapes he somehow managed to fall into. Carlos Bustamante, film historian, after viewing the film at the 1997 Pordenone Silent Film Festival in Italy, praised Florence's control as she rapidly changed emotions, purposely bringing about comical results. He summarized her motions from *The Joneses Have Amateur Theatricals*, describing how she employed classic histrionic movements with a few touches of pure Florence:

> Florence Lawrence enters the shot from the left and discovers Mr. Jones and Mrs. Trouble (John R. Cumpson and Marion Leonard) in an embrace. Florence steps back, faints into a chair, then recovers quickly. In rapid order, she kicks Mr. Jones in the bottom, separates him from Mrs. Trouble, all the while sweet-talking Mrs. Trouble (using her hands most expressively), then briefly changing her bodily expression, jabs quickly back at Mr. Jones' belly with her elbow while giving him the most evil stare, continuing her sweet and loving caresses of Mrs. Trouble's face, until Mr. Jones is left in a chair convulsed in pain and Mrs. Trouble in a chair on screen right sweet-charmed into submission. Florence, now center-stage, takes command. She seems to straighten her dress, almost unnoticeably, and with a quick hand movement also checks her hairdo. Suddenly she is shy and almost unsure of herself as she has won the attention of the play's director. As he moves toward her, she is surprised at being offered the leading part.[30]

Another favorite co-star of Florence's was Arthur V. Johnson. Johnson, the son of an Episcopalian minister, tended to be cast into wholesome or dignified roles. Johnson, unfortunately, was actually an alcoholic. His carefully developed on-screen demeanor usually hid his problems, especially later in his career. Florence enjoyed working with him despite his faults. "He is even funnier off the stage than on. When he gets one of those sanctimonious parts,

From left, Florence, Arthur Johnson and Clara T. Bracey in the 1909 Biograph film *The Resurrection*, based on Tolstoy's novel. The placement of the letters AB on the sideboard at Bracey's feet helped to prevent pirating of films by duplication. Photograph courtesy of the Museum of Modern Art.

which he just delights in, he keeps the whole company at a roar."[31] Lillian Gish recalled Griffith's opinion of Johnson was that he was "handsome, well educated and lazy."[32] Mary Pickford said that he drank even on their brief lunch breaks.[33] Florence did not seem to care about his off-screen behavior; to her, he was "such a delightful artist that it always was a pleasure to be cast to play opposite him."[34] Crossing his path in the future would be an excellent opportunity to expand upon their good acting kinship.

Florence played Katusha to Johnson's Dimitri in an adaptation of Tolstoy's *The Resurrection*, released on May 9, 1909. This stunning work amazed audiences and critics both. Fan mail mentioned the role even years later, and it was revived as late as 1917 for fund-raising benefits. The story, familiar to audiences then, is a simple one of class separation in imperial Russia, where the peasant woman is seduced by a prince and loses everything. In the end, the prince sacrifices all to be with her, only to be righteously rejected. Florence loved her role. "Mr. Johnson seemed so earnest and looked so handsome, and I so poor and ragged ... that the play appealed to me greatly." At the climax, when Prince Dimitri repents of his sins, reciting, "'I am the resurrection and the life,'" Florence said a strange atmosphere covered the set and the players: "Our souls seemed to rise above our earthly thoughts and surroundings."[35]

The reviewer for *Moving Picture World* could not have been more complimentary of the work as a whole, but especially of Florence's recognizable skills:

> We were curious to see how the Fourteenth Street Company interpreted Tolstoi's melancholy story. The public opinion on the film when we saw it echoed our own interest. As the picture started to move, there was a sudden hush in the theatre, which always indicates concentrated interest. And that hush continued right to the end of the film, when the afflicted girl kneels at the foot of the cross on the Siberian steppes. In these same scenes, where the fallen girl is on her way to Siberia in company with other unfortunates, and is knouted by Russian soldiers, there is an aspect of unreality, excessively sharp modeling and not particularly convincing snow, which we suppose could not be avoided owing to the exiguity of space at Fourteenth street. But in the preceding scenes, in which the peasant girl and the prince are shown in the urban environment, the pleasant sin and its penitential punishment for the girl and the unmolested freedom of her betrayer, the Biograph staging is quite as convincing as that of an ordinary play. And then the acting of the leading woman and the prince—how fine and tragic the former is! how excellent the latter! We do not know the lady's name, but certainly she seems to us to have a very fine command of her emotions and to be able to express these emotions before such an unemotional thing as a camera. A very ordinary person indeed can act before a crowded house of interested men and women, but it takes a genius to do so with real feeling on a moving picture stage.[36]

In 1917, the film was shown at a Red Cross fund-raiser in Westwood, New Jersey, in Florence's honor. The writer covering the event commented on the unbelievability that the whole of Tolstoy's drama was "crowded" into a 15-minute film. "Yet in the Griffith production the story is clearly outlined and the meat of the drama has been extracted."[37] If an audience a mere eight years later was dubious, then an audience over 80 years later is downright incredulous.

The Resurrection was one of Griffith's most far-reaching attempts. During the time that Florence was there, he also directed *A Fool's Revenge*, based on Rigoletto, and *The Necklace*, an adaptation of the Guy de Maupassant story. Other subjects are so insignificant that a half-reel seems infinitely long for them. *The Wooden Leg* is one of these; Florence was Claire, a girl who successfully rebuffed an unwanted suitor by pretending to have a wooden leg.

Florence continued to receive accolades for her anonymous work in the pages of *Moving Picture World*. In its lengthy review for *Lady Helen's Escapade*, the reviewer first gave Florence the nickname "the Biograph Girl." The review also highly praised the entire company for their work in this charming comedy. "The acting in this film is superb. Each character stands out by the Biograph players with unflinching decision and conviction.... Of course, the chief honors of the picture are borne by the now famous Biograph girl who must be gratified by the silent celebrity she has achieved. This lady combines with very great personal attractions very fine dramatic ability indeed."[38]

Several of Florence's films under Griffith are still regarded today as breakthroughs in technique and style. The November 3, 1908, release, *After Many Years*, a very free adaptation of Alfred, Lord Tennyson's poem "Enoch Arden," involved a waist-high close-up of Florence, intercut with a scene of her lost husband (Charles Inslee) which indicated that they were thinking of one another. Tom Gunning points out that Florence's expressive movement of holding open her arms, shown immediately after Inslee kisses a picture of her in a locket, transcends the usual melodramatic expectations of the gesture. Griffith uses the parallel of these actions as an exclamation point in course of the narrative; "Through editing, Griffith creates a space of the imagination in which these gestures meet in a phantom embrace."[39] Gunning's understanding of the film is different from Linda Arvidson's. She remembered that Frank Woods adapted the scenario, that the Biograph management thought it would flop, and that *After Many Years* was very emotionally quiet. "It was the first movie without a chase ... [It] was also the first picture to have a *dramatic* close-up—the first picture to have a cut-back ... It was the first picture to be recognized by foreign markets." Linda's memories were at best generous. Griffith himself barely remembered the film by 1916, remembering that his rivals called the close-up work a "silly revolutionary method." His rivals also claimed that his work would probably ruin the film industry.[40] Florence does not mention *After Many Years* at all in her memoirs.

She did not recall *The Barbarian, Ingomar* either, though it contained another protracted cut back, where Paranthia (Florence) is being held at sword point, interspersed with a shot of Ingomar (Inslee) running toward her location. Griffith remembered *Ingomar* as a film "that went far toward sustaining all of my ideas which had been used in its making."[41] This film, made and released before *After Many Years*, was a practice run for Griffith. The cut used here did not have the psychological punch as the one used later, but it still contributed to the flow of excitement in the story line.[42]

Griffith used alternating scenes in *The Song of the Shirt* (November 17, 1908) to show how the two halves in society lived, a theme he continued to work on throughout his career. Kay Sloan, watching the film from a socially conscious standpoint, said that Florence's face "projected both strength and fragility" in the telling of two poor sisters, one dying and the other trying to earn a living by sewing. The tenement squalor the young women were forced to live in was depicted in scenes that were intercut with depictions of the factory owners dancing and drinking wine. "The contrast among the three merrymakers, lifting their champagne glasses, and the heroine, treading away at her sewing machine, needed no words to explain that, in Griffith's eyes, the wealthy did not care about the plight of the poor."⁴³ The review in *Moving Picture World* accuses the film company of abusing its storytelling license by distorting the original source of the story and its title, a poem by Thomas Hood. "The last scenes are a bit overdrawn and the notion that all people who have money must needs be dehumanized, the film makers must have borrowed from the cheap melodrama; they never found it in Hood." Perhaps the reviewer was not as familiar with the poem as he indicated, for even the last stanza of the poem clearly censures the wealthy:

> With fingers weary and worn,
> With eyelids heavy and red,
> A woman sat in unwomanly rags,
> Plying her needle and thread—
> Stitch! stitch! stitch!
> In poverty, hunger, and dirt;
> And still with a voice of dolorous pitch—
> Would that its tone reach the rich!—
> She sang this "Song of the Shirt!"⁴⁴

Despite this erroneous rebuke, the reviewer praised the acting and the staging—"This is a good film."⁴⁵

The Biograph Company finally began allowing field trips further abroad than the "wilds" of Fort Lee, New Jersey, where all of the Westerns were filmed. Cuddebackville, New York, hidden in the Shawangunk Mountains, was an ideal spot to photograph many outdoor scenes that could be worked into interior shots taken in the studio. Eight years later, even Griffith was reluctant to reveal its exact location for fear of spoiling its natural beauty. "Cuddybuckville [sic] is a place where Goldsmith could have written as he did of Auburn; which Tennyson would have peopled with the lovely majesty of romance; and where in our small way we found the perfect 'location,'" he said. "There is a quality about the light there, particularly a twilight that I have never found elsewhere."⁴⁶ Florence particularly enjoyed being out in the country, not just at Cuddebackville. She fell in love with Commodore Benedict's home on Long Island Sound where the Biographers were frequent guests, writing under a picture of it in her scrapbook, "The most beautiful place I have ever seen. I wish I owned it."⁴⁷

The importance of the Biograph Company in these early years of filmmaking must be emphasized. The vast amount of amazing talent and the output of excellent films have earned it a rightful place in film history. Many of the actors who worked for Griffith from 1908 through 1913 became famous and productive stars in the years to come—Mary Pickford, Mabel Normand, Marion Leonard, Blanche Sweet, Lillian Gish, Dorothy Gish, Mae Marsh, Henry Walthall, Charles Murray, Flora Finch, Owen Moore and Florence

LaBadie are but a few who made good careers based on their work with Griffith. And also not surprisingly, Griffith also produced a record number of directors who claimed to have been under his tutelage—Harry Solter, Mack Sennett, Thomas Ince, George Nicholls, Frank Powell, E.V. Stanner Taylor and Billy Quirk, among others. One writer in 1913 thought that even without his wonderful film work, Griffith's gift of spotting and developing great players would have been memorable. "Probably the best service he performed for the art in America was the training he gave to the actors and actresses who worked with him and who now occupy lucrative positions by reason of that experience."[48]

Spring 1909 brought yet another new face into the Biograph fold. A young woman with a long list of stage experiences, a pert face and long golden curls appeared at the door of the studio, seeking extra work until she could land her next Broadway job. Mary Pickford, formerly Gladys Smith of Toronto, Canada, brought with her a mastery of the new style of restrained acting, plus a quick and creative mind that Griffith used to its fullest. Florence liked her from the beginning. "From the first, Mary won our hearts with her charming ways," Florence said. "She possesses a pout and a frown all her own, which are irresistible." Florence, Mary and Gertrude Robinson began a long-running joke among the three of them about who was the tallest and who was the shortest. Florence remembered, "Mary did not like being called little and Gertrude claimed to be taller than Mary and me." Finally they realized that a wardrobe dress that Florence wore did not touch the ground as when Mary wore it, establishing Florence as at least taller than Mary. "Whenever I meet Mary we always start that same old argument," Florence laughed. In 1914, Florence summed up her feelings about Mary Pickford most favorably: "I am glad of Mary's success, and hope that she will always remain just as unspoiled, as little and sweet and dear as she really is today."[49]

However kind Florence was in print, there must have been some jealousy between the two talented actresses. Florence no doubt recognized the greater abilities Mary possessed when acting before a camera. Mary was ahead of her time in terms of acting style and place in the film world. The younger girl was also paid more than Florence was. Of course, Mary was soon to rise to superstar status within a few years, separating herself from the rest of the world, mentally and physically, for the rest of her life. Florence was only one in the legions of fellow actors who would end up in Mary's dust.

Mary was the biggest threat Florence had faced yet in her career. This "elfin like little girl" now was taking the roles that Florence had been used to getting. In the June 28, 1909, release *The Way of Man*, Mary even ends up on the arm of Arthur Johnson at the end when Florence appears to have committed suicide after having an accident that left her face scarred. Florence, playing the sympathetic protagonist in that film, still received the high accolades that she was accustomed to in the reviews: "The famous Biograph heroine suffered patiently under her temporary disfigurement ... a very excellent Biograph comedy subject which did not end in tragedy."[50] Florence used mostly verisimilar actions when displaying her dismay at seeing fiancé Johnson with cousin Mary. Roberta Pearson analyzed her actions in the scene:

> Retreating to the next room, she leans over the back of a chair for a few seconds, her arms straight down the chair back. Then she walks slowly to front center, hands at sides, staring dully ahead. She picks up a hand mirror, looks at her reflection, puts a hand over the mirror, and shakes her head. She then puts an arm to her forehead. With the exception of the last gesture, Lawrence does not use her customary histrionic gestures, but embodies her character's thoughts through body posture, a slight movement of her head, and the look in the mirror.[51]

Florence's restraint played well against Mary's, generating even more sympathy for her character by reacting as a woman would, not as an actress would. Audiences grasped the meanings instantly. "'You can see them thinking,'" announced one viewer within earshot of a *Moving Picture World* writer as *The Way of Man* unfolded.[52] Somehow even the campy ending is easier to swallow with the simple character identification; instead of living happily ever after, Florence's character fakes her death in order to work anonymously and satisfactorily at an orphanage. Florence's own life would eerily parallel parts of this story line in the months to come.

Another snag in the Biograph life was evident from Florence's 1914 memoirs. She began to resent the speed with which she and the other actors were expected to deliver their scenes, whatever the emotions to be displayed. Griffith's official response was that the exhibitors wanted action, not "illustrated song slides." Slow scenes to them meant money was being wasted. Florence, an avid student of film even in those days, dreamed of making films like the French actresses she so admired. Without directly criticizing Griffith, Florence praised the Pathé imports released as Film d'Art brand names. "In naturalness, they were far ahead of anything yet produced in this country, and largely for the reason that the important artists portraying the chief roles were permitted to do things as their training had taught them." Florence lamented about how things were being done at Biograph. "We made our work quick and snappy, crowding as much story in a thousand feet picture as is now portrayed in five thousand feet of film." A scene which should have taken four minutes to truly enact was crammed into 40 feet of film (or about 20 seconds), according to Florence.

Florence did not like this rushed acting style that Griffith was pushing on them, as a result of pressure he was obviously feeling from the Biograph office. Florence said that "nearly all of the Biograph players asked Mr. Griffith to be allowed slow acting, only to be refused." Given Griffith's huge contributions to film, Florence's comments border on treason, or at least disgruntlement. But Mary Pickford too refused to overact a scene, as did Lillian

Gish. Both of these actresses would take the art of hidden emotions and subtlety to new dimensions in the next few years under the direction of Griffith, while Florence retained her own natural, open style. At the very end of the Biograph installment of her memoirs, Florence conceded that Griffith had finally begun to allow his actors slow acting just as she was leaving the company, adding, "American film manufacturers woke up to the fact that they were on the wrong track in producing pictures showing human beings doing things at about four times the speed of real life."[53]

The sheer number of films that Biograph was creating at this time probably had something to do with Griffith's "official" response. When viewing the films Florence made for Biograph in 1908 and 1909 back-to-back, keeping in mind that audiences then were seeing them week-to-week, the output is dizzying. A modern viewer can believe the latter-day pronouncements of critics who claim all Griffith ever did was create last-minute rescues and switch-backed chase scenes, for these do stand in the mind after seeing many of these films. What tends to be lost are the little things—the caress between mother and child, the glance between lovers, the look on a face when an idea enters the mind—that made Griffith great, regardless of the innovations of exactly where the camera was placed or how often he cut from one scene to another. Early in Griffith's career, *Moving Picture World* noticed how detailed and precise his work was, even though they were not supposed to know his name. In 1913, just before Griffith trumpeted his successes in advertisements in the *New York Dramatic Mirror* and *Moving Picture World*, writer Louis Reeves Harrison tried to pinpoint his success: "His best interpreters give us the essence of this or that emotion instead of moving around like a lot of lay figures worked by invisible strings. He peels away the rind of human character; tears away the mask and bares the soul that has been hiding behind it ... He will fasten attention with immobility and suddenly transform silent mystery into tremendous revelation."[54] Viewing the master's work is awe-inspiring; seeing the master at work must have been unbelievable.

Harry Solter felt that he had learned enough to become a director just by watching Griffith's unique techniques. Between his wife's unhappiness and his own ambition, he hatched a plan that would give them some freedom to do as they wished. He wanted to go to another film company to apply for a director's job, and Florence could take the leading actress position. Before, when Florence and others were switching companies, any actions came at the company's request. Daily extras without guarantees or contracts may have had some freedom, but established members of the stock companies simply did not move around at their leisure.

However, what seems easily enough done was actually fraught with intrigue and involved other people's plans. While the Solters had been at Biograph, in September 1909, the film manufacturing companies that agreed to honor Edison's patents on the moving picture equipment had joined together to pool these patents and their assets. They were known as "licensed" companies, or members of the Motion Picture Patents Company—the Trust. Biograph had been a holdout for some time, claiming its camera was different, but eventually it joined Vitagraph, Essanay, Kalem, Selig, Lubin, Pathé, Méliès, Kleine and of course Edison. With these resources, the Trust could hold the industry firmly in check. No one but the licensed companies could buy film, for the Trust had an agreement with Kodak. An unspoken hierarchical system was established, from the heads of the Trust through the presidents of each company through directors, then with the actual actors taking the bottommost rungs of the ladder, second only perhaps to errand boys. By approaching another company on their own, the Solters would remove some of the power that these licensed companies had over a player. Such an action was unheard of at that time.

No sooner than the plan was put into motion than the Solters found pink slips in their pay envelopes. They were unemployed.

Chapter Four

LAEMMLE'S IMP

We are just grinding out sausages, Billy, and will continue to do so as long as we remain here.
—D.W. Griffith to Billy Bitzer

Why were Florence and Harry fired from the Biograph Company? One historian has called it "presumption,"[1] but the answer is deeper than that. The Trust saw itself as one ideally unified organization, with each studio as a factory and each actor as a daily-paid worker. The output of the Trust was not yet in direct competition with the legitimate stage, but thought to learn a lesson from the expansive star system already developed by the theater and, more recently, vaudeville. Artists competing for top billing, negotiating more elaborate contracts, and demanding royal treatment by vendors were items that the Trust could avoid by keeping their actors in the dark—literally. No names on the screen, no names in the press.

Modern Americans are used to seeing and knowing actors from films, television and other media, plus the oftentimes intrusive knowledge of an actor's private life. The idea of going to a movie, not knowing who was in it or anything beyond the movie's title (except maybe the production company), is completely foreign to us today. In the early days, the novelty of moving pictures brought people to the door the first time; the talent or appeal of a certain performer within a certain company may have had a lot to do with bringing them back again. And again.

Florence knew all too well the power of the stage and what top billing was. She recognized the specifics of what the public—her public—was seeking. She also knew what she was capable of and what she liked to do.

Essanay Film Company, formed in February 1907 by George K. Spoor and Gilbert M. "Broncho Billy" Anderson, had begun making Western pictures as early as 1908 in Golden, Colorado, and San Rafael, California.[2]

Anderson, actor-author-director-producer, could barely ride a horse when beginning his seven-year reign as king of this genre. But the Western explosion was just beginning. George Spratt said producers initially thought the Western "lowly" at first, "but Westerns represented nonetheless a steady source of income."[3] Ever since 1903's *The Great Train Robbery*, crowds packed little theaters to see more cowboys and horses. According to Spratt, the first big year of the Western was 1910—not a coincidence for Florence Lawrence.

More than likely, Florence had seen Essanay's output over the last year or so. She probably recognized the fact that Anderson was not a true equestrian. She almost certainly had noticed that he went through leading ladies rather quickly. Spratt explained in *Image* magazine that Anderson traveled with as few as possible—extras, including the ladies, were picked up along the way. All too often, stunts led to accidents, which took out its fair share of Anderson's actresses.[4] Florence knew what Essanay needed—herself. She could ride and travel and grub with the best of them. "I'd rather ride a horse than eat," she told the *St. Louis Post-Dispatch* the next year. "When I am riding before the moving picture camera, I really forget the picture and everything else. And I always act better in such scenes because I am not acting at all. I am just having fun."[5] Even four years after her brush with Essanay, Florence was still wistful about her lack of Western themes: "Of late the pictures I have appeared in have not called for much of this kind of work, but that fact has not dampened my ardor for galloping 'cross country at breakneck speed. Also, I intend working in some pictures soon in which my equestrian abilities will be needed and then you shall see."[6]

So with a dream of saddles and mountains, Harry and Florence wrote a letter to Essanay Studios offering their services as director and actress. If Essanay had accepted, Florence and Harry would have been among the true pioneers of the tiny town of Hollywood. Someone else would eventually have taken up Carl Laemmle's challenge to be his "IMP Girl." Florence Lawrence would have become one of the thousands of forgotten silent film stars swallowed up in Hollywood glitter.

But Essanay turned the Solters down. Was it Trust fear? Trust loyalty? Unwritten Trust policy? Whatever the "presumption" that Florence and Harry displayed, Essanay felt that they could not take the chance of hiring away one of Biograph's brightest stars. Florence, a proven player with box office appeal, had a rather famous face. Perhaps that fragile, anonymous fame that she had been granted as the "Biograph Girl" made Essanay afraid they could not afford her or keep her. At least one modern writer has suggested that Essanay was afraid that other Trust studios would try to hire away their own stars.[7]

Florence's last film with Biograph was in late June or early July 1909. In her book *When the Movies Were Young*, Linda Arvidson Griffith used a photograph of the open registration book from the Caudebec Inn in Cuddebackville, New York, dated July 20, 1909. No Lawrence or Solter was listed.[8]

This was D.W. Griffith's second trip to the rural locale; during the first, the company filmed *The Mended Lute*, among others.

When the door shut behind them at Biograph, Florence and Harry found the doors of the other Trust companies shut as well. None of the licensed manufacturers would hire them. Whether they attempted to find work at one or all of the other film studios is unclear. In 1924, *Photoplay* called this the industry's first case of blacklisting,[9] although Florence's crime today seems trivial considering the studio-jumping to come.

Florence, undaunted, fell back on her oldest resource for help—her mother. With her help, Florence secured a position with Ezra Kendall to tour with a new play. What Harry did is uncertain. One very modern source, the sprawling and undocumented Internet Movie Database, gives Harry credit for four Biograph films during 1910. His old friend Griffith may have been able to sneak the rubbery character actor in for a few roles while Florence worked at IMP. Just how long Florence worked for Kendall is also confusing; one interview claims she was just about to start when Laemmle's call came,[10] another says she was on the road for a month.[11] Kendall died in February 1910.

The length of time that she and Harry were out of work is also confusing. To the layman's eyes, and to a great many movie historians, she was out of the pictures until her big splash back into the limelight with IMP in February 1910. But a closer look shows that Florence began work after only a few idle months, possibly by September. A small notice in the *Variety* of October 16, 1909, shows Laemmle's claim that "Miss Lawrence, the former star actress with the Biograph's stock company, has been with the Laemmle firm for the past six weeks."[12] *Love's Stratagem* is generally accepted to be Florence's first IMP release, on November 1, 1909. The first IMP film was released the week before: *Hiawatha*, starring little Gladys Hulette, Vitagraph's young actress from *Princess Nicotine*,[13] and Leah Baird.

Going independent was a considerable risk, because outside the Trust, American independent filmmakers simply were not allowed to exist. Independent films that were shown were imported from foreign producers. Names such as Harstn, Warwick, Méliès, and Itala show just where these films originated. Independent films, however, had begun to take on a life of their own in March of 1909 in *Moving Picture World* when their reviews were listed as separate from the "Licensed Films."[14]

Enter Carl Laemmle.

Laemmle was recognized by the film industry at that time as one of the most successful film renters imaginable. A January 9, 1909, *Moving Picture World* interview, written by Laemmle's partner Robert Cochran, elaborated on his great success as a start-up theater owner from Chicago after a highly profitable career as a clothing store manager in Oshkosh, Wisconsin. Terry Ramsaye's lighthearted account of the bonding between Cochran and Laemmle reads like Laemmle's airy advertising strategies. Laemmle, burned out from selling men's clothes, turned to adman Cochran for advice. Cochran tried to steer him back into clothing when Laemmle noticed the number of dimes flowing into a movie theater. Patiently Laemmle kept track of the storefront's profits and traffic, then turned all information over to Cochran for his perusal. "There is no suspense to the story," Ramsaye assured his readers. "Laemmle effectively sold the motion picture idea to Cochran that afternoon."[15] That was 1906. At a remote site on Milwaukee Avenue, Laemmle set up shop. His first week's profits were over $100 and kept climbing.

"The thing that bothered him most was his inability to secure the very best pictures," Cochran said of Laemmle in the *Moving Picture World* interview. "So he decided to take the next step upward and become a 'lessor' himself."[16] Six months after opening his Chicago theater, Laemmle became a distributor, loudly advertising his products and services. Business boomed, and he opened seven branch offices within a year. Because this interview should generally be regarded as a press release from Laemmle himself, the figures of $10,000 per week profit should be taken with the proverbial grain of salt. Nonetheless, Laemmle was a giant in the moving picture distributing game, and in June 1909, he went one step further and became a film manufacturer. His plans were vaguely alluded to in the May 22 *Moving Picture World*, but he went public in June with full-page advertising and a small formal announcement that he was becoming a manufacturer: "He is set about the business in the best possible manner—that is, a business-like one. He will have the best equipped plant and the best available talent for working it. He will also produce American pieces by American writers. Moreover, he will personally supervise the production of the pictures."[17]

Laemmle conveniently left for Europe soon after this announcement to escape the public and private wrath of the Trust. Early in July, he was evidently back and in full force, announcing the name of his new company as IMP, short for Independent Moving Pictures Company of America, complete with the soon-to-be overexposed devil trademark. (In an advertisement, Laemmle bestowed a $25 prize to Mr. Charles M. Mapes of New York City for suggesting the name and making a rough sketch of the trademark.[18]) Laemmle did not immediately begin production, taking his time to put together the best that he could afford. *Moving Picture World* again was his forum when he declared that he "was willing to spend $50,000 to carry out his ideas and would not publish a single film until it was technically and artistically beyond criticism."[19]

The talent that Laemmle assembled was indeed impressive. William V. Ranous, Florence's former director at Vitagraph, was among the first to come aboard. George Loane Tucker, John Brownell and J. Farrell MacDonald were the other directors Laemmle hired. Players eventually included Hulette, Owen Moore, John "Mr. Jones" Cumpson, Thomas Ince and King Baggot.

The hiring of King Baggot was considered quite a coup. Laemmle biographer John Drinkwater extolled on his talent: "An upstanding young man of good looks ... was persuaded to put on grease paint and try a small part as a screen test. This proving satisfactory, he was invited to join the company. William De Mille, also impressed with the novice's possibilities, stepped in with an offer of a hundred dollars a week in the theater from which he had not yet extended his activities to the screen, but with no guarantee as to its duration. Laemmle offered seventy-five, but on a fifty-two-week contract, and King Baggot signed up as the first IMP leading man."[20] Baggot, born in 1879 in St. Louis, was embarking into motion pictures rather late in his career. A real estate agent, semi-professional soccer player and popular regional theater actor, Baggot had founded the Players Club in St. Louis in 1900, an early incarnation of his 1912 Screen Club. In 1909, Baggot was scheduled to be on the road with Margarite Clark and William Dempster in *The Wishing Ring* through its November finale in Chicago. At its end, Baggot returned to New York immediately to take up Laemmle's offer.

A striking photo of handsome King Baggot, Florence's leading man at IMP in 1909 and 1910. The two remained friends throughout her life. Photograph courtesy of Sally Dumaux.

Baggot's memory of coming into motion pictures varies slightly from Laemmle's. For a 1915 magazine, he told interviewer Selwyn Standhope that he chanced upon old stage friend Harry Solter in a Greek shoe-shining parlor. Baggot said Solter seemed "just a little ashamed" to be in moving pictures and had himself personally dismissed them as much of an art form: "I was amused at the violent gestures and jumping about of the players, and mentally characterized the industry as a fad."[21] After some soul-searching, Baggot went over to motion pictures. His first IMP film was *The Awakening of Bess*, released the last week in December 1909.[22]

Florence remembered becoming an IMP player in the summer of 1909, according to her 1914 autobiography. She there claimed to have been on the road with Ezra Kendall for a month when she received a telegram from William Ranous: "'I am helping to start a new moving picture company and want you for my leading lady. Come to New York at once.'" Florence went.[23] Mindful of the IMP's delicate position as an independent, Florence and Harry approached the new company with some trepidation. Laemmle's fight with the Trust was not only hard on him, but also on the employees. Florence remembered Laemmle's battles well: "At times it looked as though he would lose every dollar. This legal battle prevented him from tying up any great amount of money in IMP productions until they became popular with the public."[24] King Baggot said, "We had a lot of trouble producing a picture."[25]

The struggle to make IMP films marketable was also recounted by Florence: "At first our photography was poor, and we experienced many difficulties getting suitable settings."[26] Props and scenery were hastily improvised on even more improvised sets. Florence claimed that *Love's Stratagem*, her first IMP release, had no interior shots because there was no studio, almost impossible to believe knowing Laemmle's planning. The shoddy working conditions were a far cry from Biograph's precision, but evidently continued even after Florence left in 1910. When Mary Pickford left Biograph in late 1910 for IMP, she stayed only nine months. Mary told *Ladies' Home Journal* in 1923 of her dissatisfaction with the IMP films: "The pictures taken by the 'IMP' company were not good. The photography was poor, and they did not light the pictures properly."[27]

Reviews for the earliest IMP films in *Moving Picture World* were lukewarm. "No American film manufacturer has more openly invited criticism or shown more willingness to profit by it than the 'Imp'. The first releases of the Independent Moving Picture Company were naturally the weakest technically, and we pointed out that this was only to be expected in a new concern. But how quickly they have improved. The third 'Imp' film was better than the second, but the photographic quality of the fourth places the 'Imp' far up among the older manufacturers and decidedly in advance of some who have been longer in the business."[28] Clever storylines or clear scenes were the only praiseworthy items in the earliest IMP films. By the middle of January, *Moving Picture World* could not be kinder to the upstarts: Referring to the January 17 release *The Tide of Fortune*, "The story is clean and ennobling—the acting is good and then some—the photography equal in quality to the best work of much older firms. All this should be encouraging to the 'Imp.'"[29]

The first IMP films had some extraordinary story lines, an interesting mixture of comedies and dramas that the reviewer of *Moving Picture World* liked. *The Tide of Fortune*, released January 17, 1910, was a strong drama of a prodigal black sheep son that brought down the house: "There were few dry eyes in the old Fourteenth Street Theatre on Monday while the changing scenes in *The Tide of Fortune* were being flashed across the screen. Women had us for their handkerchiefs and strong men were visibly affected."[30] The March 7 release *Mother Love* sounds absurdly morbid, but audiences of the era loved the pathos in a mother's insanity: "If the 'Imp' continues to give us pictures of the kind and quality of *Mother Love* the independent exhibitors will not lack headliners for their programs."[31] *The Eternal Triangle*, the May 23 release, left only one after a murder and a suicide: "The unfortunate thing about this film is that it is much too true to life."[32]

None of the IMP players are mentioned by name during that first year; in fact, if the actors and actresses are noted at all, they are mentioned as a group. The photography and the plot were first on the reviewers' agenda. Articles outside of the reviewer's column revealed other fascinating stories of life on the IMP set. In *Mother Love*, the mother loses her senses after the death of her baby. An article in *Moving Picture World* tells how the death of the baby was credibly shown: "It is a trick with moving picture producers, when it is necessary to show a dead baby on the sheet, to cover a dummy and lay it on the bed as required. But now, for the first time in the history of motion picture making, the feat of using a real baby has been accomplished ... The picture shows the infant on a little bed, face to the camera, with nary a quiver of an eyebrow to destroy the illusion that it had just passed into the land of angels, nor did it move a muscle all through the scene."[33] Harry Solter, credited by some with directing this picture, took two hours to get the child to sleep for the few moments' scene on film, an extravagant measure that made an impact. Later that month, *Transfusion* was released, with an interesting story regarding the treatment of hospital scenes: "The director called in two physicians, who, besides supplying the appropriate surgical instruments, were given carte blanche in superintending the setting of the scene."[34] The cast then enacted a scene showing an actual blood transfusion, a relatively new procedure in medicine, where a man gives blood to save a woman's life, and they fall in love.

IMP kept Florence busy while turning out a one-reel film per week. In February, Laemmle announced in his usual fashion that two reels per week would be done: "Thank Heavens! We're Ready To Release Two Imp Reels A Week! In spite of frantic letters and telegrams from exhibitors and exchanges, we've been holding off on this double release plan until we were dead sure we could maintain our high standard of quality. And <u>now</u> we're dead sure of it. Our new studio is working gloriously, every member of the staff is enthused to the highest pitch and we think you'll be just as daffy as we are over our next two releases. Monday and Thursday will be our release dates."[35]

This additional reel each week probably suggests when Harry Solter formally took over directing Florence's films and career. Whether he directed any of the IMP films up to this point is debatable. King Baggot said that the director of *The Awakening of Bess* was William Ranous,[36] which makes sense. An experienced director such as Ranous would have been used before Laemmle would have turned over the control to Solter, who could have only had limited exposure to actual directing under Griffith. Solter, an actor at heart, may have been as deliberate about learning from Griffith while working at Biograph as Mack Sennett apparently was; Sennett remembered following Griffith around everywhere to pick up directing skills. "So far as my knowledge of motion-picture technique goes, I learned all I ever learned by standing around, watching people who know, by pumping Griffith and thinking it over,"[37] Sennett wrote in his autobiography. Whether Solter observed Griffith as closely remained to be seen. A production still of *The Eternal Triangle* shows Solter in the cast;[38] Solter probably did not possess the capability of directing himself at this point, and he rarely appeared in Florence's pictures after it is positive that he did begin directing. And again, the Internet Movie Database puts Harry in several Biograph films during 1910. If he was not directing, he may not have been completely idle.

The IMP was technically a success from the start. Laemmle had proved his point. Now what remained was securing more than his share of the business. He wanted real fame and exposure. His chance was coming, for, unbeknownst to him, the moviegoers had begun to notice that the new IMP Girl and the old Biograph Girl looked strangely alike.

Chapter Five

St. Louis

The lantern was about to create a new kind of human being on the face of the world, the movie star, a demigodlike person who would be worshipped by dime-store girls and farm hands, millionaires and Society. Come to think of it, no emperor, king, president, or prime minister had ever known the worldwide fame or the affection enjoyed by a full-blown movie star.
—Mack Sennett

Carl Laemmle's publicity campaign for Florence began at the beginning of 1910, soon after the idea of using performers' names in marketing became a hot topic within the industry. Kalem, a member of the Trust Company, began offering distributors photo-lobby cards of their stock company in the January 15, 1910, issue of *Moving Picture World*. A week later, Florence's name was used in an IMP advertisement in *Show World* magazine: "[*Coquette's Suitor* is] a picture that gives Miss Lawrence the best opportunity she has had for months to work up some hilarious comedy."[1]

Performers were not yet expected to sell a film to the distributors; film relied mostly on the name of the manufacturer, then on the genre, then on length (whole or half reel). Combinations of films were supposed to be carefully screened and put together in a way that created a flow of events—drama, travel story, song slide, comedy—to make up an evening's entertainment. Distributors relied on industry magazines such as *Moving Picture World*, which was in a class by itself, to help put together the strongest program possible to draw in patrons. Performers were simply not a factor in this process. Laemmle's statement using "Miss Lawrence" was an industry first—one that was not duplicated immediately.

The idea was slow to start. When Kalem began advertising their lobby card art, *Moving Picture World* covered their proposal with their usual mixture of journalism and commentary: "The idea is an old one as applied to the regular theaters and would no doubt make good in the picture field, but it is very doubtful that it [is] in hearty accord with the exhibitors in the project, and so are the manufacturers." *Moving Picture World* went on to blame the actors and actresses themselves with holding back the publicity flow. "They have an undisguised impression that the step from the regular productions to the scenes before the camera is a backward one." If the actor was publicly advertised as being in moving pictures, regular ("legitimate") theater managers and the public would not want them, because "the speaking parts are cut out [in films], so far as the audience is concerned, and in spite of the fact that some remarkably clever and effective work is done these days in the pictures, the fact that it is in reality pantomimic work makes the people playing the parts feel that their artistic reputations would suffer should it be known they were playing parts in moving picture studios." But even the biased *Moving Picture World* writer conceded, "Conditions will eventually change and the performers will not feel they have as much at stake as they do now."[2]

But the lack of publicity about the players did not dim the enthusiasm of film goers. Florence's absence from Biograph had already been noticed by the fans, a fact driven home by the offhandedly honest letter by P.C. Levar from Coos Bay, Oregon. Printed originally in *Daily Coast Mail* in January 1910 and reprinted in *Moving Picture World* the next month, Mr. Levar's letter reveals how much the early stars meant to their public:

> Dear Sir,
> I have the honour to announce that your man who writes "Comments on the Films" is as crazy as a bedbug. Through the courtesy of manager Keller of the Orpheum here, I have just seen what you say in your issue of the December 18 about "Through the Breakers" and "The Biograph Girl." That picture was shown here during the past week, and—that isn't the Biograph Girl at all. She is all right; she is the handsomest girl (or lady) on the moving picture stage; she is a superb and charming actress; she is in every way adorable; we are all glad to see her appearing here regularly, for we thought, a while back, that we had lost her—but she is not "the Biograph Girl" not THE Biograph Girl.
> The Biograph Girl who won all the hearts, male and female, in this neck of the woods was the one who used to play Mrs. Jones in the Jones comedies. I could mention a lot more of her parts, but that one is the easiest to clearly and briefly designate. She has been gone from "the bunch" for months and the Biograph people should be lynched for letting her get away. She is, or was, with the IMP and appeared in "The Forest Ranger's Daughter" which dropped in here on a special occasion. Look in the IMP ad in your issues of the above date and you will see a horribly poor picture of her. Now that is, or was, the Biograph Girl—and I am confident that you could find about 8,000,000 people in the United States who would agree with me. You could find a lot of them in this town, and only one who would agree with you in liking the Beauty better.
> But that girl was simply out of sight—unapproachable. She was in a

class by herself. In every part she played she was an exquisite delight. Whether comic, pathetic, dramatic, tragic or any other old thing, she simply took the rag right off. The power of expression that lay in her features was nothing less than marvelous, and the lightning changes were a wonder. In fact, she was a wonder altogether, and her versatility would be unbelievable, if a fellow hadn't seen it. To see her play Mrs. Jones in a tantrum and then see her as the Russian nihilist girl, for instance, in a drama of which I have forgotten the name; as a young girl; as a mother; to see her as a highly polished society lady, one time, and at another time see her straddle a cayuse as a Western girl and ride like a wild Indian—to see her take these widely varying parts and play each as though she were in her native elements, with every pose and motion and expression in perfect harmony with the character—all this was a revelation. And to see her in a love scene was enough to draw a fellow right across the continent, if he were not fifty years old, and married—and broke.

And now you think someone else is the Biograph Girl! If you think I am off my base, you go and see that girl in some IMP picture where she has some chance—if they make such. And that is the deuce of it. She doesn't belong anywhere else but with the Biograph people. They are the only ones who have regular plays that call for and bring out her grade of talent. But look it up anyway, and see if I am not right.

Yours very truly,
P.C. Levar[3]

The offices of every Trust company had to have noticed and taken seriously Levar's letter. So should have other players; after all, Florence *was* one of them, a refugee from the stage in front of the camera. If the Trust companies were unwilling to provide names for their players, and the players were unwilling to provide photographs, where would the push for publicity come from other than the fans? The answer may simply have been from the distributors. "Managers of picture theaters and nickelodeons all over the country are making repeated requests upon the producers of moving picture subjects for photographs of the principal actresses and actors taking part in them," *Moving Picture World* said in January 1910. "The managers of the places now see a big advertising advantage in the display of such photographs in the lobbies of their theaters."[4]

If the requests were truly numerous—and Laemmle, with his fingers on the distributors' pulse, would know—and the Trust that unwilling, what else could Laemmle do but to take advantage of the opportunity? Advertising the players would go against one more Trust grain, but Laemmle did not mind. Perhaps the Trust considered Kalem's experiment with lobby cards just that—an experiment. With such a halfhearted attempt, the results were naturally limited as well.

Florence Lawrence was obviously willing enough to use her name unflinchingly and unsparingly. Her exact role in the whole new publicity game was unclear—instigator, partner or victim. Regardless, she cheerfully went along with Laemmle's plans, presenting a pleasing personality in person and an even more charming actress in print. She had proved already that she was more than a replaceable, fleeting image on the screen. She had fans—fans who not only recognized her lovely face, but fans who also recognized her great talent in the many roles she played. Trying to make someone else the "Biograph Girl" did not fool anyone; making Mary Pickford the "Biograph Girl" worked only after Florence was firmly established as the "IMP Girl" or as Florence Lawrence. Tom Gunning proposes that this confusion over Florence's identity may have been what gave Laemmle the idea for the publicity campaign.[5] What Laemmle had wanted to do was replace the sobriquet of the "Biograph Girl" with that of the "IMP Girl." What he wound up with was Florence Lawrence, a star in her own right.

Florence remembered the early months of 1910 as ones of change. She claimed to see her own obituary in a New York newspaper on February 19, 1910: "I ... was startled to see a likeness of myself staring me in the face, topped by a flamboyant headline announcing my tragic end beneath the wheels of a speeding motor car."[6] A refutation appeared in *The Billboard* in early March, datelined Chicago, February 26; "Miss Lawrence has a one hundred percent health certificate that should keep her with us a long while, and Messrs. Laemmle and Cochrane are too solicitous for her safety to allow her to even take a street crossing without having traffic stopped until their star is transported to the safe side of the curb." *Billboard* treated the story gently, relaying copies of telegrams St. Louis theater owners sent to Laemmle and quoting a poem a fan supposedly sent to Laemmle when he heard of Florence's passing. One stanza ran:

> As a loving and faithful wife,
>   Or a maiden full of grace,
> She has made us laugh and cry,
>   And in our hearts she's found a place.

Even *Billboard*'s sub-headline has a unique ring—"Florence Lawrence has the exquisite if rare privilege of testing the love and loyalty of her friends; Incidentally Carl Laemmle grew excited." The article refers several times to Florence as the "queen of moving picture actresses," humorously adding that she had been "very busy assuring her host of friends that she is very much alive" since the rumor began. Florence's name had moved from IMP advertising copy into articles about the IMP Company.

Years later, Laemmle stuck to the story of amused innocence. John Drinkwater, Laemmle biographer, stubbornly asserts, "A rumor was released from ill-disposed quarters that she had been killed in St. Louis. It was poor, half-witted ruse, intended in some nebulous way to unsettle the independent public ... The New York press made a feature of the report which merely had to be left alone to discredit itself, since Miss Lawrence was at the moment showing her best form in the IMP studio."[7]

The "ill-disposed quarters" were probably not very far away from Laemmle's and Cochran's desks. Film history has been very quick to say that Laemmle was probably the source for any rumors about Florence that were circulated, even though he tried to pin the blame on the Licensed film companies. *Moving Picture World*, as early as the very next month, called the rumors and subsequent publicity in St. Louis the "unique and clever stunt of the press agent."[8] Few were fooled, but the guise worked. Laemmle had to begin planning his next steps in February, which included advertising exploitation and a road trip to St. Louis. Laemmle assumed that a personal appearance by Florence would enhance her image and the studio's. St. Louis was probably chosen because it was King Baggot's hometown and possessed a good movie-going population. St. Louis may have also been the home to some of IMP's major financial backers. The city turns up again later in Florence's career when she was starting the Victor Company in 1912, which may not coincidentally have been a lure back to the Independents from the Trust.

Laemmle began March by stepping up the advertising, using Florence's name in an advertisement in *Moving Picture World* for *Mother Love*, the March 7 release. "In this picture Miss Lawrence, known to thousands as 'Mrs. Jones,' does the most excellent of her remarkable career [sic]. She enacts the role of a young mother whose reason has been temporarily dethroned by the death of her baby ... Take it from me that you MUST have this "Mother Love" picture. Talk about your film d'art! This is a film d'peach, film d'great, a film d'magnifique!!!"[9]

Just in case readers did not remember exactly who Biograph's "Mrs. Jones" was, Laemmle reminded them vividly the next week in another advertisement, the famous "We Nail a Lie," cited by film historians as a turning point in film publicity.[10] The now-familiar devil caricature is holding up a rather unflattering mug shot of Florence, followed by the text, "The blackest and at the time the silliest lie yet circulated by enemies of the 'Imp' was the story foisted on the public of St. Louis last week to the effect that Miss Lawrence (the 'Imp' girl, formerly known as the 'Biograph' girl) had been killed by a streetcar. It was a black lie because so cowardly. It was a silly lie because so easily disproved. Miss Lawrence was not even in a streetcar accident, is in the best of health, will continue to appear in 'Imp' films, and very shortly some of the best work of her career is to be released."[11] A short article (accompanied by two photographs) appeared in the March 6, 1910, *Louisville Courier-Journal*, both planting and dispelling the rumor by reprinting the "gist of two telegrams that passed between St. Louis and New York last Friday ... It can be conceived, therefore, how much of a blow to the producers, renters, exhibitors and patrons of the 'Imp' pictures was the report circulating throughout moving picturedom the other day that Miss Lawrence had been killed while 'posing in the streets of New York for a new film.'" The article further announced a souvenir show at the IMP theater, the Hopkins, where each "feminine patron" would receive a series of character poses.[12] The upcoming avalanche had just barely started.

On March 6, 1910, readers of the *St. Louis Post-Dispatch Sunday Magazine* were surprised to find close-up photographs of several popular film actresses with their names directly beneath them. There were also several still film scenes from popular and recent moving pictures. "Heroes and Heroines of the Moving Picture Shows" blazed the headline, adding in smaller print, "'Silent Film Fiends' Now Demanding Personal News of Their Favorite Actors and Actresses." The article itself is quite lengthy, with a pleasingly knowledgeable stance toward moving pictures and the arts in general.

Suprisingly, most of those highlighted are Trust players. Eleanor Gaines with Lubin, Rolinda Bainbridge and Mrs. Bernadine Reisse with Edison are prominently pictured, as is an unusual photograph of the Edison stock company. Selig Films' *The Senorita* and *Wife of Marcius* also are displayed and discussed. The A.G. Whyte Stock Company also had photographs printed of Marjorie Thornton, Constance Powell and Grace Graham.

Florence does not have a photo accompanying this article, but she is mentioned with great reverence. In italic print under the headline before the article begins, the *Post-Dispatch* reports,

> What American actress is most popular with the people? Whose face is the most familiar to the greatest number? At once the names of Maud Adams, Ethel Barrymore, Julia Marlowe, Margaret Anglin and other stage celebrities will occur to the reader in competition for first place in the affections of the great amusement seeking public, and as the one with whose features the public is most familiar. There is one actress playing in the silent drama, who is seen acting every night in every week simultaneously in the theaters in nearly every town in every state in the Union whose face is known to 10,000 people to the one who knows Maud Adams. Her name is Florence Lawrence, and she is a member of the stock company of a New York firm of moving picture manufacturers.

Florence is mentioned again as the one whose death had been reported in New York papers "a few days ago," an event termed "an awakener" to the popularity of the players in moving pictures. The Independent Moving Picture Company is mentioned with as much emphasis as the Suburban Stock Company where King Baggot played the summer before. The other actresses whose photographs surrounded the article also merit a few lines apiece, listing their stage careers if appropriate. (One unique talent also mentioned was French pantomimist Mlle. Pilar-Morin, yet her film affiliations were not listed.) The article gives a thumbnail sketch of the history of moving pictures in America, how the foreign stars were introduced first, then American stories and players were gradually brought onto the scene. "One good trait of the moving picture actors and actresses, is they do not consider it beneath their dignity to play before a camera instead of an audience," the article stated, contradictory to what is considered now the norm for 1910 player attitudes. But another statement rings with much more truth for the era: "The names of these actors or actresses are known in the picture trade, but have seldom got beyond."[13] Whoever wrote this article did know what he or she was talking about.

But just what this article means in the big picture is not clear. Florence was mentioned as the most popular, but did not have a photograph so that people could clearly link name to face. The subtlety displayed in this article is not like IMP's usual publicity, and Laemmle may have only had limited input, if any. No credits are given for the photographs — where did they come from if the Trust companies were not issuing photos?

However, a week later, the same *St. Louis Post-Dispatch* readers were treated to a front-page spread in their Sunday magazine of America's favorite and highest-paid moving picture artist, the Girl of a Thousand Faces, Florence Lawrence, complete with over a half-dozen photos and illustrations.[14] This interview was the first of its kind in a non-trade publication. Alexander Walker, in his book *Stardom*, said that the article was probably a "trailer" to advertise the upcoming visit.[15] The piece itself was extremely enlightening and revealing, serving to introduce the star and her name to her fans. Since there was no byline, the actual source of the interview is not clear; perhaps it did come from the pen of a St. Louis reporter, but more than likely the entire article and photographs were a carefully orchestrated press release from Laemmle. If it was indeed an IMP creation, this would explain the exaggerations, but not the inaccuracies.

Her age was listed as 20, a golden example of youth, which was fudged a few years. "Her name at home was Florence Solter" was included, saying the name Lawrence was adopted for the stage. Solter was of course her married name at that time; her name back home was Bridgwood.

Her salary at several points during the St. Louis trip was reported to be $15,000 per year, which breaks down to an incredible $300 per week. Only the year before last had she been lured to Biograph for $25 per week. Mary Pickford was making five dollars a day at Biograph in 1910 and $200 per week with David Belasco on Broadway in 1912.[16] But also to contrast this to the largest names on the vaudeville circuit, Anna Held (Mrs. Florenz Ziegfeld) was making $2,500 per week in 1912, and Eva Tanguay was bringing in $3,500 per week in 1910.[17]

The nickname "Girl of a Thousand Faces" evidently was sufficiently well known to movie fans at the time for it to be used often in reference to Florence. The *Post-Dispatch*'s statement, "There is no question that she is the most popular of the moving picture players in this country," would ring truer if indeed the article was not a Laemmle invention. The *Post-Dispatch* also claimed that the numerous photos used of Florence were the first ever published in a newspaper, which may not have been true, if photographs accompanied her "obituary" in the New York papers. Also, two of these same shots were used in the *Louisville Courier-Journal* article earlier in the month. These photographs certainly were to be used again and again, describing Florence's wonderfully effective expressions: piety, coquetry, determination, sadness, concentration, horror and hilarity. One that was not used, which Daniel Blum mislabels in his book *A Pictorial History of the Silent Screen* as the piety photo, is a sad-faced Florence looking upward with her hair braided around her face. That photo was the one used in the "Nail a Lie" advertisement; it was neither the best nor the most identifiable of the group. Why Laemmle or Florence chose to highlight that shot is unknown.

The article was an interesting insight about how motion pictures were made, a curious blend of stage techniques and modern technology. Without voice, it was emphasized, the actor's body language must do all the work: "A movement of the lips, a glance of the eye, a contraction of the facial muscles, a gesture of the arm or hand or a swaying of the body."[18] These were the ways a moving picture actor could contact the audience "across the footlights," to borrow the stage term. Florence also revealed how the actual acting was rehearsed with and without the camera. When asked how many rehearsals were need for the "average film play" (to adapt another stage term), Florence said two. The first was a dry, technical run, which she called "mechanics," where the stage director shows what he wanted in the shot. "Next we go through it 'with feeling' as the saying goes. Then we are ready for the camera," she explained. Crowds gathering about to watch the films being shot didn't bother her, although this attitude was to change in upcoming years. Florence denied feeling stage fright before the camera, admitted that she talked while performing, and expressed surprise that motion picture acting was to be "criticized and judged as severely as that of the regular stage."

Florence did seem to recognize her own star power even before the publicity began. She said she often went to the theater to see herself, which Linda Arvidson remembered vividly: "When [Florence] wasn't working on a picture, she was at some movie theatre seeing a picture,"[19] Florence told the *Post-Dispatch* that on one occasion when she was recognized in a theater, she was "'fairly mobbed for autographs.'"[20] Like it or not, Florence had quite a following. This was further evidenced by the "bundle after bundle of letters, notes, picture postcards and what not" that Florence kept with her: "It may seem foolish, but I keep them all."

The last "fact" in the article was an often-quoted figure regarding how frequently Florence was photographed. If a film had 14 frames per foot and there were 1,000 feet per film, the writer reasoned that Florence was photographed 14,000 times per day, for a total of 4,000,000 times annually. In truth, this would assume that Florence was present in every single shot of every single film that IMP produced, and that she did actually make 300 films per year as the article claimed. IMP was actually only distributing two reels per week at that time, with Florence starring in one of them.[21] In a more realistic view, the article the week before claimed that Florence put in about six minutes into each of her 15-minute films, averaging about $25 per screen minute.[22]

After this lengthy interview, St. Louis needed just one more incentive to see Florence. On March 25, 1910, the *St. Louis Times* printed a small notice in the classified advertisements that was to be clipped and presented to Florence: "March 25, 1910, Miss Florence Lawrence, Twentieth Street Entrance, Terminal Station, St. Louis, Mo., Dear Miss Lawrence—Kindly give me an order on the *St. Louis Times* entitling me to one of your autograph photographs, taken by their Staff Photographer, Burton. Wishing you and your company great success, I remain AN ADMIRER."[23] Whether anyone in connection with Florence's trip thought that a few people would show up at the station holding these notices is pointless; they should have known better. The front page of the *Times* that day invited the city to come and meet her, with a personable article of her career history and several photographs.[24]

There is no doubt that when the train carrying Florence and King Baggot pulled into the station in St. Louis, movie history changed permanently. Historians have also correctly shared Florence's spotlight with her employer, the mastermind behind the scheme, Laemmle. John Drinkwater called the reception "highly favorable emotional circumstances."[25] Laemmle had no trouble exploiting the circumstances, as Drinkwater explained: "The stars were received at the station by a crowd in a stampede of excitement, and St. Louis became a riot ... The enthusiasm of Miss Lawrence's admirers did its best to confirm the rumor which she had come to dispel [her death] ... they demonstrated their affection by tearing the buttons from her coat, the trimmings from her hat, and the hat from her head."[26]

This, of course, is the way Laemmle wanted to remember St. Louis after many years, with his own twists along the way. He had nothing to lose from a colorful retelling of the story. And it does make a good story.

The truth does not seem to be too far behind. Florence's arrival was scheduled at 5:25 P.M. Friday afternoon at Union Station. The Saturday *St. Louis Times* reported that crowds began to gather before 5:00. "The crowds compared in numbers and equaled the enthusiasm that which greeted Commander [Robert] Peary, and even that which greeted President [William] Taft on his last visit to this city,"[27] but was not as large as those for Dr. Frederick Cook after his supposed discovery of the North Pole in 1908. Not surprisingly, the majority of the crowd was women.

Ready to meet Florence's train were Laemmle; Frank Talbot, the local theater manager; Frank Daeheel, president of the Moving Picture Men's Association; and Fred Wehrengerg, secretary of the same association. The train arrived seven minutes early, causing a rush to the platform: "Hundreds of women and men succeeded in passing the gateman."[28] Talbot managed to board the train to fetch Florence and introduce her to the local press. Upon leaving the train, Florence was shocked at the crowd awaiting her. "'I had no idea that so many people were interested in me,'" she told the *St. Louis Times* reporter. "'I appreciate this honor, and it seems so strange that so many people would gather at the train to welcome one they had never seen, only in pictures.'"[29]

The actors remained on the observation deck for a few minutes, then attempted to go back into the car. "If the crowd was embarrassing to the 'silent actress' within the gates, it was many more fold so when she, between the huge form of Talbot and King Baggot, attempted to make her way through the crowds," reported the newspaper. When they passed through the train gates, another wave pressed close: "There were enthusiastic shouts from female voices, and a rush of well-dressed women to get a closer view of the little woman in a close-fitting blue dress whom they instantly recognized as Miss Lawrence, their heroine."[30]

If the men had not been surrounding her, Florence would have been swept off her feet. She apparently became highly agitated. Drinkwater reported that she fainted,[31] but the newspaper claimed that she was merely "frightened."[32] After a struggle, Florence, Talbot and Baggot made it to the car, but that was not the end. The crowd surrounded the vehicle, making it impossible to move. The unknown reporter explained: "The women ... felt repaid for the journey to the Station, and for the exertion they had been compelled to put forth for the mere privilege of seeing for a fleeting moment the form of one they felt so familiar with."[33]

The balance of the article is a personal interview with Florence regarding her career and the motion picture industry. She said that she had visited St. Louis as a child actress with her mother and that she had had a varied entertainment background before entering motion pictures. This article was where she claimed to have attended Loretto Academy in Toronto in her childhood. The article ends with a trite physical description: "She is of medium size, of graceful figure and carriage, and has a charming personality. Her voice, low and cultured. Her eyes, large and blue, are particularly expressive."[34]

This report of Florence's visit to St. Louis is mundane by today's standards. Star arrives, is mobbed by adoring crowds. But in 1910, this type of fanaticism was restricted to explorers and politicians. Stage celebrities were restricted to performances at the theater; their very work was a personal appearance. The theatrical gossip page was tame even by 1910 standards. Florence's visit was extraordinary for this era. Drinkwater aptly called it "revolutionary."[35]

Florence and Baggot were scheduled to speak at two theaters in St. Louis during the weekend. Advertising for these events was unusual as well. Sandwiched between an advertisement for the American Theatre's production of

George Barr McCutcheon's *Beverly* (seat prices ranged from 25 cent matinees to $1 premiums) and an advertisement for the Mississippi Valley Kennel Club's Fifth Annual Dog Show (admission 50 cents, children 25 cents), the Gem Theatre ran a small ad for the "first and only appearance in St. Louis of Miss Florence Lawrence and King Baggott [sic]." The advertisement further reminded readers, in case they had missed the Friday St. Louis newspapers, "You've Seen Them On The 'Screen,' Come See Them In Person." Talbot, owner of the Gem and Grand Opera House, promised different shows at each theater in the ads. The admission price was ten cents, the same as regularly attending a movie, still a bargain as compared to St. Louis' legitimate stages.[36]

The weekend's press was entirely devoted to Florence. Surprisingly, King Baggot was not interviewed at all in his hometown during this media event; his name was misspelled in most of the publicity. The Sunday *Post-Dispatch* followed up its interview of the week before with a small notice, on their "Across the Footlights" theater gossip page, regarding Florence's and Baggot's appearance at the Gem, where "they will give a talk concerning their work in the moving picture world."[37] Florence was credited with being the former leading lady with the Biograph Company, but was also credited, incorrectly, as being with the Independent Company "about a year now." Interestingly, another theater in St. Louis, the New Bijou, added and advertised a Florence Lawrence Biograph film in its program to their vaudeville offerings of Mlle. Coretta and Little Lord Robert, the smallest performers in the world.[38] So Laemmle's attempt at a personal appearance was not all-inclusive. This little notice for the New Bijou shows the public that even though they could not have Florence in person, they could still have her on film. With the magic of movies, she could be in two places at once, which no theater performer could boast.

The *Times* did not have an exclusive with Florence either. The *St. Louis Star* also ran an interview with Florence on Monday, March 28, 1910. The article, by Anita Moore, was a cloyingly ingratiating piece, with the focus on staying youthful. "If you want to retain the facial semblance of youth, or if you want to remove all the wrinkles and crow's feet which are beginning to show around the corners of your eyes, pose in dramatic and comic and sentimental scenes for the moving pictures. This is the belief and the advice and the practice of Miss Florence Lawrence ... a woman whose face is more familiar to the people of the United States by 500 per cent than that of the wife of the President of the United States, or for that matter than that of even so famous an actress as Sarah Bernhardt or the noted beauty, Lillian Russell."[39]

Hidden within the exaggerations are several truths: Moore reminds readers that they have seen this "mere slip of a girl" in many different roles. Her face, tranquil and young at the time of the interview, could be "seamed with care, trouble, distorted by horror, fear and anger, representing laughter and tears." Moore also pointed out that Florence's face was not that of classic beauty (as did Mr. Levar in his letter), but that she had a "fascinating," rather than pretty or handsome, countenance. Her coloring, however, was perfect for a blonde: small, expressive blue eyes, eyelashes and eyebrows "in their natural state" and lots of sandy, wavy hair.

Moore must have thought she was posing an important question when she asked Florence, "Don't you fear that 'making faces' will cause premature wrinkles?" Florence dismissed the question with her usual bluntness. "Why, it will keep me young. If you would retain your youthful appearance make faces. Use every muscle in your face and neck. It is the very best massage." She likened the facial workouts to an athlete keeping in shape: "If the circulation is not good the color becomes poor and the tissues waste. If this applies to the body, why should it not apply to the face?"

The remaining part of the article shows how Florence dealt with the moving picture business as a player. Unconsciously she displayed her knowledge of the theater and how she applied it to her present work, even acknowledging that the best stage actors do not make the best screen actors. "The actor depends upon his voice. In moving pictures, a strong personality is required." She also added knowingly, "The moving picture business is trying on the nerves ... much more than theatrical work." Moore assured her readers that Lawrence did not look as if she suffered from nervous ailments: "She was as serene and merry as a June day."[40]

Again, Florence Lawrence was showing just how good an actress she was.

Chapter Six

MOVING ON

> *By the time you get your name up in lights you have worked so hard and so long, and seen so many names go up and down, that all you can think of is: "How can I keep it up there?"*
> —Billie Burke

"I shall never forget that trip to St. Louis. It simply overwhelmed me," Florence said in *Photoplay* four years later. "For two days and nights I made short talks—'Clever little speeches' so the newspapers said—telling how I came to enter motion pictures. Events came so thick and fast that I was dazzled."[1] Florence's nerves must have been completely frayed at this point in her career. Within a year, the Solters had left the comfortable and systematic Biograph system for a life that Laemmle now seemingly controlled. Every public move of Florence's was carefully planned. She had been declared to be dead, she had been proclaimed to be alive, she was the property of her fans.

The publicity stunt had not only been noticed by her St. Louis fans, but by other film manufacturers as well. The Vitagraph Company quickly countered with a reception for Florence Turner, popularly called "The Vitagraph Girl," at Saratoga Park (moving picture theater) in Brooklyn. In mid–April, Florence Turner made an appearance, making "a very naive and fetching little speech" which the audience loved. She accepted a huge bouquet of flowers, and the audience heartily sang the chorus of a song written especially for "The Vitagraph Girl" in song slide fashion.[2] *Moving Picture World* cautiously began presenting interviews and feature stories about the players. Turner had a lengthy article and several photographs in July 1910, causing at least one film historian to give her credit for being the first movie star.

Florence seems to have put more of her energy into her work after the St. Louis trip. Her IMP pictures were the usual mix of drama and comedy, with the drama extremely high-pitched and the comedy less-than-farcical.

Trade papers such as *Moving Picture World* picked several of her early 1910 films to rave over, such as a January release, *Tide of Fortune*, and March's *Mother Love*. On the surface, the reviews and commentary describe wonderfully made and enacted pictures; to turn the focus around, these pictures and others of the same caliber must have been extremely difficult to make, under any circumstances. As released within the first three months of 1910, Florence had made at least ten seriously engrossing dramatic one-reel appearances, each with a completely different and difficult character and plot. There is little to compare with this today; an actor working in a weekly half-hour television show can at least expect a developed character, with typical responses within the parameters of the show. Florence had little control over script selection, yet had to adapt into any given persona via bodily and facial movements, wardrobe selection, and director's orders within minutes, hours at most, for a role that would last less than 20 minutes upon the screen.

Someone, probably Harry, noticed Florence's stress with these highly emotional roles, for the rest of her IMP work was noticeably lighter in tone. A few were dramatic, but lacked the distressing punch of emotion at the end; the story may have been more or less effective while also helping Florence to continue working for as long as she did in the trying atmosphere. Most of these melodramas were favorably reviewed; several were not. *The Eternal Triangle* and *The Mistake* were highly praised by the *Moving Picture World* critic, but *The Irony of Fate* was not ("The outcome of the film is not natural and as it disappears one has a dissatisfied feeling which seems rather to increase as one thinks of the pictures."[3]).

Florence's IMP comedies were universally liked. Old friend John Cumpson was brought into the IMP fold for at least one film, *The Nichols on a Vacation*, released in June. Ironically, Florence apparently played his daughter in this story. At the very end of her IMP career, Florence was in a short series of comedies with King Baggot and either Harry Solter or William Daly, portraying the romantic interest between two friends, Gerald and Percy.

Florence did take one step toward her favorite characterization of the lovable tomboy in the August film *The Taming of Jane*, a role that she would become quite popular doing in years to come. Her lover "uses somewhat vigorous measures in his wooing. Finally it takes her father to help in the taming process. It is accomplished by making her believe that she has shot her lover." Not unexpectedly, the review adds, "The wedding ceremony follows," but does add the following notice of Florence's work without mentioning her directly: "The picture is a characteristic study of more than ordinary interest."[4] Other 1910 romantic comedies well-liked in reviews were *A Reno Romance* (May 30 release), *Old Heads and Young Hearts* (July 11), and *Pressed Roses* (September 26).

The film industry continued to learn and grow as it entered its third decade. IMP was gradually accepted as a bothersome but necessary force

Florence in a still from a Lubin film, probably *His Chorus Girl Wife*. The common vanity table with individual mirror lighted by electric bulbs, plus the women doing their own make-up, was very typical of the theatrical dressing rooms of this era. Photograph courtesy of Joseph P. Eckhardt.

within its confines. The growing number of independent filmmakers did well if their films were at least comparable to the licensed manufacturers. But the eyes of the Trust must have been jealously watching every move that Laemmle and others made. Florence, as a defector, was obviously scrutinized as well. Her personal star power was becoming more and more evident; in May, *Moving Picture World* noticed an announcement in an Illinois newspaper that featured a picture of Florence as an advertisement for an individual theater. "This is bringing the personal element as the attraction," *World* intoned, "and while it has the feature of a novelty, yet we believe in featuring the subject of a film or the work of the artist rather than the personal equation. After all," the writer smugly added, "it is the work that counts."[5] The Trust took notice. At least one historian has theorized that Florence's popularity and Laemmle's success, especially after the personal appearance in St. Louis, goaded at least one licensed manufacturer to go after Florence and her husband to see if they could be tempted away from IMP.[6] That man was quiet, honest, influential Siegmund Lubin.

When Lubin first approached the Solters is unclear, but he certainly began making overtures for their services well before they left Laemmle. In August, Harry wrote a disheartened and melancholy letter to Florence, who was evidently on vacation to see her mother in Toronto:

> Am tired out with this job. Cochrane has got on my nerves and I am going to have it out with him. I am going to tell him we will quit the first of Sept. We will take a chance and go somewhere else. We can go to England and get a job as they want us over there. We can try Lubin first and if there is any trouble, we can do the other. What do you say to a trip to Europe. This strain is too much with the I.M.P. If I had some assistance it wouldn't be so bad, but this continually bucking Cochrane is too much.

The Solters evidently had already begun having marital problems; Harry asks twice if she will be home when she said she would: "Wondering if you will take the train you promised."[7] In another letter written that same week, Harry begs, "For the love of heaven Mike [his pet name for Florence] come on home. It's lonesome." After using weak romantic wiles for a few pages, he used a last tactic that would likely bring Florence running: "I have to retake some of the scenes from 'Among the Roses' and will be held up until you get back so don't fail to get here by Wednesday night."[8]

The Solters broke their contract with IMP in September 1910 and left for Europe almost immediately, sailing on the American Line *Merion*, on September 10. Lubin was still courting them, as Florence wrote to her mother on that day: "Received a beautiful box of flowers and Harry got a box of cigars from Lubin. Wasn't that nice?"[9] Florence's rambling letter covered the day-to-day activities of the ship as they crossed the Atlantic; little of interest until the following Saturday when the passengers held an after-dinner concert in which Florence took a part. "I was very much surprised, because the talent was exceptionally fine. I was the last on the bill. They would hardly let me go—I was the hit of the evening. Whistled—sang 'Irish Wash Woman'—and 'Irish Stump Speech'. They thought it great." Despite Florence's film popularity—the upper-class passengers of the boat would not have been frequent patrons of nickelodeons—she was an unknown onboard. ("They don't know I am an actress, and yet they all said they knew I was going to be the best.") In her typical pessimism, Florence added, "I thought I was punk,"[10] slang at that time for poor or inferior.

By the end of September, the Solters were lodged at Horrex's Hotel in London, entertaining and being entertained before they left for Paris. They were fortunate to have missed the record-setting 100-degree weather London experienced the month before. In mid–October, they were at the Hotel zum Reichstag in Berlin with Lowder and Sarah Layton, new friends from Philadelphia. Lubin met them there with a blunt but friendly note, "Dear Mr. Salter! Mr. Lubin is calling at the Hotel 3½ o'clock this afternoon to take you and Madam and Mr. and Mrs. Layton out for sightseeing in his carriage and beg you and your friends to have tea in his house afterwards."[11]

Lubin's charm worked. Florence was deeply attracted to Lubin's work ethic, his history in motion pictures and his cheerful outlook on life. "Mr. Lubin is one of those rare lovers of wisdom who follow the precepts of Montaigne and practice what they preach," Florence said of him later. "He is a man of peace, averse to strife of any kind, and it was this happy disposition of his that won me away from the Imp studio." Florence also cheerfully admitted in seeing a father-figure in the big man: "Mr. Lubin called me his 'pretty daughter.' I liked him immensely for that."[12]

Florence's mail was sent to the Lubin Studios in Philadelphia as early as November, but her first Lubin release was not until late the following January. And Laemmle did not turn his back without a fight; he sued Florence and Harry for not fulfilling their IMP contract. In a letter to the Motion Pictures Patent Company's office, Lubin conveys the unusual request that the Solters' attorney made on their behalf:

> The "Imp" Co. obtained an order against Harry L. Solter and his wife, Florence Lawrence, seeking to compel them to carry out their contract with the "Imp" Company, which Solter declared expires on March 5th, 1911, but which the "Imp" Company contend expires on March 5th, 1912. The strength of their case lies in the affidavits that they have filed, that Solter is an unusual man; that as the Manager and Director of Productions, he has the power to inspire and stimulate actors and actresses beyond any other man in the trade; that he is so unusual and his abilities are of such an especial and striking character, that he cannot be supplied by anyone else; and also the further statement that Mrs. Solter is an actress of world-wide fame, that she is the greatest woman known to the Profession, and that to lose her would mean a loss that it would be impossible to replace.

The Hon. Mr. Moon of Philadelphia is their Attorney. He has obtained affidavits that show these statements are ridiculous and untrue. He has obtained affidavits from the Biograph and the Vitagraph Co. that show the success of a Picture depends upon its mechanical execution, studio surroundings, upon a perfect photographer and that the Director of Productions performs only the duties of a Stage Manager, which consists in grouping the actors, arranging scenery and these in accordance with the play to be produced and that the present state of the art is that individual actors and actresses are not "starred"; that the public know and care little about their personality or their names and that the Profession is full of men and women seeking occupation and that no man or woman in this field is indispensable and that other Managers are employed in this work who render service with equal if not superior skilled [sic] than that of Solter; that there are other Manufacturers who are not employing either Mr. or Mrs. Solter whose product has a far greater sale than the films of the "Imp" Company, who are at present employing them.

Mr. Moon states that an affidavit from Mr. Edison to this effect would be well nigh conclusive of this suit. His great name and reputation would be controlling with the Court. I have told him that Mr. Edison would probably make such affidavit as he is doubtless familiar with the situation ... You will do me a great favor to do this for me as it would be of great benefit to Mr. Solter and his wife and to me personally.

Very truly yours,
LUBIN MANUFACTURING CO.[13]

The ideas behind this letter are both amusing and disturbing. The idea of Harry as the most powerfully effective director in the industry after a scant year's work was ludicrous, yet he may have been the best director for Florence, a point that was not stated. Florence may well have been the "actress of worldwide fame" as they claimed, but that field must be narrowed somewhat when passengers on an American boat not two months before failed to recognize her. Her acting abilities were only alluded to, rather than emphasized. Statements regarding the impact of the director and the actor within a moving picture from the Biograph and Vitagraph companies are not surprising; Biograph still clung to some of the oldest ideas about the role of the actor by not allowing names to be released, although they did have the best and most innovative director working for them. D.W. Griffith may not have agreed with Biograph's official description of a director's duties, but he was still caught within the confines of Trust policies.

Lubin had to realize he was stretching the truth when he stated that the public did not care who the actors or actresses were; the daily arrival of fan mail would have indicated this. But he was telling the truth when he said other firms were doing better business than IMP; Laemmle's company was doing well to excellent, but the older, solidly established Trust companies were still commanding the best box offices. And Lubin's statement about Thomas Edison's "great name and reputation" borders on the absurd until Trust control and power are understood. Within the licensed moving picture world, Edison's word was evidently law, but how far did that reach beyond the boundaries of the Trust proper? Edison's control of the Trust would seem to only refer to the patents that he held. He personally had been out of the film production loop for some time. Could Harry and Florence expect him to help—help with current knowledge of the genre, and help them despite their former renegade independent status?

The lawsuit dragged on for months. In January 1912, Florence's brother Norman commented in a letter to her, "I do not imagine you will stay in Philadelphia very long if you dislike it so much. Don't the Lubin's people treat you as they agreed, or is it just the law suit with the I.M.P. is having with you, that worries you so much? I should think Lubin would fight your law suit and pay you also, as they were the first ones to tempt you to leave."[14]

Florence was having her share of troubles with not only the film and legal world, but in her personal world as well. She and brother Norman were trying to renovate or build a house on one of several lots that Florence owned in the Blasdell suburb of Buffalo, with Florence providing the funds and Norman subcontracting out the actual labor. After the first contractor vanished with their money, the house burned down the day before Christmas 1910. Norman was distraught that someone other than himself had notified Florence: "You don't know how I felt when I heard the house burned down ... I did not want you to know anything about it until I had everything settled in regards to insurance. There was not a bit of use in telling you about the fire, I have enough trouble without you having it too."[15] Only one of Florence's letters to her brother survives from this time, but just the responses from Norman reveal much about their relationship. Florence wrote and sent money to her brother on her own terms, often not to Norman's liking. Over the course of three months he asks for money to pay for an outstanding bill from before the fire; Florence evidently ignores him. She disputed everything regarding the fire, from the insurance policy she herself had held to Norman's handling of the situation. Less than a week into the investigation, Norman irritably tells her, "It is necessary for me to ask you to trust me and abbide [sic] by what I say or else have someone else attend to it for you, I cannot please you or nobody else could, if you do not trust me, and I do not purpose [sic] to have you think that I cannot do this settling with out half a dozen telling you what you can do and what you cannot do with an insurance company."[16] Florence evidently did not trust him much; on January 14, friend and Lubin co-worker Albert McGovern carried a letter with him to Buffalo that served as an introduction to Norman. "Mr. McGovern has kindly condescended [sic] to stop off in Buffalo on his way to Chicago and look over my affairs, I want you to take up the matter with him from the bottom and work with him." In case "dear Normie" did not notice that Buffalo was not typically en route to Chicago, Florence added, "In the event of your being convinced that he is better suited to the same than yourself, place the matters with him solely."[17]

Their squabbling continued throughout January, when a settlement was reached and money distributed. Florence apparently did not have faith in anyone, even her own brother, as was evident just from his letters to her. This instinctive distrust of others came from deep within her character, and it showed in her career moves, but seldom in her actual work. Her work remained one of the few constants in her life, one that she grew to depend upon more and more.

Even as much as Carl Laemmle loved publicity, his lawsuit against Florence and Harry did not make it into the papers. Even his biography, published years later, does not mention it directly; his given reason for Florence leaving IMP in 1911 was to raise flowers, based primarily on the wild reception at St. Louis. "The incident, doubtless, inclined her thoughts to the cultivation of roses."[18] Her departure was shown to be fortuitous for Laemmle, for he could hire Mary Pickford away from Biograph to replace the leading lady who had, derisively, "departed to her roses."[19] Pickford stayed even less time than Florence did, just long enough to marry Owen Moore and make the hazard-filled working trip to Cuba that Laemmle felt forced to make in early 1911. Florence's co-star King Baggot stayed with Laemmle throughout most of his career as an actor and, later, a director. He and Florence remained friends throughout their lives, even living near each other in Los Angeles during the 1920s.

The lawsuit was either dropped or settled privately before the end of January. Florence may have begun filming with Lubin before that, in hopes of being vindicated professionally by appearing on the screen as quickly as possible. Regardless, Florence's actual onscreen career with Lubin began with the release of *His Bogus Uncle* on January 30, 1911, a "lively" but dismissable comedy.[20] After this and several other films with Albert McGovern and a few with Harry Myers, Florence was teamed with former Biograph co-star Arthur Johnson, himself a new recruit to the Lubin forces. Arthur's first film with Lubin was either *His Friend, the Burglar* (released March 9) or *The Actress and the Singer* (released March 13); the *New York Dramatic Mirror* gives Arthur credit for the latter. The ensuing series of romantic comedies were and are universally praised. Edward Wagenknecht remembered them best of any of Lubin's output ever.[21] *Moving Picture World* declared that "moving picture lovers will be glad to see these two picture stars working together again."[22] Even *Photoplay* asked its readers in 1914, "Who among you who witnessed these charming comedy dramas but would not like to see them again?" reminding them that "the Lawrence-Johnson team prov[ed] the greatest box-office magnet ever known to filmdom."[23]

Before many weeks had passed, the already-high quality of Florence's films increased noticeably. The cause was her on-screen chemistry with Arthur Johnson. Most of these films were formulaic romantic comedies, with neither actor making serious nor varied characterizations. Either the two portrayed fractious sweethearts about to be married or a married couple at trivial yet maritally threatening odds, with only a few exceptions. Florence did take a turn into melodrama in March with *Her Child's Honor*, where a second marriage after the supposed death of her first husband made her a bigamist with an innocent but illegitimate child. In *Her Humble Ministry*, released in May, her character reforms a petty thief with her forthright honesty. *The Little Rebel*, released in July, was a rare period piece dealing with the Civil War, a quick mixture of a spy drama and reuniting romance.

The Two Fathers, released April 22, 1911, could be considered a typical dramatic story for this era even though it was entirely standard for the Lawrence-Johnson team. One of Florence's very few surviving Lubin films, a complete copy of *The Two Fathers* is at the National Film Archive in London. Florence portrays Johnson's daughter, a child he was forced to give up for adoption because of poverty. He later takes a job as the butler in her new home so he can see her growing up. In the end, he gives her up again, this time to her new sweetheart (Harry Myers). Joseph Eckhardt, after seeing this film and comparing them with other earlier Lubin films, understands why Siegmund Lubin had wanted the actress: "Florence Lawrence comes across so strongly and with such warmth and genuineness, it is easy to see why she was so popular." Arthur Johnson, too, had a keen sense of how much emotion to put into a role—"acting without seeming to act." When the two are combined, the quality of Lubin films unmistakably rose. "Their abilities to convey feelings without the extremes of histrionics made their Lubin films quite different from all the Lubin films which had gone before."[24]

Florence portrayed her favorite lovable tomboy in *The Hoyden*, released April 24, 1911. The *New York Dramatic Mirror* practically raved over Florence's work: "The manner in which Miss Lawrence works out her role in this sprightly and entertaining comedy is a delightful drawing of the development of a tomboy to womanhood, and again shows the power that this lady has of bringing out the inner thoughts of the part she may portray."[25] Even the usually demanding actress found approval of her own work: "Did you see *The Hoyden*," she asked her mother in a May letter. "I do wish you would see it before it gets rain streaked and old, because it is my pet picture." Unconsciously furthering the pessimistic image of herself, she added, "You know I don't often rave over anything."[26] The character showed up again two months later in *The Professor's Ward* when the *New York Dramatic Mirror* noticed that her portrayal of the ward was "reminiscent of The Hoyden and quite as delightful."[27]

Florence's name began appearing in reviews of her films in the *New York Dramatic Mirror* in early February 1911 and in *Moving Picture World* by that June, and it appeared regularly from then on. Whether Lubin began submitting Florence's name with their advance advertising to the trade journals or whether the reviewers simply began to recognize certain actors is not clear,

A late 1911 Lubin film, *One on Reno*, has Florence and co-star Arthur Johnson's characters headed for a quickie divorce until they finally kiss and make up. Photograph courtesy of Wisconsin Center for Film and Theater Research.

but not every company's leads were mentioned in the reviews. Biograph, the usual example, but also Pathé, much to the industry's initial amusement and eventual annoyance, refused to identify actors or directors of any of their films, but almost every other company, licensed or independent, was doing so by the end of 1911. Oddly, even as little as five years would pass, and movie histories and commentaries would forget that actor's names were commonly used even before then: Vachel Lindsay remarks in *The Art of the Moving Picture* that 1911 was "before ... that of any actor in films was advertised,"[28] which is simply not true. Eileen Bowser felt that most films from 1910 to 1912 "were released without any naming of the players on the film itself or even in their advertising," but mentioned that at the same time, theater owners were selling or giving away calendars with Pearl White, or postcards with pictures of Florence Lawrence, Arthur Johnson, Maurice Costello, Edwin August, Florence Turner, Marion Leonard or Gertrude Robinson.[29]

The movie-conscious public was growing. Fan magazines came into being February 1911 when the Trust organized the *Moving Picture Story Magazine* (later known as *Motion Picture Magazine*) which publicized only the licensed companies' stories from the films, using many still photographs and no identification of the actors and actresses. The concept of this magazine is almost lost on modern moviegoers; *Story* was practically a supplement that summarized the entire film, leaving no surprises to see in the theater. *Story* was, in fact, the scenario writer's dream, for background, dialogue, and details could be revealed or even invented about a story line without wasting precious film space with intertitles. For example, Florence's film *Art Versus Music*, released December 20, was covered in the January 1912 issue of the magazine. The introduction of her and Arthur Johnson's characters' backgrounds sounds prosaic and charming, but would have been visualized in less than 20 feet of film: "The house of the Vernons fronted it [the only street of Dosebury] from the north, and here lived Ethel, an only child, with her fond father. Across the common, the Whittler dwelling stood, quite as well tended, with flankings of boxwood hedge and flowering shrubs. Herein dwelt John with his doting mother."[30] This type of magazine did not stay in vogue for very long; the first true fan magazine, *Photoplay*, began in 1912 mainly for the independents, followed by numerous others.[31]

The star system for advertising individual films and studios was firmly established by this time in film history. Fan mail was regularly received and responded to. Autographed photographs were sent out by stars, studios and publicists. Florence apparently had young fans who sent gifts: "I am sending you some flowers. I hope they are fresh when they reach you,"[32] ran one letter from a New England girl. Other fans took to following her career seriously: "If it is not too much trouble, I would like you to answer these few questions: What lady played the lead in Lubin's *The Test*, and if you know what lady played the leads in the following Biograph productions of a few years ago, *The Reckoning, Lady Helen's Escapade* and *The Taming of the Shrew?*" The writer, a Florida attorney and theater owner, was so positive of his identification that he claimed to have made a "ten thousand dollar bet ... against a nickel."[33]

Motion pictures were expanding the cultured definition of the arts.

Daniel Blum, in his book *A Pictorial History of the American Theatre, 1900–1951*, said that 1911 was the first year that fewer than half of the top ten plays had actors or actresses with star billing. The years 1910 and 1911 can be seen as catalytic for the movement from stage to screen. In 1910, the names that filled Broadway programs were Laurette Taylor, Billie Burke, Maude Adams and Helen Hayes. The names destined for 1911 stage fame were also destined for film success: Julia Dean, George Arliss, Alice Brady, Douglas Fairbanks and Mary Miles Minter.[34] Even vaudeville, a medium destined for a gradual downslide in both popularity and quality, needed the outrageously startling or extremely talented by this time to attract audiences. Julien Eltinge, Harry Lauder, Texas Guinan and Grace LaRue were all popular in vaudeville in the early teens, as well as perennial favorites May Irwin, Eva Tanguay and Anna Held. Some vaudeville stars did make films during this period—some with success, such as Fannie Ward; others with less, such as Lillian Russell.[35]

Unexpected and unusual combinations within other artistic genres were beginning to appear as well. Irving Berlin's "Alexander's Rag Time Band" was composed and released in 1911 as was Strauss' "Der Rosenkavalier." Edith Wharton's *Ethan Frome* was published and sold alongside D.H. Lawrence's *White Peacock* and H.G. Wells' *New Machiavelli*.

Audiences were being introduced to more and different concepts and intellectual pursuits, each more appealing than the last month's. Moving pictures, at first a novelty, were adding an exciting aspect to the already fascinating artistic melting pot. Newsreels, first run by Pathé in August, brought fresh news into theaters daily. In the realm of fiction, relatively few stories were admittedly based on other works. Companies feared a repeat of the 1908–1911 Kalem-*Ben Hur* lawsuit which ultimately cost the Trust $25,000. The idea of selling movie rights was still new. Even if the story was an old or borrowed one, usually something unique set it apart from its predecessors. *Moving Picture World* frequently pointed out superior acting, stunning scenery or clever adaptations that livened often-used plots.

In the middle of 1911, *Moving Picture World* began making more noise about the quality of films. Their editorials recognized the fact that audiences would not be satisfied with the mere story that a film showed. Audiences wanted to spend their time—and their money—wisely. In June 1911, *Moving Picture World* editors pointed out that people wanted comedy rather than the overwhelming number of dramas being presented. "They are hungry for a laugh ... They want relief from the seriousness of the day, and it is not to be expected that their feelings are going to be much relieved by putting them through thrills and tears."[36] Two months later, *Moving Picture World* writer Louis Reeves Harrison deplored the mediocre productions that some manufacturers were satisfied with releasing. "The intelligent portion of our people is only partially attracted by the picture shows and many who were enthusiasts a year ago are growing weary of the tiresome strumming of a few stale

Six — Moving On

A still from the 1911 Lubin film *The Snare of Society*. Florence is shown here playing cards with Jack Standing. Photograph courtesy of Wisconsin Center for Film and Theater Research.

tunes." Harry Solter's work was elevated to high levels when Harrison recognized him with the best directors of the day, but, as usual, his name was misspelled. "Men like Mr. Griffith, Mr. Blackton, Mr. Porter and Mr. Saltor could undoubtedly contribute much valuable information on this subject [of inferior films], but their messages of the world are sent out in the pictures they produce; they are less men of words than of deeds."[37]

So with Harry's able direction, Florence Lawrence's work was accepted as better than the rest. She rode along the established wave of one-reel films with relative ease and increasing fame. The year 1911 was a great time to be a good actress in motion pictures. Even established companies such as Lubin had to adjust to the ever-growing popularity. In July 1911, Lubin added an additional reel to be released per week, from two to three, to accommodate the demands of the distributors. Lubin advertising promised "a high-class drama, a genuine Western and a snappy comedy," sometimes splitting a reel with an educational snippet.[38]

Florence, like any creative soul in this changing environment, was growing restless. She was falling into the familiar rut where the only way out was to drastically change her life once again. Lubin, dear to her heart as he was, did not seem to be on the cutting edge of the industry. Philadelphia was not New York, which even by 1911 was losing some of its moviemaking ground to sunny California. Florence's growing fame was coupled with envisioned mediocrity. Her personal life was less than fulfilling.

Independence tempted her and Harry. The thought of her own money tempted her. And somehow, through all of her dreams and speculations, Carl Laemmle was there to tempt her again.

Chapter Seven

INDEPENDENCE

> *Producers don't make stars. God makes stars, and the public recognizes his handiwork.*
> —Sam Goldwyn

Florence's displeasure with herself gradually became more apparent not to just those closest to her, but to her co-workers as well. In this time of primitive fan magazine writings and limited public exposure, Lubin forces could control what was said about Florence in the trade papers and other press. Her marriage, for example, was never acknowledged in 1911 press releases, something that may have contributed to marital disharmony. All interviews that did make it to print were carefully structured to only give the positive side of Florence Lawrence, the lovely and talented actress.

The little fish-big pond syndrome was beginning to affect Florence once again. Her temperament got the best of her time and again. One Lubin extra, former Buffalo Bill cowboy Harry Webb, remembered that Florence would "flop down on a 'Society' set and beat a tattoo with her head and heels for an hour" to relieve her anxiety.[1] Right after Arthur Johnson appeared on the set to work with her at the end of January 1911, Florence abruptly disappeared for several weeks. She may have taken a steamer across the Atlantic, then back immediately, in an attempt to settle her jangled nerves.

Florence was willing to try anything to get herself back into a solid groove. In May 1911 she wrote to her mother, "Since I started this letter I have had an osteopathic treatment," referring to a possibly holistic approach to her ailments that may have included massage or chiropractic therapy. "I think they are helping me a great deal." That very letter itself indicates just how much anxiety Florence could work herself into. In relating some speculation about her future in the film business, her handwriting becomes more and more illegible, practically scribbled after a graceful and neat opening page.[2]

Lotta was not much help to her confused daughter. Her letters tended to be both understanding and aggravating. "I am always glad to sympathize with you when you feel blue or downhearted as we understand one another as no one else can," Lotta wrote to open an October 1910 letter, but peevishly dropped into criticism by the third page. "I wish, Florence, you would pay more attention to your writing and composition. These are matters you can improve on yourself ... you can practice on mother."³ And she unintentionally confirmed Florence's depressions quite often. "I know how you feel that you are the banker for two in your family," she said, referring to Florence's constant money-worrying compulsion. Lotta weakly tried bolstering Florence's self-esteem by adding, "I appreciate your good heart and common sense."⁴ Florence's heart may have been big enough for three at that point; she was evidently sending her mother money as well. When she failed to send a payment, Lotta wrote back in peeved amusement, "I see you are bound to force me into matrimony."⁵

The weekly grind of filmmaking continued. In the summer of 1911, Florence and Harry went to Portland, Maine, for a month with a crew from Lubin. They made several beautiful pictures along the shores of the Casco Bay, incorporating the rugged scenery well into the background of the stories. Yet the working vacation had little lasting effect; by the end of August, Lotta was urging her daughter to "go to the country and take a good quiet rest and treatment ... let everything go." She knew as well as Florence did that a major change was needed to improve her stamina and work-enthusiasm. "Remain long enough to feel that it is a pleasure to anticipate work ... then you will return with renewed energy able to cope with mountains of work that now are impossible."⁶

Well before the end of the year, Florence and Harry knew that they had done all that they could with Lubin. While reviews were still good and press positive, they did not renew their contract with him, choosing to remain unattached for several months. They anxiously watched for what their future might hold. Even as early as May 1911, Florence wrote to her mother, "We haven't settled anything with Lubin yet ... There are several people after us to start up a concern of our own. Of course they furnish all the money and we would get thirty-five thousand a year and an interest in the firm."⁷ Florence did not specify here or in any other correspondence who offered them the cash to start their own firm.

Florence's last Lubin film, *The Surgeon's Heroism*, was released on January 8, 1912. Within a few years, Florence looked back at the parting with Lubin as a complete necessity. "As is not generally known," she admitted in a newspaper interview, "I haven't the most robust health in the world—several years ago while with the Lubin Company I had a complete nervous breakdown and since then it has been a problem to keep myself sturdily on my feet."⁸ Her mental health was challenged yet again at the end of 1911 when her grandmother Ann Dunn died after a long illness. Lotta wrote to Florence of her own exhaustion and grief and added, "Am glad I did not let you come as you would have been upset."[9]

Spring of 1912 found the Solters aboard a boat for Europe once again, returning in mid-April on the White Star Line's steamer, the *Arabic*. The White Star Line's *Titanic* went down on April 15, 1912, taking over 1,500 people with her. If that tragedy had happened before the Solters had planned to return to America, Florence would have probably opted nervously to stay in England longer. The day they anticipated their return to the States was April 19, the same day that the *Titanic* survivors were brought in by the *Carpathia* into New York. Florence would never set foot on an ocean-bound ship again.

Fortunately, this European vacation had been one of the most restful that Florence and Harry had ever experienced. They toured France and studied French language and customs. They also toured Italy, concentrating their attentions in Rome on the recent excavations of ruins, but also taking time to attend Mass on Palm Sunday at St. Peter's. Crossing the Mediterranean to Egypt, the Solters mixed in with the Kalem Company, filming far down the Nile at Luxor. Florence wrote to her mother that Gene Gauntier had been ill and did not travel with the rest of the company, so Harry gave up his berth for her, bunking with Sidney Olcott in second class as they cruised northward on the Nile.

The group arrived in Cairo for several genteel evenings of dances and parties. "The second night Thurs a dance was given at the Continental Hotel in our honor ... had a grand time," Florence wrote home. Another evening, a ball was given at the legendary Shepheard's Hotel, but by this time Florence was miserable and ill with what she thought was malaria. "The least little slight on any one's part, I become dispondent [sic] ... I was feeling very badly, didn't want to go, but I went." She wound up on a bench by herself all evening until the others came to fetch her. "[They said] they were looking all over for me, I said something very short, about they didn't look very far. Anyway I went home in a huff."[10]

Florence pulled herself together admirably well in the remaining days of her vacation. She boarded the boat home happy and relaxed. "I feel much better and look very good or rather I must look good for I seem to be the marvel of the boat," she wrote back to her mother. "I have been taken for 15, 16, 17 and 18 years old, and Harry is either my father or brother and Miss Greenfield who is only 27 is taken for my Mother or step-mother and Harry's wife." Florence enjoyed sorting out the truth for those who asked, basking in what people thought to be a honeymoon, even though she and Harry had been married for three and a half years.

She was rather anxious to return to the United States and get back to work. "At first I didn't think I ever wanted to see moving pictures again," she admitted in a letter. "Thought I could go on site-seeing forever, but I have

got the fever now, can hardly wait to get back."[11] Upon their arrival home, they kept quiet to the press about where they would be working, and speculation about where Florence would show up next was evident even in the often-hilarious "Inquiries" column of *Moving Picture World.* Accidentally saying she would be with Powers in a previous issue, the "Inquirer" sought to cover his tracks on June 1, 1912: "For the purposes of record it is stated here that Miss Lawrence will be at the head of her own company on the Independent side and not with the Powers players." In the same issue, Owen Moore's screen presence was missed: "Owen Moore is unplaced at present, but we should not be surprised to learn of his connection very soon."[12] A mere two weeks later, they announced that he would be the leading man with the newly formed Victor Company.[13]

The Victor Company, which Florence always considered to be hers even though it probably never was, actually came into being in the late spring or early summer of 1912. The business address was 575 11th Avenue in New York City, but some of the filming was done in Fort Lee, New Jersey, or the surrounding area—a short commute for the Solters, who had bought a home in River Vale, New Jersey. Their studio was eventually located on the "extreme west end of Forty-second street," but as one interviewer found, "where odors are not the most pleasant in the Spring of the year."[14] The first film released was *In Swift Waters,* on July 12, filmed the month before on location in Cuddebackville, New York. Universal Film Manufacturing began releasing their films very early in the Victor's life, with advertising showing the Universal name by the end of June. Laemmle's advertising for Victor Films, as usual, does not disappoint. In his house organ, *Universal Weekly,* full-page ads repeated Florence's name over and over, interspersing accolades about her acting talents between her name.[15] Advertisements in *Moving Picture World* were only slightly less obnoxious, with Harry's name appearing as her director in much smaller type below her name bannered across the top of the ad.[16] The California Film Exchange printed large photos of Florence with a challenge for Californian exhibitors to "Take Notice: Every man, woman and child know Florence Lawrence who now appears exclusively on our program."[17] Film stardom had indeed arrived.

Carl Laemmle used Florence's face and name to her own advantage in the advertising and in his weekly magazine, aimed at distributors. Several articles about Florence do stand out, however, as more true admiration for

---

Opposite: Florence and Harry Solter's post–Revolutionary War farmhouse in River Vale, New Jersey. Today the porch has been removed, the chimneys are non-functional and the beautiful stone wall once surrounding the house is almost gone. Interior photographs reveal the Solters' taste as being rather eclectic, yet artistic, with her piano a focal point in the drawing room. Photograph courtesy of Wisconsin Center for Film and Theater Research.

Florence as an actress, rather than mere counsel of how to get more people into the theaters. Thomas Bedding, a former reviewer with the *New York Dramatic Mirror*, now editor of *Universal Weekly*, clearly remembered her work with Biograph, IMP and Lubin, claiming to have been the one to first call her the "Biograph Girl." Bedding pointed out that Florence had worked hard to get to where she was, but was now reaping the rewards of it. "For it is unquestioned that her hard work in the business has made Miss Lawrence the most popular motion picture artist in the world. This is not exaggeration or hyperbole. It is a clear fact, evident from the consensus of public opinion." Florence, he said, represented not only the best, but his "ideal" of film acting ability. "She was graceful, expressive; she was emotional, she was talented in many degrees."

The fact that she was the first screen star to be known by name does not escape his attention either. "At one time it was doubted whether the personality of a moving picture actor could be conveyed by the medium of the motion picture screen to the minds and hearts of the public in front. Florence Lawrence was the first to demonstrate that this could be done."[18] Several weeks later, Bedding continued to praise her in a follow-up column, based on the positive responses to the first one. "If I were to draw a comparison between this lady's work to-day and that of three years ago, I should say that while not abating one atom of her personal charm as far as the screen picture is concerned (for she looks just as nice and attractive as ever) her art has deepened and intensified to a remarkable extent." Bedding goes as far as pushing aside the work of co-star Owen Moore to show that Florence is the "greater drawing card." In *Not Like Other Girls*, he said, "It is just an Owen Moore part and Owen Moore plays it like Owen Moore." He adds dismissively, "He looks good to the eye." But Florence, he said, "is entirely good."[19]

Other publications noticed the fledgling company and its star attraction. The *New York Dramatic Mirror* reported on the inception of the company in early June, crediting Harry Solter, P.A. Powers and Joseph Engel as the organizers. Patrick Anthony "Pat" Powers, founder of the independent Powers Company (later known as Powers Picture Plays), was a colorful character in the early wheeling-and-dealing days of the independents versus the Trust, then of the independents versus themselves. Powers and Florence may have known one another when she was growing up in Buffalo—Powers had owned a phonograph store not very far from Florence's neighborhood—but they were definitely friends by the time the Victor came about. Engel had most recently been with the Rex Company in 1912, and became one of the industry's leading producers in the 1910s and early 1920s. Giles Warren, a scenario writer in great demand during the 1910s, was announced as head writer.[20]

One unexplored facet about the Victor Company and its early connection with Universal is just where the Victor Company and its name originated. Why did Florence and Harry not name the company Florence Lawrence

Pictures, an easy drawing card? However, the Victor brand name may have been owned by either Laemmle or Powers as early as 1910. Victor was listed among the dozens of companies represented by Motion Picture Distributing and Sales Company (of which Laemmle was the president and Powers the vice-president) in their inaugural advertising in May 1910. At this early date, Victor as a production company may have just simply been a hollow name, since no releases are listed for the company until Florence began to use it in the middle of 1912. However, the Victor Film Company, a business that sold moving picture machines and supplies, was located in Buffalo between 1910 and 1915 and was managed by Arthur Schmidt and Frank Hopkins. Schmidt previously was in the phonograph business in Buffalo, a tenuous connection with Powers. Powers of course could have owned Victor Film Company, too, eventually lending or selling the name to Florence.

The Motion Picture Distributing and Sales Company was the funnel used by the independents to get their products into the hands of the independent exchanges, who could then get into the struggling non–Trust theaters. Independent manufacturers such as Nestor, Thanhouser, Bison and Powers sold films to the Sales Company, as did importers for Hepwix, Cricks and Martin, Film D'Art and Itala. But a few of the names listed in the 1910 advertising (such as Carlton, Motofilm, Owl and Uncle Sam) never released anything. The Solters may have simply bought the Victor name and its previously established rights from Laemmle or Powers, effectively buying into Universal on the eve of its formation, or Laemmle may have just given the name to them, reserving the rights for himself.

Regardless of just how it had happened, Florence was one of the first women in the field to have her own film company. The first is traditionally regarded as Helen Gardner with a company that bore her name, as announced in *Moving Picture World* in early June 1912. Gardner's company focused on much longer features—five and six reels—a phenomenon that the industry was only thinking of readying itself for. Rather than using the feature-length as an artistic creation, however, Gardner's works were merely elongated single-reel stories, and her venture eventually folded. By 1914, Gardner was back working with her original company, Vitagraph; then she too went to work at Universal.[21]

The Mirror followed Victor's progress at the end of July 1912 with a full-page interview with Florence. Again, she was recognized as being one of the first film actresses of importance, and again, her height and weight, hair and eye color (5'4" and 106 pounds, light golden and blue) were dutifully reported. The majority of this interview, however, is Florence's opinions on opera ("I don't care much for Caruso"), censorship ("They do not look at the whole [work]") and her appearance ("I always feel that people are so disappointed in me, when they see me for the first time"). She lightly alluded to her depression and how she handled it: "I am taking up music now as a sort of recreation, and then it cheers one up so when one gets a little glum," she said, adding that she tried to make time for automobiling and outdoor sports as well. "When I am working I don't have much time to think of anything else."

She related that her favorite roles in the past were *The Slavey, The Professor's Ward, The Hoyden* and *Mother Love*. When she was not on the set, she was retired to her cheerful dressing room that she herself had decorated. Her dressing room figured in many of her upcoming Victor interviews, each reporter trying to see something different in the blue and white "boudoir." The *Mirror* interviewer noted that Florence, seated upon her little sofa, made "an attractive picture of a rather sensitive little creature in whom the spirit of youth and sentiment prevail." In an interview that was apparently not scripted by Laemmle or his word-man Robert Cochran, Florence came across as witty and charming.[22]

Moving Picture World dutifully included reviews of Florence's fledgling company's output with their "Independent" films, erring once in calling the company Lubin. Florence was the highlight of most of their reviews, the films themselves usually not causing very much commotion in the industry. The review of *The Chance Shot* opens, "Another Florence Lawrence-Owen Moore drama that proves that 'class will show.' There is perhaps nothing remarkable in the scenario as to plot ..."[23] In another, the reviewer calls Florence "she who so bewitchingly portrays the tomboy—not the unruly, the hoydenish sort, but the gentle, the wholesome."[24]

Many of Florence's early Victor roles were hardly stretches of her acting abilities. The tomboy, the sweetheart and the young wife were true to character, making the exceptions more memorable. In September, Victor released *The Advent of Jane*, where Florence portrayed a new doctor coming to a rural community. The reviewer liked Florence's work especially: "There's a thread of fresh and acceptable sentiment as the story develops into a melodrama ... Miss Lawrence is a master in subtilly [sic] portraying the situation. Her work lifts the value of the offering above what the scenario would have by itself without her."[25] The same month saw the release of *Flo's Discipline*, which the reviewer thought to be weak.[26] Unfortunately, this Victor film is one of the few that survives, presenting a rather narrow perspective of her work during this time. *Flo's Discipline* is in the archives of the Library of Congress in Washington, D.C., as is *Not Like Other Girls*, the July 26 Victor release.

Flo's Discipline is a good example of how silent short films can be misunderstood and underappreciated. Florence portrays the recently returned headmistress of a boys' school. Owen Moore is the assistant director who has allowed some laxness of the rules, but developed a strong following among his pupils. Flo finds them to be an unruly, disruptive crowd and dismisses Owen, hoping to instill some discipline of her own into them. The lads rally around Owen, sneaking out of a window to meet with him. Flo eventually locks the students in an ice house to bring them around, sending in hot coffee

Seven—Independence

so the boys will not freeze. She then traps Owen on a ledge above the ice house by moving a ladder, hastening negotiations. When all is resolved, Owen prepares to leave, but Florence cajoles him into staying ... by stealing his hat.

Florence is wearing her own clothes for this silly short: a white suit with a low-slung black belt and big black bow tie with a matching soft hat. This dress also appears in a series of publicity photos Florence had taken sitting in a window sill. In *Flo's Discipline*, her acting is somewhat stilted; several scene-closing shots consist of Florence standing and glowering, arms akimbo. These repetitions should have been caught and corrected by the director. Also, twice Florence rips off her hat and throws it during the story's short span. The story is hard to follow, with few subtitles that reveal any real action.

The bulk of Florence's 1912 Victor films may have been made by August, although they were released through November. In August, Harry and Florence had a fight large enough to cause them to separate; it was evidently caused by Harry saying something dreadful about or to Lotta Lawrence. Florence left without him for Cuddebackville with a filming party on August 6. Harry left by the middle of the month for Europe aboard the German steamer *Dampfer Prinz Friedrich Wilhelm*, sending Florence a stream of pitiful letters claiming that he was going to commit suicide. "Everything will be accidental, at least it will appear so," he wrote. "No one will ever need know, so it will not interfere with your career." He repeated often that he wished to spare her the details, but told her in his second letter, "I have a bottle of mureatic and nitric acid, which will gently but surely eat away one of the rails, soon I shall lean upon that rail."

Harry had left behind a paper trail that on the surface indicated that he was serious. Florence may have known better. He made out his will on August 9, 1912, but signed it with no witnesses. He left one-quarter of his estate to a nephew and the rest to Florence, so long as she did not remarry. He also left a detailed set of instructions for Florence regarding the mundane details of daily matters, such as rent and gas bills, peppered with advice. "Do not get too friendly with Powers ... Keep all of your relatives away from the studio if you wish to be a success." He had sold their car to Powers for $1,400, half of which was due to Florence. He also cautioned her against signing any contracts that Lowder Layton, their attorney-friend in Philadelphia, had not approved. "Powers tried to put one over by trying to have you sign a contract made out to him, but I have had a contract drawn up for you with the Victor, signed by me." Harry's ramblings probably just meant more confusion and problems for Florence, especially since he had sold their car out from under her.

The letters continued. Harry soon said in his third and fourth letters that he was saved from killing himself by an opera singer traveling on the same ship, a lady who had a sadder story than his. She had planned to leave her husband until she suddenly received a telegram saying he had been in an accident. The summons made her realize how much she loved him, and she rushed to his side. Ever the scenario-builder, Harry remembered the story and used it four years later when he and Florence separated again.

By the fifth letter he was telling her that he had thrown away the bottle of acid and was playing chess with a college president. He spent most of each of his letters moaning about how he had ruined his life, her life and her mother's life. "Darling Florence, come to me—we will build a home together upon some beautiful lake, we will have music, we will have flowers, we will have laughter, and each day, we will grow younger, and younger, and we shall be lovers and playmates."

At first, Florence was not as receptive as Harry had wished she would be. In Paris on September 2, 1912, Harry wrote to her, "I had hoped, and prayed, and had only lived upon the hopes that your messages would have just a little word of love." He had wandered all about Paris, remembering when they had been there before, sitting on a park bench and crying. His desperation began to take on some hilarity: "I'm going to learn how to smile (have begun already), I'm going to strangle dull care, learn to dance and sing, and honey I'm even going to grow hair, and even outshine you in uptodate dress … Shall I come to New York? Will you give me a job with the Victor? I will write you some beautiful stories, comedy or tragedy. You shall be Mamselle La Directress and I shall be Monsieur Le Property Man." He summed up his plea with, "You can get me very cheap. I will work for love, love."[27]

Florence forgave him at some point, and Harry headed home. In a letter dated September 27 (no year written, but it has to be 1912), from the Hotel Marie Antoinette in New York, Harry wrote to Lotta, "Florence and I are once more together and I am so happy." He explained to Lotta that the Victor was in serious trouble, partly due to bad photography and partly due to Universal's independent status. "After 14 releases there is not one cent of profit from our American sales," he said. "Now if I continue with the Victor, what will I have to offer for my hard work—nothing. The independent field is in worse shape than ever, and always will be. Here in New York it is impossible to find out where a Victor can be seen." This fact is rather telling of how the independent filmmakers and distributors survived or failed during those early, lawsuit-filled years. Laemmle was engaged in actions against both the Trust and other independents; the latter caused by the split of the two-year-old Motion Picture Distributing and Sales Company in the second quarter of 1912. Almost like a divorce settlement, one party took some of the Sales Company's brand names and the other took what was left. When the dust had settled, Universal had been formed, and beginning on June 8 it was the sole distributor of films made by IMP, New York Motion Picture Company (101 Bison), Powers, Rex, Champion, Republic, Nestor and Victor. If no profits from the U.S. distributions of the films were forthcoming, then Harry had every right to be worried about their future with Laemmle. Harry also told Lotta that only one of Florence's Victor films had even been released in

Europe, though that apparently was part of the contract with Universal. In the same letter, Harry explained, "The selling qualities of a picture in Europe depend about 50 percent on the quality of the photography, as the Victor photography was the limit, the only sales will be from the fact that Florence was in the picture." He knew many other things hung in the balance at this point: Florence's unsteady health, their now-rocky marriage, and her unswerving preoccupation with perfecting her craft.

Harry seemed a bit nervous about the whole independent side of things, based on his negative attitude toward staying with the Victor Company. He favored returning to Lubin in Philadelphia, subtly attempting to win Lotta onto his side. "She will lose none of her popularity," he said in the September 28 letter to Lotta. "How could she, when she can sign a contract for any length of time at a salary of at least [$]500 and maybe more ... She won't have to work every day, in fact not more than 3 or 4 days a week."

Harry also gave details about how Florence's delicate nature interfered with her work. "She now works very hard every day, and it is only a question of time before she will break down." Harry had noticed too what the reviewers had often repeated about the Victor's films: "She practically puts on the pictures her self."[28]

Whether they realized it or not, both Harry and Florence were having serious problems in dealing with their day-to-day lives, their work and their relationship. Between Florence's unstable temper and mental health and Harry's threatened suicide, the two were a marital time bomb waiting to go off. Things came to another crisis less than a month after their reconciliation. Harry saw Florence in a car one evening with her friend, IMP actress Isabel Rea, and Pat Powers. Harry jumped to conclusions and ended up chasing them down the street with a gun. Lotta criticized Harry's actions, and Florence wrote a particularly nasty letter back to her, surprisingly siding with Harry without explaining herself. "I made up my mind that Harry is too fine a fellow to be thrown over for any one, and any one that isn't nice to him doesn't need to be nice to me ... You seem bent on keeping me riled about Harry, if you don't care to be friendly with him, <u>I don't give a dam</u> [sic]." Florence raved for several pages about how Lotta should and should not treat Harry. "I am sorry I have had to write to you this way Mother but you carry things too far some times."

Florence hinted that someone other than Harry was directing her in Victor pictures during Harry's absence, which only makes sense. "If you could see the papers now coming out now and panning my picture and me. It goes to show how dam [sic] wonderful I am and how far I could go with out a good director," she said sarcastically. "You talk to me as if I were about ten years old, and don't know any thing about the business I happen to be in. I think I have studied this business about as well as any one and must use my own judgement."[29] Florence was probably referring to the lackluster reviews for

Flo's Discipline, one of the worst received of her 1912 films. Harry could not have directed this and several before and after it, especially any of the work done at Cuddebackville in August. Florence makes no reference as to who might have so weakly directed her.[30] *Moving Picture World*, however, commenting on the noticed absence of Harry Solter, said that Giles Warren was doing Harry's work while Harry took "a vacation to look after some private business matters." Universal, seeking to assure viewers that Harry was still employed by them, nearly botched the effect by adding, "He will be back at the studio when he gets ready to return."[31]

Somehow all of the crises passed, and life returned to what passed as normal. Florence and Harry tentatively remained married, and he returned as her director. But the fight and fire for films were once again gone. Florence took stock of her life and did the best thing for herself—she decided to retire for good.

Chapter Eight

AMONG THE ROSES

If you had two or three years of motion pictures you were a pioneer, a veteran. You'd really been through the mill. You might have made a hundred and some pictures in that time.
—Joseph Henabery

Florence intended her last Victor photoplay to be *The Lady Leone*, only the second two-reel film she had ever done, which was released November 15, 1912. She had made at least 18 films from July to November, a dizzying amount of work, especially for Florence. Then she and Harry gave up their New York apartments and moved to their "country home" in River Vale, New Jersey. For Florence, this was her dream come true. No more touring, no more studios. She had a place that she and Harry could call their own.

And it was some place. The eighteenth-century house, located on River Vale Road in the Hillsdale Township, was considered a mansion, a sprawling two-story fancified farmhouse with plenty of space—five bedrooms, billiards room, a living room, two drawing rooms, a breakfast nook, a sunroom and a large wraparound porch. Outside the house, Florence had 50 acres to grow her favorite flowers—roses—less the space that tennis and croquet courts occupied. "It is a sweet place, this estate of mine," Florence told a British magazine. "The farm is all but inaccessible to anything except an automobile, and this is the only method I employ to reach it. Of course there is a railroad connection a few miles away; but really, the service of trains is too uncertain to bother about—so I never bother!"[1]

The exact dates that the Solters owned their house on River Vale Road will probably never be known; an early 1960s fire destroyed most of the local tax records. River Vale Township was formed in 1906, beginning as a laid-back farming community that has evolved into a recreation-oriented small town, complete with three golf courses for its 9,000 inhabitants. When the Solters were there, the population numbered in the mere hundreds, mostly farmers.[2] The closest film studios were in Fort Lee, less than 20 miles away, but then considered distant. In 1912, Fort Lee had satellite studios for many of the day's biggest production names—Selig, IMP, Famous Players-Lasky and Essanay—plus plenty of the smaller names, such as Eclair, Peerless, Solax and Lincoln.[3] If Florence had that film itch again, relief was only an hour's drive away.

Harry and Florence may have tried to settle into some semblance of domestic happiness. During his string of letters from Europe the autumn of 1912, Harry promised to devote all his energies and time to mending their marriage and his relationship with her mother. He also spoke about their future family, referring often to their "baby." Florence could have been pregnant at some point, possibly even causing her retirement from film work. The idea was never far from even her family's thoughts; Norman wrote in 1911 about meeting an old school friend, "Alice McCormic ... asked about you, and wanted to know if you had any little Solters yet." Norman assured Alice that they did not, "as yet."[4] Florence evidently never ruled out the possibility, and Harry made provisions in his 1912 will for any future offspring (another sign that his suicide threats should not be taken seriously, unless he had left knowing Florence was pregnant). Despite their plans and hopes, Harry and Florence never had any children.

Florence tried to immerse herself in the cultivation and care of roses, a tricky avocation that can become consuming. In many of her interviews during the 1910s, she mentions the roses with loving care. "I have always been passionately fond of flowers and flower-culture," she said once. Her goal was to create a new rose, to be named after herself. *Moving Picture World* reported in the magazine's usual style, "A pretty story is told of her efforts to produce a rose of distinctive character and it is said that she has been successful."[5] Of course, Carl Laemmle saw the gardening as Florence's escape route from what she really loved best—acting.

Film fans took a few months to realize that Florence was not among their weekly quotas. A cute poem in the September 1913 issue of *Moving Picture Story Magazine* wistfully asked, "Who is the girl we no more see?/Florence Lawrence. Oh, where can she be?"[6] Other magazines such as *Photoplay* ran contests to gauge the popularity of the players, with each subscriber receiving a certain number of votes to cast for their favorite. The readers often sent poetry or letters to illustrate their feelings. A Baltimore fan wrote in late 1912:

> Of all the girls in the picture shows,
> There are few that compare with the smiling Flo,
> Her eyes are bright and her teeth like pearls,
> And her hair is a mass of flowing curls.[7]

Bad verse abounded. Within the same issue, someone else wrote:

> Here's to Miss Lawrence, the brightest star of all,
> May she be with us through winter, spring and fall.
> So long live Miss Lawrence, I wish her blessings by the score,
> I know the boys are longing to be Mr. Owen Moore.[8]

Florence still received lots of fan mail, and she apparently tried to answer much of it, carrying on correspondence with several of the more persistent. She also kept clippings of the poetry from fan magazines or the original letter itself if the magazine gave it to her.

And no doubt she kept up with the film world even from her garden in New Jersey. She would have seen that Mary Pickford had again left Biograph in late 1912 (after having left IMP) and joined Famous Players in early 1913 for an astonishing rate of $500 per week. She would have noticed that dainty blonde who had joined Biograph in the last year was rightfully receiving better roles and much attention for her work, even though no one knew her yet as Lillian Gish. In December she probably saw the first Keystone Kop movie, produced and directed by her old friend Mack Sennett. And then only two months later, she may have read with interest the debut of a new toy of Edison's, the Kinetophone, which tried to meld film with voice.

Bigger but somewhat subtle changes were happening to the industry during this time as well. The moving picture was gaining a new attitude, and subsequently being perceived as somehow different to the American audiences. More people were starting to go to the movie theaters, which were now springing up in the nicer parts of town. Distributors and theater owners toyed with the workings of the system, giving better film choices to the nicer theaters that attracted a more desirable clientele. The nickelodeon, with its gaudy storefront everyman image, was showing its last film.

In the years between the death of the nickel movie in 1912 and the birth of the two-dollar film in 1915, when Griffith released *The Birth of a Nation*, movie history has much of a void. William K. Everson pointed out that these years were highlighted by the orchestrations of the star system, the organization of big production companies, and the evolution of the palatial theater, but also acknowledges, "Many film historians see this period as essentially one of commercial rather than artistic growth."[9]

What happened? Gradually the one- or two-reeler was replaced by the five-plus reel film, creating an hour's worth of engrossing entertainment, similar in form to a night at the theater seeing a play. American distributors learned in 1912 that American audiences could stand for it when Adolph Zukor successfully showed the four-reel French film *Queen Elizabeth*, Sarah Bernhardt's bid for immortality. Audiences sat still even longer in 1913 for *Quo Vadis?* at nine reels. Of course these were exceptional films, with length not being the main draw. Hundreds of single- and double-reels were still being produced and still being enjoyed. In 1912, anything longer than two reels merited special attention in the review pages of *Moving Picture World*; there simply were not many of them. And as Everson made clear, those features that were made were not very good, citing Helen Gardner's *Cleopatra* (1913) and Edwin Porter's *The Count of Monte Cristo* as examples. *Cleopatra* dragged with "its static posing, lack of action, and cardboard interior sets." *Cristo*, he thought, was not even actually directed: "A number of sets were provided and the actors let loose to go through their paces."[10] Still, these films were considered to be successful in their day, this time being novel as a lengthy feature. And just as one-reel films were strengthened and improved upon over the years, so were features. The process took more money and time than producers ten years before would have ever dreamed of, but the feature soon began to stand on it own, not as a specialty or oddball appearance. And again, the lawsuit-plagued Trust (now seen as General Film Company) helped the process right along by sticking up its collective nose at distributing features, even withholding D.W. Griffith's four-reel *Judith of Bethulia* for two years after he had secretly made it.

Florence's uninterested eye must have been caught again and again by these changes that only someone close to the industry would have seen. Now clearly moving pictures were not only here to stay, but they were changing the way people lived. The old-fashioned theatrics that she had known as a child were gone forever. The early days of film where she had worked, anachronisms and all, were disappearing. A story that needed two reels had two reels in which to tell it. The acting styles had changed as well; no more broad pantomime, just simple little feelings and gestures.

Retirement did not last much more than six months. Florence suddenly could not wait to get back to work. Not being on the screen was torturing her; knowing Mary Pickford was, and making $2,000 a month, was the ultimate humiliation. Besides, she could justify her return by picking up just about any fan magazine (and now there were plenty to choose from) to find her name with question marks after it. Her fans missed her; the industry needed her.

Harry and Florence made careful arrangements with Laemmle about how Florence would work so as not to overtax her. They agreed to a one-year contract for 26 two- or three-reel films, one every two weeks, with Florence making $350 per week. With this arrangement, they could remain in their home in New Jersey with only brief stays in New York at the studio. Their former Victor writer, Giles Warren, had left Universal during their absence to work with Marion Leonard and Stanner Taylor at Warners. Other writers, Leslie T. Peacock and Charles H. Hoadley, were assigned to create Florence's scenarios. The question of a leading man was temporarily solved by using Universal's fill-in man, Alexander Frank, for one or two films before they brought in Matt Moore, the handsome talented brother of Owen, to be Florence's leading man.

The Victor Company was still considered theirs, although her leading roles had been taken over by Fritzi Brunette. She and Owen Moore were paired soon after Florence left and together garnered usually good publicity and created a solid screen chemistry. The Victor brand, distributed through Universal, also expanded to several reels a week, including weekly releases from Biograph veterans James Kirkwood and Gertrude Robinson. The reviews for their films were surprisingly only fair on average, with most comments on the film as a whole rather than the work of the actors. Victor needed a boost only Florence could bring about.

Florence's return was covered in several magazines, with much publicity flourishing throughout her big year at Universal. *Moving Picture World* started the October 4 review of her first film *The Closed Door* with the words, "Florence Lawrence has come back," praising her work and the film: "Not only has she come back, but stronger and better than when she deserted the screen." The work of Harry Solter as director and Frank as her "foil" were also noted; "If all the coming releases measure up to the standard of the initial production, picture lovers may be content."[11]

Gladys Roosevelt interviewed Florence just as she was returning to work, a candid and airily open piece that appeared in *Moving Picture Story Magazine* in October 1913. While some of it is hopelessly dated, several tidbits of good information come out of it. Roosevelt claims that Florence is not only a suffragist, but "a banner-bearing, street parading suffragist!" aligning her with Mrs. Alva Belmont, a noted millionairess who enjoyed spending her ex-husband's money for the cause. Florence truly did believe in votes for women, however most notably from the standpoint that actresses would benefit from the equality.[12] Florence was not shy about her opinions, and she did know how to use them to her advantage. She had appeared on horseback in a Kinemacolor newsreel in March 1913 that covered a Washington, D.C., suffragists' parade, allowing the supporters to freely use her name for the cause. However, Florence did frown upon the radical tactics used by their English sisters. She told the British fan magazine *Pictures and the Picturegoer*, "I wonder you British people put up with them as you do." She knew that the British people were much more passionately angry about the way their women were protesting, and added a placating statement, "Men rule the State, yes; but women are the *mothers* of men—isn't that a higher responsibility?"[13] In America, though, she could appear to be, in Roosevelt's words, "short and light and slight and sensitive" and still be opinionated without much harm to herself professionally.

Photoplay noted that Florence was "probably the only 'star' who could retire at the height of her popularity, drop out of sight for a year, and then return to the pictures and immediately become as popular as before."[14] There had to be some truth to that; in the October 1913 *Photoplay*, with the votes tallied up through August 30, 1913, Florence was named one of the top 15 most popular players. This was before the release of *The Closed Door*; Florence had been off the screen for almost a year.[15]

The Victor family began to grow. Matt Moore continued to provide wonderful on-screen companionship that seemed to delight the audiences. The Victor Company also added more talented players as the year progressed. *Moving Picture World* announced in November that Lenora Von Ottinger had recently been recruited from the legitimate stage and would appear in "second leads and heavies" for Victor.[16] Earle Foxe, who had a busy career during the 1910s, ultimately co-starring in *The Fatal Ring* serial with Pearl White, appeared in many late 1912 Victor films with Florence. But sadly, as often happened in these years, many actors and actresses who appeared in these productions simply vanished after a few films. The boil of the star system had already begun, somewhat to Florence's dismay. "I like the people I meet and work with in Motion Pictures," she said. "They're frank and honest and sincere." She liked having a constant circle around her; the changes of studio life were one of the things that frustrated her so easily.

Florence's now-famed dressing room was attended by a black maid identified only as Rosey; Florence built it up as a homey little corner of the Victor studio that was hers exclusively. For interviews, Florence arranged herself in her suite to her best advantage, usually working at needlepoint, the very picture of goodly womankind. Interviewers ate it up. Teddy bears competed with dolls for space atop the piano, cushions and pillows were piled upon the floor, boxes of chocolates were within easy reach, and Florence's own needlepoint was safely displayed on tables under glass. One reporter prattled on, "Once in the suite of two rooms ... it is easy to forget that anything but daintiness ever existed in this bad old world."[17] Such an escape was something Florence had to have while doing her film work; evidently Harry was barely allowed inside the rooms.

The Victor films were well-received by audiences and viewers. Florence did try to move away from the girlish story lines which she was so well known for doing; many of these new Victor roles were more mature, involving Florence's broad range of emotions. Of course by now, the histrionic code had been completely replaced by the verisimilar, and Florence's natural abilities flowed well. After *The Closed Door*, Florence released *Girl O' the Woods*, probably filmed in Cuddebackville. Critics continue to praise her: "The strong personality of Miss Lawrence [is] being shown to the best advantage," *Moving Picture World* said of *Girl*.[18]

Florence did manage to jump on an industry trend for one film, *The False Bride*, by appearing in a dual role, using double exposures to portray two women who unwittingly changed places. This film was three reels in length, the first of several Florence did for Victor. Another role where Florence did not need double exposure, but where she played dual roles, was *A Mysterious Mystery*. She played herself as an actress and also a madwoman bent on impersonating and following her. Florence's use of doubles in this case was interesting and rather unique given the plot.

Not all of the stories were completely original. *A Girl and Her Money*, released in December 1913, had the same plot as the long-ago *Lady Helen's Escapade*, where a wealthy woman changes places with her maid and continues the charade even after the maid's death. A January 1914 release, *The Coryphee*, was pointed out to be based on the stage play *The School for Scandal*, only brought up to date; Florence portrayed an actress who takes the blame when her married cousin's lover appears at midnight. The "theatrical girl" assuredly could have looser morals than a married woman; "It is handled delicately and with good suspense."[19] Florence may have tried to balance out this stereotype with the earlier release, *The Spender*, where the vaudeville actress she portrayed cured her boyfriend of overspending.[20] Another story seeming to have been taken from a Biograph short was *The Bribe*, released in May 1914. This story, showing a young woman hypnotized into stealing from her father's safe, ran along the same lines as *The Criminal Hypnotist*.

Florence's portrayals of her youthful-maiden roles were offset by several strong performances in dramatic stories. She brushed the Jewish religion with *Unto the Third Generation*, showing a young woman's struggle with the decision to marry outside her faith. Florence also convincingly played a mother whose child has died, probably her tenth reprisal of such a role, in *Influence of Sympathy*. This time, the bereaved mother finds peace in caring for a lame child. In February 1914, the plot of *The Stepmother* was called "one of the strongest two-reel stories of domestic life we have seen in a long time."[21] A mature role of another kind came with *Diplomatic Flo* in March. Florence portrayed a woman caught up in a modern-day foreign arms intrigue, a rare sort of role for the day. Another different role came at the very end of her year in a sophisticated comedy called *The Man Who Was Never Kissed*. *Moving Picture World* struggled to define the highbrow plot: "an amusing two-reel story which verges on the 'spicy' without giving actual offense ... a commendable offering of the smart, breezy type."[22]

Florence's famous hoyden roles were revisited in *Her Ragged Knight* and *The Mad Man's Ward*, both released in the summer of 1914. Even in the confusing story line presented in *His Wife's Child*, Florence's characterization shows through: "A pleasing touch of humor appears in the scene where the waif mistakes the wax model in a department store for a living being."[23]

Because the viewers (and reviewers) expected so much of Florence, any time she did not act completely convincingly, she heard about it. June 1914's *A Disenchantment* was seen as entertainment "in a mild sort of way, but does not represent this company at its best."[24] *A Mysterious Mystery*, released in September 1914, was "quite entertaining," but Florence's work was "not as strong as some things we have seen her in."[25] The worst criticism may have come with *The Honor of the Humble* in August 1914. "The girl [Florence] would have gained more interest if she had not thrown herself at the Count so violently." The plot was faulty, the ending hasty, but *Moving Picture World* still assured viewers that it "will hold the interest."[26] Upon closer examination, the less-than-glowing reviews all appear at the end of her contract, when she would be tired of the grind. With her physical and mental health impaired, her performances were simply not as good as they should have been.

The decline in her work is also attributed to an on-set accident that somehow permanently disabled her career. If a stunt double had been used, there is no telling where Florence's career would have gone. She could have continued in her on-again, off-again cycle of filmwork, or she might have actually created a successful features career for herself. But her injury coupled with her frame of mind was enough to take her out of the spotlight for good.

Stunt doubles were not unheard of—after all, Harry had entered the film business as the acting double for J. Stuart Blackton at Vitagraph—but usually players were expected to do their own work, except of course at times when a dummy would do. An interview with Matt, Owen and Tom Moore in 1915 showed that the players were usually proud to do their own risky footwork: "Some of their stunts as you will have remarked in the movies require just about as much nerve and involve as much danger as if they were true-true perils devised for the wicked for the obfuscation of the pure and innocent."[27] Anthony Slide points out that while many silent film performers did their own stunts, there were exceptions, but since the stunt man was not credited with the work, especially in these days when the actor was just beginning to get credit, the public happily assumed the player did it all.[28] Writer Creighton Hamilton, in a 1916 *Picture-Play Magazine,* pointed out that fewer stunt-filled movies were being made that year than in the past because the public was learning how some stunts were performed. "The exposure of many of the tricks ... made the people who saw the pictures skeptical about believing the real thing." Florence was not considered to be one of the wilder actresses in films, not with the likes of Helen Holmes, Helen Gibson and Cleo Madison, who did stunts that seem impossible even today.[29]

Florence, perfectionist that she was, certainly would not have allowed anyone to double for her for any reason, and at this point, she would have expected that Harry would know her and her capabilities well enough that he would not place her in danger. Fortunately her particularly favorite type of story—the dramatic comedy—did not usually require much in the way of actual jeopardy. Her luck ran out at the end of March 1914, when Harry asked her to perform a dramatic scene in *The Pawns of Destiny* that involved her carrying a supposedly unconscious and blind Matt Moore down a flight of stairs in a fire. Florence gamely tried to comply.

"We had to do it three times, and I was supposed to faint on the second landing," Florence told an interviewer two years later. "I was very near fainting in reality when we had finished the picture."[30] In an interview published on April 4, 1914, just after the incident, she introduced Matt as the "huskey that I dragged down stairs in the picture, and nobody will believe I did it."[31]

Her exact injuries are unknown. In the dawning age of Hollywood journalism, the accident did not make the newspapers. It may not have even appeared to be much of an accident at that time; Florence apparently continued working with little or no time off. The stories of horrible facial scarring and debilitating back injuries do not seem to have happened at this time. She made ten more films in 1914 (all two or three reels) after *The Pawns of Destiny*. Nothing about her physical appearance or mobility was noticed, although reviewers cited her slightly disappointing performances.

A biographical article in *Films in Review*, perpetuates this myth: "She was licked by flames, her hair was singed, and she suffered a serious fall. She was in shock for a month, and when she was able to return to work, she had a long scar under her chin, some burns on her face, a terrible back problem and, the worst part for someone as sensitive as she—shattered nerves."[32] None of these statements are true, even the last at this time. If Florence had truly collapsed, no amount of inducement or pressure could have made her continue working for another four months. She and Harry both had broken contracts before; Laemmle in particular would have been used to it.

Another myth that has arisen from this accident was that she returned into a burning building to save her co-star Matt Moore. A nice angelic sentiment, particularly for Florence, but again this was probably not true. Florence did care enough for her friends to have done just about anything for them, and doubtlessly she would have tried to save someone from a fire. But since this fire was completely staged and Florence's character was saving Moore's character, this is how she and others chose to remember the scene. She probably did fall at some point, trying to carry the 175-pound actor.

"I found afterwards that my back had been injured," she said in 1916. "The pain grew worse as the days went on, and when it spread to the back of my head I gave in to it and went to bed for long weeks." She gamely worked out the rest of her contract, even participating in the July release, *The Great Universal Mystery*, starring King Baggot and featuring just about every other Laemmle employee. When she had made the number of films that she needed to, she then went home to New Jersey with Harry and tried to figure out what to do next.

Despite her assumed ill health and injuries, she managed to write a lengthy four-part autobiography serialized in *Photoplay* magazine from November 1914 to February 1915. Monte Katterjohn, whose scenario career spanned from the earliest IMP days, through Paralta, Famous Players, Metropolitan and finally ended up with Paramount as sound came in, began the project, intending for it to be a book called *Growing Up with the World's Newest Art*. Katterjohn told *Moving Picture World* that he was struck by the

Florence, in her private dressing room, around 1914. Cosmetics and mirrors are on the vanity table, a bearskin and family photos are on the wall, and needlepoint pillows and pom-pom edged drapery decorates the furniture. Photograph courtesy of Fort Lee Public Library, Fort Lee, New Jersey.

wonderful career that Florence had already had. "Few people, even in the busy production realm of the film play, know that Miss Lawrence has enjoyed the most remarkable experiences within the wish of any motion picture actress, for she is the only picture star of today who has been continuously before the motion picture camera since the photoplay stepped out of the novelty class."[33] The *Photoplay* editorial that introduced the series echoed Katterjohn's statement, dating picture plays back to the beginning of 1907. *Photoplay* added that the editors felt that Florence's story was "the most valuable contribution to motion picture literature up to this time—the authentic life-story of the most remarkable motion picture actress of today, Florence Lawrence, whose following throughout the civilized world is far greater than any star of the legitimate stage."[34] Strong words for a woman who had been fired or retired from motion pictures at least four times since she began.

The series started very strongly, only to taper off to only a few pages closer to the back of the magazine by the conclusion. Florence's last Victor film was released the same month as the first installment; interest would seem to wane as her screen activity diminished. The first part, written and labeled as such by both Florence and Katterjohn, tells of Florence's childhood and career up through her first movie role with Edison. The second tells about her work at Vitagraph. The third is about her time at Biograph. The last manages to squeeze her years at IMP, Lubin and Victor into about five pages. Guest writers such as Harry Solter (never identified as her husband, only her director) and J. Stuart Blackton contributed short "interludes," to liven the story-telling. Each article is well illustrated with studio shots and still photography from films.

The series is fun to read, even more so with a knowledge of early film history, and if indeed Florence did write the parts attributed to her, she seemed to enjoy turning her memories into print. The sentiment, slang and honesty characteristic of a novice writer are there. She closes the series with words that could only have come straight from her: "And now I say good-bye. I love you all—love you with all my heart and soul. When I look from my window at night I wonder if there is anything I have ever done to cause you pain. I hope not. So again, good-bye!"

In the brief space that she devotes to her work with the Victor Company, Florence does not mention her accident, saying only that she currently intended to remain at her farm for a few months before coming back to work. "And what are my plans, do you wonder?" she asked whimsically. "Dear readers, have I not told you that Fate shapes our destinies, leading the oldest and most experienced of us where she will?"[35]

In spite of her carefree words, Florence was not one to let Fate have its way with her. She liked being in control of her life and her career. She was used to doing what she pleased. But this time, she found herself losing a battle she barely had begun fighting.

Chapter Nine

COMEBACK AGAIN

> *You're only as good as your last picture.*
> —Marie Dressler

Florence did not have a new film out between November 1914 and April 1916. However, the now constant re-releasing and showing of the acclaimed Biograph split- and one-reel "classics" helped maintain her popularity. During this year and a half, Florence was not completely at leisure, even though later she would claim to have been handicapped with pain. In some ways she was very busy. In March 1915, one year after the accident, she released a press announcement through Unico News Service that detailed her career and recent activities. No mention was made of Harry, but her "country residence" was mentioned, as was her mother, with whom a fresh relationship had been created. "In her mother she not only finds all mother, but also a loveable friend and intimate pal. It has been whispered that Florence Lawrence and her mother intend to tour the continent in their automobiles, and their destination is San Francisco."[1]

This press release, complete with instructions to news editors to "file for quick reference," gave much nonspecific information about her career, possibly to be seen as an announcement that she was essentially "at liberty." Unico could have been part of Universal, but this does not seem likely; Carl Laemmle would have had his company's name entangled with hers. Laemmle may have been miffed that Florence was trying to strike out on her own.

Her absence was again noticed in the pages of the fan magazines. Unfortunately, the answers to the question of "Where is Florence?" often brought many more questions. The August 1915 question-and-answer column in *Photoplay* admitted for the first time that Florence was married, but gave her husband's name as Leigh B. Trafton. This name appears several times in *Photoplay* over the next few months as her husband. The August question-and-answer column also contains the following: "Miss Lawrence was recently operated upon, but is now out of the hospital and contemplates a return to the screen very shortly. She and her husband make their home in New Jersey, and he will undoubtedly appear with her in the pictures."[2] *Moving Picture World* reported in August that Florence Laurence [sic] was seriously ill at her country home in Milford, Massachusetts. The journal attributed her retirement from moving pictures (from Lubin and Victor) to ill health and gave her husband's name as Harry L. Salter.[3] A month later, *Moving Picture World* reversed itself and said that Florence, "in spite of reports to the contrary, is neither sick or ailing." She had been in a recent automobile accident, but "no ill results followed, however, more serious than a shock to the nerves of some members of the party that were being conveyed to her country home for a week-end outing, and considerably added to the debit side of her day book, for repairs to the injured car." This time her retirement from acting was called temporary; the magazine added that she had "grown more sylph-like and roguish than ever" during her recent stay in New Jersey.[4]

At Christmas of 1915, she told of having a great party and her first Christmas tree ever. "You see," she told a reporter, "I have so often been working on Christmas, and before that we were nearly always traveling." She does not say whether her husband was there or not, but Florence obviously had the time of her life. "We played games—hid a prize in a stocking, you know, and hunted the whole farm for it. You should have seen us, climbing up on the hay mow and in and out of the stall of the horses and cows, and up in the attic!"[5]

Few to no personal papers from this year seem to have survived, so what happened when is speculative. Her strained back may have finally given out a year after the accident, needing surgery. Her mother may have moved into their house in New Jersey since there was, unusually, no correspondence between Lotta and Florence. Florence and Harry may have formally separated during the year, or they may have made another effort at saving their marriage in 1915.

The marriage, however, was essentially over. In March 1916, she shrugged off the matrimony problem. "I have been busy at being married. Oh yes! I'm married still, but I'm not working at it any longer."[6] Enough said; the Solters were headed for a personal and professional break.

Despite these problems, Florence let it be known at the end of the year that she intended to return to the screen. *Moving Picture World* cheered her decision. "There is much to be gained by the manufacturer as well as the public by the return of a favorite star, especially at a time when the moving picture is making such rapid strides, and the quality of the work demanded by an intelligent public requires that only the best talent be supplied to them." Florence, the paper reported, had not made the decision about what firm she would work for; "Several offers are pending."[7] The Florence Lawrence cycle was beginning once again.

Speculation about where Florence would work did not last long. "Carl Laemmle for the Third Time Corrals the 'Girl of a Thousand Faces,'" proclaimed the January 1, 1916, edition of *Moving Picture World*.[8] "Florence Lawrence, First and Most Recent Star of the Universal," read the January 8, 1916, cover of *Moving Picture Weekly*. *Photoplay* ran her image in March, with the cutline, "A photographer's recent grab at Florence Lawrence, who had scarcely time to pause for her picture while *coming back*. She is returning by the door at which she made her exit, many months ago: Universal."[9]

A hint of the changes that were coming in Florence's career was hidden within the *Moving Picture World* article. "One of the best directors in the business will guide her screen efforts," the Laemmle camp boasted. Evidently this was not to be Harry Solter. Stuart Paton, a new director at Universal, was soon selected to put Florence's face back upon the screen. A week after declaring that they had her, Universal announced that her first project would be a picture based on Marie Corelli's novel *Thelma*. However, she began working instead on an adaptation of *The Elusive Isabel*, a novel written seven years earlier by the late Jacques Futrelle. (Futrelle, known as the American Sherlock Holmes, had perished on the *Titanic* in 1912.) The story is an interesting tale of a conspiracy by Latin nations to rule the world. Florence played Isabel Thorne, a diplomatic aide to a prince, who falls in love with an American secret service agent.

Surrounding Florence were old friends such as Inez Ranous, wife of her former Vitagraph and IMP director William Ranous. William Ranous had died the previous April in California, and Inez gamely tried to keep working in motion pictures for several years. Another favorite player was her one-time Romeo Paul Panzer, playing a secondary love interest to Florence's Isabel. Her former Victor co-star Jack Newton added to the troupe. New friends rounded out the cast. Sydney Bracy, Wallace Clarke and William Welsh were all supporting players to Harry Millarde, the romantic lead.

Myths about her existence during the preceding two years began almost immediately. One article claimed she had been traipsing about Europe and the Holy Land,[10] a risky venture given the war now raging. Another said she had merely looked "to the affairs of her household, tended her garden and romped to her heart's content."[11] Only in one place does she discuss her accident from almost two years before. "I have spent most of the time in being very ill and trying to get over it," she told Gladys Jones in *Feature Movie Magazine*, referring to her time off the screen. "I hope it is all over now, but they say I must still be careful."[12]

Once in the spotlight, Florence did all she could to stay there. When *Jeanne Doré*, a Universal import starring Sarah Bernhardt, was pre-released in early January 1916 in New York City's Proctor theaters, Florence attended the premiere and appeared onstage before the film was shown. To her delight, the audience greeted her with enthusiastic applause.[13] Florence also sat for many interviews and photo shoots. She managed to appear as both an all–American girl hovering between "where womanhood and girlhood meet" and a worldly connoisseur of the best of European fashions and trends. Several photos from early 1916 show Florence dressed in exotic French negligees, speaking of how sensible the French were when it came to dressing. "Miss Lawrence has traveled so much abroad that international clothes customs make an interesting topic of discussion with her,"[14] one reporter cooed. Another proclaimed, "Miss Lawrence is a globe-trotter, and can tell you how the moon looks rising on the Sphinx in the Egyptian desert, or how the 'dawn comes up like thunder,' out of China, 'cross the bay,'" but declared also that Florence was just "a little figure, more like Alice-in-Wonderland than the first Universal star."[15]

The film industry pulled itself together for a party in late February, dubbing it the "Movie Costume and Civic Ball," commandeering Madison Square Garden for the weekend. Members of the Screen Club and New York Exhibitors Association were the coordinators, and an estimated 16,000 people attended. In March 1916, Universal Film Manufacturing held its own party for its employees. Florence was a member of the reception committee for the masquerade ball held at the Grand Central Palace in New York City on March 18. Her costume was not identified, even though Violet Mersereau's Little Lord Fauntleroy and Carl Laemmle's old woman disguise both made it into *Moving Picture World*'s article about the event. Florence's importance to Universal, however, was not forgotten. *Moving Picture World* reported, "One of the enjoyable features of the evening was the appearance of Helen Coyle in a song and dance number, the music for which was written by Emma R. Steiner. It is called 'Florence Lawrence.'"

The song "Florence Lawrence" followed a musical trend of the early 1900s of dedicating or writing compositions to popular persons or events. The instructions for the song included that it was to be "Sung Whilst Dancing," and the dances could include the fox-trot or waltz. Florence's photo graced the cover, one from the series taken in a pale lavender French gown. The song itself could have been written for anyone, but did certainly suit Florence, opening with:

> Light as a fairy, quite as contrary
> Golden and pink and white
> Eyes like the Violet, Lips like the cherry,
> Cheeks that in summer grow brown as a berry.
> Voice that is trilling, Now gently thrilling,
> Softly and sweet and low.

Steiner was a dear friend, a frequent visitor in Florence's dressing rooms where she played the piano in accompaniment to Florence's whistling. Emma

Steiner had been an important figure in the American musical world in the last years of the nineteenth century, being one of the first successful career woman conductors. She conducted, composed and played several instruments during her life, creating such works as "The Burra Pundit," "The Man from Paris" and "The Flag—Forever May It Wave." Only three years before her 1928 death, Steiner conducted a concert of her own works at the Metropolitan Opera House in New York City.[16] For such an honor to have been presented to Florence at the Universal Ball must have certainly been a high point in her career, if not her life.

And then there was actual work. Many scenes for *Elusive Isabel* were taken on location in Washington, D.C.; *Moving Picture World* seemed to delight in relaying anecdotes about the company's doings. Even Stuart Paton was mentioned for having celebrated his fifth wedding anniversary with a party in April. The year 1916 was the highest point of Paton's career, even though *Isabel* was not it. He adapted Jules Verne's *20,000 Leagues Under the Sea* for Universal; produced, directed and released the undersea science fiction by the end of the year. When *Elusive Isabel* was completed, Florence then began work on another film, *Spring Time and Tillie Todd*, the manuscript of which she kept for many years. A writer for *Moving Picture World* caught her working in Fort Lee, New Jersey, wearing "the woeful attire of a slavey, torn red calico bodice, black skirt of a rather rapid fit on an already slim form, much beholed stockings with yellow tops that started a bit below the knees."[17]

Elusive Isabel was released on April 24, 1916. It was Florence's first full-fledged feature film. Even after all the hype surrounding her comeback, the reviews were only lukewarm. *Moving Picture World* expressed sympathy that a better vehicle was not provided for Miss Lawrence to make her re-debut in the film world, in its usual way, never blaming Florence for any bad work.[18] *Variety* dismissed the picture with only a few words: "The feature in six reels is a very much jumbled up affair that runs along in halting fashion and finally ends up nowhere... The picture is just about a third-rate feature."[19] After the hugely emotional uprasing not a month before, Florence had to have been humiliated by the dull reviews.

More than likely she quit rather than risk being fired. *The Billboard* headlined their April 1 Pictures section with "Florence Lawrence Out of Universal's Employ." The article said that Florence had quit the Universal Film Manufacturing Company "vowing she will never return" and explaining her departure with a "complicated narrative of friction and internal disturbances."[20] The other film press publications commented on her departure briefly and matter-of-factly. "The corporation side of it was that the actress had an attack of temperament; the other side is mum," *Photoplay* said, comparing the "loud noises" that Universal had made when Florence arrived and the "whisper" when she left.[21] *Moving Picture World* agreed with the rumor that "Florry Lorry" had been volatile, but added that "she had no written or

Florence in a signature beaded negligee and feathered boudoir cap. In this photograph, like others from the mid–1910s, Florence has a bracelet pushed up tight on her arm, a sign of nervousness.

verbal contract with the Universal President, Laemmle had no means of making her stay at the big new Fort Lee studio."[22] Perhaps not coincidentally, Bluebird Productions announced in June that the company would stop hyping the names of the stars in their productions, commenting in *The Billboard*, "Too long has the public followed names in picture houses, only to meet with disappointment time and again because the name was all that the entertainment vouchsafed." This so-called "break away from moving picture tradition"[23] did not help Bluebird very long; within a year, the company had vanished from the vast picture world.

Elusive Isabel was six reels, the longest film that Florence had ever made. This of course was becoming a norm for the industry at this time. The industry had changed so much that Florence may have barely recognized what was going on around her when she returned to work. From the last part of 1914 to the first part of 1916 marked several specific changes in the way movies were made, the way they were shown and the way they were watched.

The movies were moving west. After years of making shorts in California, producers had taken the permanent step of making features there as well, and gradually Los Angeles was losing the battle to keep Hollywood a quiet, harmless suburb. All the major companies had western offices by 1915, and the eastern filmmaking scene was quickly losing its glamour. Places like "Universal City" were springing up, taking 250 acres of sandy patch outside Los Angeles and creating a fantasy moviemaking place.

The second change was the birth of the movie palace. When Samuel Rothapfel opened the doors at the Regent Theater in New York in 1914, he introduced a new era of movie theaters, with the usher wearing a tuxedo, the 16-piece orchestra in tune, and the song-slide not in unison but by a soprano opera soloist. His efforts and vision were applauded—and copied. Soon going to the movies was no less than a night of symphonic music or Broadway show or classical ballet. And just in time, too, for the moving picture was flexing its little muscles, and films such as *The Birth of a Nation* were showing.

No single history of silent film, or even film in general, can omit D.W. Griffith's opus. The work of a genius, the propaganda of racism, the distortion of history, the timelessness of love—*The Birth of a Nation* is all this and more. *Birth* carried the potential of film from elementary school to high school in two hours, 40 minutes. Historian Gene Brown sums it up well: "Aesthetically, with its advancement of the craft of editing, multiple camera angles, and close-ups to tell a story on an epic scale, it is a stunning, landmark American film."[24] And yet, *Birth of a Nation* is much more than just the stunning visual. *Birth* reaches into personal thoughts and expands the memories; history, at least from one person's view, comes alive.

Birth does seem to overshadow everything else from 1915, but other things happened while Florence was off the screen. Theda Bara was the seductive (and very bad) vamp in *A Fool There Was*, opening in January 1915. Rules for women seemingly changed overnight, as did the definition of "star." In his book *Movie Star*, Ethan Mordden has drawn a good comparison of the popularity of Theda Bara and Florence Lawrence: "They typify the two most basic elements of stardom, the public's interest and the producer's engineering." The difference, he said, was that Bara's star was developed, Florence's star was spontaneous. Bara was seen "as an institution before anyone even knew who she was." Florence, on the other hand, had already been "virtually acclaimed by her fans"; Laemmle's push in her publicity merely "centralized" all those who knew her face but not her name.[25]

Stardom was not restricted to the birth of the vamp character in 1915. Charlie Chaplin pulled all of the right clothes and mastered the waddle to make "the Tramp" his trademark, and Harold Lloyd became a hit as Lonesome Luke in *Just Nuts*. Other soon-to-be-famous players with 1915 screen debuts were Douglas Fairbanks and W.C. Fields. Pearl White, hugely popular after the 1914 serial *The Perils of Pauline*, continued to endanger herself in *The Exploits of Elaine* throughout 1915. Daniel Blum estimated that over a dozen other serials were running during the year, such as *Zudora* from Thanhouser and *Who Pays?* from Pathé.[26]

And then, salary. Florence was probably right in the industry average for a solid leading lady in 1916, around $500 per week. But Florence's favorite little nemesis Mary Pickford was very publicly making $4,000 per week from Famous Players, and Charlie Chaplin signed with Essanay at $1,250 per week. The times were changing.

Another overlooked contribution to film history, attributed to Florence, was in costuming. In early 1916, Florence was recognized by several writers as "the first woman who realized the significance of clothes on the screen."[27] *Moving Picture World* gave her credit for the "first individual costuming given to any picture play ... [when] she wore new and elaborate costumes for the role of 'Lady Helen'" in the old Biograph classic, *Lady Helen's Escapade*.[28] Even as early as 1911, Lubin press releases touted the clothes specially created for Florence's roles: "The gowns ... are real triumphs of the dressmaker's art, bearing the unmistakable stamp of the Rue de la Paix. Moreover, Miss Lawrence wears them with as much grace as a born Parisienne."[29] Florence indeed had a lovely figure which was showed to perfection when wearing well-tailored clothing. The expense could be excused so long as the actress looked good and felt better about herself, something Harry probably helped her insist upon.

But Florence herself seemed to have developed a love-hate relationship with clothing. When asked about her wardrobe for her upcoming movie, she breezily replied, "When my first picture is decided upon, I shall seriously interest myself in the proper gowns for it ... Each gown must fit the situation so well that it supplements instead of detracting from the effect. My audience must feel that I look the character I am playing in every detail. That is why I must make a thorough study of my role before I dress it." Her thoughtfulness in choosing clothing changed when she was buying only for her personal self, for she added, "Out on my farm I dress to please myself. I buy my frocks in the children's department—not misses, children's. One piece frocks for ninety-eight cents sometimes."[30]

But when she was buying for her public self, Florence did not mind being extravagant. She had a full-length mink with matching muff, plus at least one fur shawl. She chose to wear imported French negligees with matching caps in her city apartments or dressing room, her outfit often becoming part of an interview. But the ultimate in her spending for clothes was highlighted in April 1916 when it was reported that she had recently purchased two genuine French gowns from the Maison Maurice. The skirt of one of these gowns was 18 yards around the bottom hem, truly remarkable even for those post-crinoline days. Florence had a series of photos made in this orchid silk ensemble, complete with hat and shoes. The other, not much less ornate, was a silver evening dress covered in hundreds of rhinestones. *Moving Picture World* amazingly devoted almost an entire column to describing these gowns, as effusively as any society writer might minutely describe a wedding dress.

Regardless of these wildly decorative costumes that Florence loved to wear, she also held very conservative opinions about dressing for other activities. She advocated a standardized dress for professional or business women, much like mens, such as "knickers and three quarter coat with golf stockings, low rubber heel shoes."[31] She relented slightly when one interviewer asked in horror if she meant to have women in trousers. "Skirts are more practical if they are reasonable designed, and far more feminine ... Perhaps this reform may be nearer than we realize. Who knows? Men's dress was conventionalized only about one hundred years ago."[32] Florence also loved hats and wore them as often as she could, both in private or on screen.

Florence returned home to her sprawling farm unemployed and unemployable, and now facing an even larger problem—divorce. The experiment that she and Harry seem to have undergone—having someone else direct her films—had failed. The Solters were back to nothing in common.

Not able to express herself before a camera, she tried to convey her feelings through poetry. A poem scrawled on an index card–sized sheet of paper mourned her pain, inside and out:

> I was hurt—but my back was a-mendin'
> It was shinin' and bright outside;
> I longed to be out in the Spring and the birds,
> And tear up the ground far and wide.
>
> I was hurt! but my nerves were much better—
> The doctors had done a good job;

> Improvin'! but not fit to work yet,
> But I'm hopin' and prayin' to God.
>
> But it isn't my back or my nerves tho
> That's causin' me most of the pain.
> My heart is just about bustin'
> But I ain't a-goin' to complain.
>
> I'd like to be out with nature
> There ain't no heart aches there,
> You don't need no doctors or nursin'
> But just a lot of fresh air.³³

Florence called this miserable poem "Broken Hearted." Its cadence lends itself better to voice than to the eye. The obvious implications are that her lingering back injuries were not as devastating as the rift between herself and Harry. Florence was not shy in sharing her words with the world; *Billboard* magazine published it in late May 1916, commenting, "During the recent inclement weather Miss Lawrence, while in a fit of the blues, wrote the following, which is an expression straight from the heart." The magazine also added that Florence was "fast recovering" from her back injuries.³⁴ Evidently the separation from her husband was not mending as quickly.

Florence and Harry had a "Hollywood marriage" before Hollywood knew that such a thing existed. Two strong careers, two very creative people, two separate paths desperately trying to merge into one. *Photoplay* looked at the divorce rate between celebrities in 1926, and Florence and Harry could have written the article ten years before then, summed up with one line from the article, "He is a director and she an actress; divorce is inevitable." Writer Herbert Howe interviewed an unnamed director who claimed that marriage and acting were incompatible. "Self-expression, taking the form of art, is naturally selfish. It does not yield to compromise, and this is a requirement of marriage."

Howe also used an example of an actress-wife and director-husband to show how the acting art tears apart the marriage: The husband acts out a part from the latest work he is directing for his adoring bride, she responds with sincerity and amusement at first, but as the performances continued, her interest and appreciation floundered. "As an audience she gradually failed to react, until, to save her home she couldn't let loose a smile or a sigh even when the occasion demanded ... She was tired of playing the audience ... For what an actor demands primarily is not a wife but an audience."³⁵ Without a doubt, the same could apply to an actress.

The Solters' combined instability created a myriad of problems that seemed insurmountable. Between insecurities and threats of suicide, Harry and Florence would have had a difficult time as a married couple whatever their professions. Harry had been instrumental in putting the roles which he felt would suit Florence in front of her, whether she had wanted to play them or not. In the 1914 memoirs, Katterjohn amusingly told the story of how Florence had become interested in a "pitifully real" story of a young girl addicted to cocaine and morphine. She desperately wanted to purchase and produce it, only to be rebuffed by Harry. "He feared nervous prostration might result from her attempting the part," Katterjohn stated. Harry finally induced Florence to do a "rollicking comedy drama ... [that] appealed to her whimsical nature more strongly than did the 'dope' story to her serious side." Katterjohn also told the *Photoplay* readers that "her director" would not allow her to do a death scene again, for "such scenes frequently grip Miss Lawrence for several days, affecting her to such an extent that she is unable to work."[36]

For all of Katterjohn's levity, Florence was more than likely not amused by Harry's heavy-handed control of her career. She knew that he threw himself into his work every bit as hard as she did; their 1912 separation had also been rooted in what Florence saw as Harry ignoring her, as well as quarreling with her mother. Harry had told his story to the opera singer on the boat as he traveled to Europe, fully taking the blame for himself:

> I was not a genius, and only the closest application to the work I had taken up, was there any chance for success. And it was this close application that led to our quarrel, for my love thought that I had neglected her, and that in my small brain, I became angry, because she could not see that it was for her only that I was working for.

Not talking and sharing may have only been part of their problem. Harry pleaded for understanding and openness in another letter: "You say I have never touched your soul, but I will, just as sure as there is a God who judges." The confrontation in which those words were spoken obviously had been full of fire. For an actress to accuse her director of not reading her well is one thing; for a wife to tell her husband he had never even penetrated the surface of their relationship is another. For an actress-wife to tell her director-husband that he had not touched her soul must have been a humiliating blow that Harry should have taken personally and professionally.

That this marriage has lasted beyond the 1912 break-up was miraculous. The inevitable occurred in 1916 when they filed for divorce. Her brother George asked Lotta in a July 1916 letter, "How did Flo come out with her divorce case?" George also suggested that he knew Florence was trying to return to work again. "So Flo is getting up another company of her own, is she, well I hope she does better than she did before. She did not seem to have the right kind of stuff with that company she had." Familial loyalty got the better of him when he added, "Of course that husband of hers may have had something to do with that part of it."[37] Even as early as April 1916, *Billboard* also announced that Florence was weighing new offers, including vaudeville, all apparently without Harry's approval or involvement.[38]

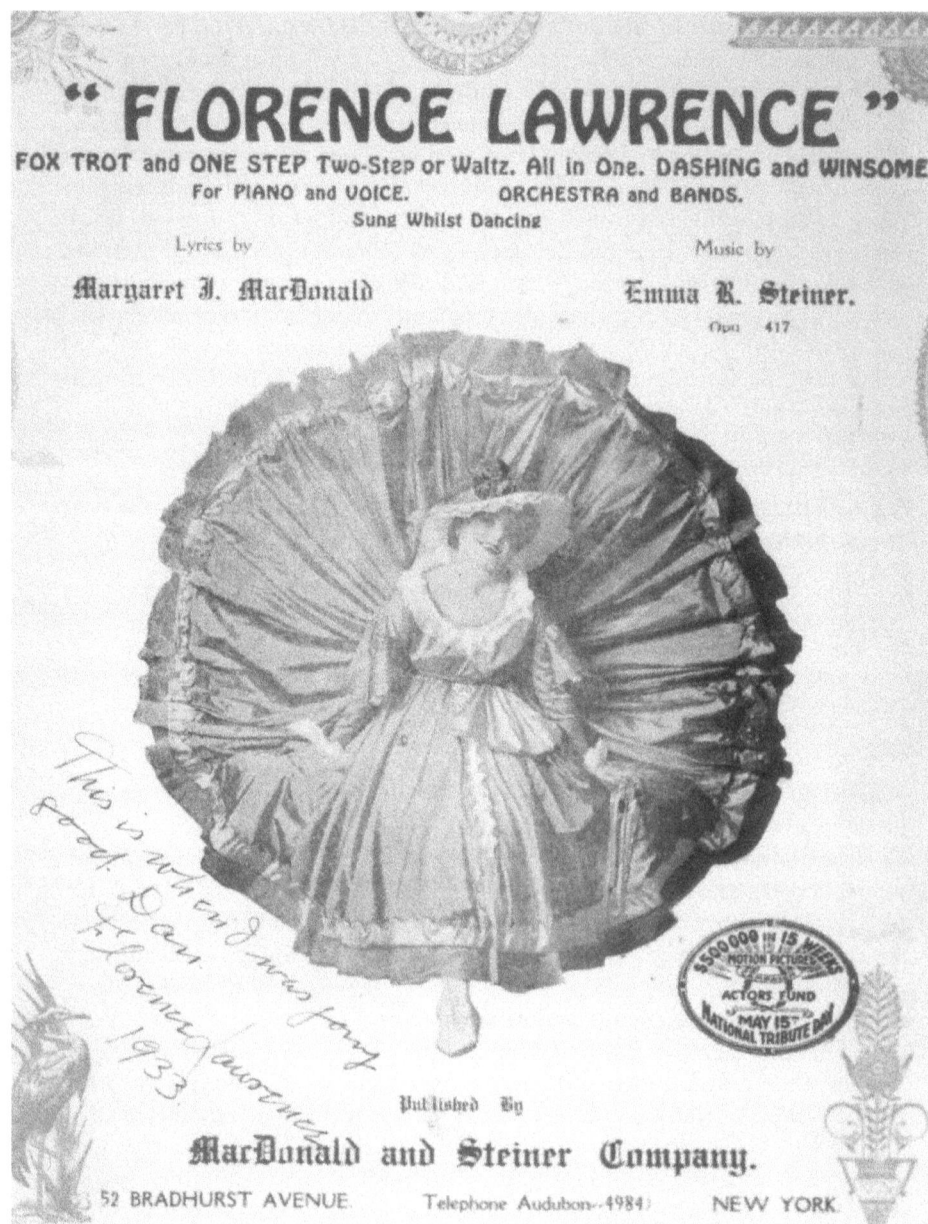

The front cover from Emma Steiner's song, "Florence Lawrence," published by MacDonald and Steiner Company in 1916. Florence presented a copy to Daniel Blum in 1933. Photograph courtesy of the Wisconsin Center for Film and Theater Research.

Harry was using the New York Screen Club mansion address, 165 West 47th Street, and stationery in autumn 1916, having either left or been thrown out of the River Vale farm. An interesting series of notes to Florence started in September, beginning with, "I am going to a hospital to have a serious operation. I should like to see you before." The next letter concerned a possible settlement in their divorce: "There are several ways of deeding the farm over to you and will explain to you when I see you." Harry told her that he was arranging for someone to inspect the farm property and make a report back to him.

The unstated nature of his operation was enough to keep him in bed, but not without a pen in his hand. "Has the man been out to the farm?" he demanded next. "I have been confined to my room most of the time and unable to get to Hackensack to see the cause of the delay." In the middle of October he wrote again: "As you failed to keep your appointment with [me] it seems you will not do the honorable thing." Their separation this time was evidently not working well either. "I have decided to come home which is as much mine as yours, and not go to a hospital and lie in a public ward. To save any unpleasantness and extreme measures you will have to get other quarters for the parties who are living in my home and on my money." Florence's replies are lost, but she may have been wryly amused to see this story unfold. It was the same tale that Harry had heard from the opera singer aboard the *Wilhelm* back in 1912 when they had separated, except the opera singer had gone back to her husband when he declared he was dying.

Without Harry and her career, she turned again to writing poetry. Sometimes, her misery was less than subtle:

> Feel blue? Don't stew! Come on have a game of ball.
> There's nothing like that American game.
> Your troubles? Forget them all!
> Ball hard! Ground soft! If you strike either, don't get mad;
> We all have ups and downs, you know, let's all be Glad.
> Friend true—game thru; What more can I say?
> If you go through life without a wife,
> Anyway, you've got to pay.[39]

Florence must have felt completely cut off from the world she had been on top of not six months before. Around the time that she and Harry were squabbling over ownership of the farm, Florence sent a passionately appealing letter to Carl Laemmle, not asking for employment, but rather for cash. Florence retained a draft of the letter in her files; the copy that she sent was, hopefully, more polished and legible.

> This is just a friendly letter to ask you to be fair with me—you know of course the *Isabelle* [sic] picture was a great detriment to me and also you

remember the offer I had from another concern, but I had given my word to you and couldn't accept it. Also you know the Victor Co. would not be in existance [sic] today but for me, and you know how unjustly I have been treated in the matter, while you have made a nice little fortune out of it. Last but not least my back was injured as you know while working on a picture which I can prove, and the shock of the unjust, unfair and inhuman way I received my dismal [sic; should be "dismissal"] was the climax to the already very much injured spine. I was hoping against hope that I would get better so I could work again but I am gradually getting worse and my left side is almost numb and joints are beginning to be enlarged and lameness has set in through favoring my left side. I am telling you all this so we can settle out of court.[40]

Even if Florence never sent this letter to Laemmle, the agony and suffering she felt she had endured are painfully apparent in this letter. Again, her emotional outpouring affected her handwriting; by the end of the letter, the characters were frenzied and illegible.

Just in case the letter had failed to get Laemmle's attention, she took the next step of retaining an attorney to act on her behalf. Her contract with Max D. Josephson, Esq., asked to sue Universal "for damages sustained by me by reason of a breach of contract and the Universal Film Manufacturing Company."[41] Since the trade papers had already announced that Florence's contract with Universal was oral, she must have known that she did not stand much of a chance.

Actors winning lawsuits against their employers for work-related injuries was a new idea in the industry, one the studios must have been afraid of. In a well-publicized case from 1915, actress Celie Ellis (aka Celie Turner) won a case against the Crystal Film Company for $4,000 damages after she broke her ankle while filming a stunt. "The sad part of the story," *Photoplay* added, "so far as the company is concerned, was that the chief evidence was provided by sections of the film showing just how the accident happened, after viewing which the jury 'found for the plaintiff.'"[42] But somehow, in these days of motion pictures, accidents were accepted as part of the job; even insurance companies generally would not grant policies to players. "Most concerns refuse a risk of this kind, owing to the many casualties in the routine of a motion picture actor's day," *Moving Picture World* stated in an article about the single unnamed insurance company that was willing to write disability contracts, plus life and old-age income policies for film players.[43] Accidents were so frequent that articles entitled "This Week's Crop of Accidents" or "Actor Injured" appeared often in the trade journals. Players with now practically unknown names such as Charles Murray, Herbert Brenon, Ruth Hoyt and Eugenia Besserer were all in the press with terrible injuries from studio mishaps during the early 1910s. In one particularly horrifying report from 1914, a very young actress named Grace McHugh and cameraman Owen Carter were both drowned during the filming of California Motion Picture Company's

A rarely-seen fan magazine, *The Moving Picture Weekly*, from the first week of 1916, announcing Florence's return to the film industry. The sagging belt in this photo shows Florence's dramatic drop in weight in the year before it was taken. In 1912, the belt fit snugly on this outfit.

Across the Border on location in Colorado. Even the very famous actors and actresses from the day were not immune; Helen Gibson, while making the *Hazards of Helen* series for Kalem, spent a month in the hospital after falling off a train "going at a terrific speed." Around this time, Kalem's railroad films were so danger-filled for the players that it was boasted they had "an accident a day"; most of the stunts were well-planned and safely executed, but a distressing number were not.[44]

The claim that Florence's career ended because of an accident may be an exaggeration at best, but it did have precedent, for many actresses who were involved in serious accidents chose to retire rather than go back to such hazardous work. So Florence not only had to deal with the physical problems that an aggravating injury brought, but she also had to resolve the tough psychological issues that arose as well. Her feelings of inadequacy in life merged with her now-apparent failures as an actress, resulting in a complete shutdown of Florence as a person. She retreated to her farm, determined to stay retired this time.

Chapter Ten

AND AGAIN

> *Notable Women of History*
> Theda Bara ... Cleopatra ... Elinor Glyn ... Teddy Sampson ... Pocahontas ... Cleo Madison ... Phoebe Snow ... Florence Lawrence ... Lydia Pinkham ... Ruth Roland ... Eva Tanguay ... Mae Busch ... Mrs. Caesar ... Lotta Miles [Norma Shearer] ... Kitty Gordon ... Xantippe ...
> —*Photoplay,* July 1916

This time, when Florence went back to her rose garden, larger events in the nation and world captured and kept her attention, helping to keep her mind, body and spirit occupied. The immediate task was the Actors Fund, a precursor to the Motion Picture Relief Fund. The player's side of the industry pooled their resources to create the Fund in 1916, trying to raise $1 million to build a retirement home for actors and actresses. Various schemes were used to amass the money, including a fair held on May 19, 1917, at Grand Central Palace in New York. Florence was mentioned in the subsequent article in *Moving Picture World* as "absent at present from the screen, but not forgotten," as she sold copies of her song on sheet music to help. She was "prettily gowned and charming as ever," the ever-faithful *World* stated.[1]

All of the fund-raising and parties rapidly became meaningless in the face of the next calamity. The Great War had broken out in 1914, consuming the lives of young European men and women at an alarming rate. The fighting escalated and ebbed seasonally, but by 1916 many in the United States were now watching every move being made for fear of eventual U.S. involvement.

The world had seemingly gone mad in a few short years. Ships were now being sunk by human rather than natural forces, sending countless civilians and soldiers to their graves. Aeroplanes and big zeppelin balloons were being used to drop bombs on the unsuspecting below. Women and children were starving and dying, lost in the chaos. Canada, being British Commonwealth, had been involved in the war for several years, heroically sending her boys "over there" to die. The Germans were particularly aware of where Canadian troops were massed, choosing to attack the lesser-trained soldiers first. Florence must have keenly felt the sacrifices being made by her fellow countrymen, even though the war was merely an inconvenience for Americans for the first few years. In January 1917, when Germany declared that their submarines would fire unrestricted on any ships in their path, the world at war was inevitable. The United States entered the fray soon afterward, on April 6, 1917.

What Florence did on a day-to-day basis from the middle of 1916 onward is not evident. She may have worked on cultivating her rose again, but the American Rose Society, a Shreveport, Louisiana–based organization which has over 10,000 historical and botanical roses registered, has no entry for a Florence Lawrence rose, and Florence was never listed as a hybridizer. So this dream of Florence's did not come true. Still, this, along with her Red Cross work, must have kept Florence busy.

But she did make a lone, brief visit on the screen in early 1917. And very surprisingly, the single-reel short called *The Face on the Screen* was directed by none other than Harry Solter. After the failure of *Elusive Isabel* without Harry, Florence must have agreed to give him one last chance as her director. However, a one-reel story, which Florence had always done so well back five years before, was not what the audience wanted in 1917. *Face on the Screen* is almost completely lost except as a footnote; neither reviews nor copies of the film seem to exist today. If this was intended to be yet another comeback, it was completely ignored save a single line in *Moving Picture World* which mentioned briefly that "Miss Lawrence contemplates an early return to the screen" on January 13, 1917.[2]

But what else Harry did in 1917 was just barely less obscure. In late 1916, he was elected to a two-year term on the Screen Club Board of Governors when former co–Biographer Billy Quirk was reelected as president. He directed two feature films for Bluebird (released through Universal) in 1917: *The Spotted Lily*, released October 1, and *The Lash of Power*, November 15. On February 4, 1918, *The Wife He Bought* was released, the last film that Harry would ever direct. These were the first films he had directed without his wife on the other side of the camera. *The Spotted Lily* starred Ella Hall, whose decade-long attempt at a film career was overshadowed by the fact that she eventually was the mother of actors Richard Emory and Ellen Hall. *Lily* also featured Gretchen Lederer and Victor Rottman. Harry's last two movies starred Carmel Myers and Kenneth Harlan, a formidable pair of rising stars. Myers, a stunningly lovely actress, had embarked on her career in films with a bit in family friend D.W. Griffith's *Birth of a Nation* in 1915. The peak of her career probably came in 1925's *Ben-Hur*, but she continued to be involved in films for the rest of her long life, even appearing in a cameo in a 1975 film,

Won Ton Ton, the Dog Who Saved Hollywood. Harlan had an equally strong career, making hundreds of films up through the 1940s with vibrant, easily identifiable roles. His stint with Bluebird came just before he signed up to join the Army in 1918, as did many other young actors. Harry's last two works also featured Helen Wright, a minor starlet who ended her career making Westerns in the 1920s and 1930s, and Howard Crampton, a stately gentleman actor who started a sparse career with *Traffic in Souls* in 1913. Other players with smaller parts were his former Biograph co-star Charles Hill Mailes, Jack Nelson and Gertrude Astor.

Maybe Florence and Harry reconciled during these years. A possibly telling factor is that no mail between the two survives, but Florence may simply have destroyed their correspondence if there had been any. Their impending divorce still lingered over their heads, but no action was taken to legalize the separation.

Florence and Lotta were still quite close during this time, even if they did not live together at the farm. They may have also been in several businesses together. Lotta, having given up the stage more than a dozen years before, had turned to real estate, mining and other mineral excavations in Ontario and New York state. Her letterhead did not reveal her gender as it proclaimed: "Farm Lands, Timber and Mining Lands ... Eastern Ontario is Rich in Iron, Lead, Mica, Marble, Molybdenite, Feldspar, Graphite, Copper and Nickel ... C.A. Bridgwood, Kinmount, Ontario, Canada." Much of her 1910s correspondence was sprinkled with notes about showing someone some land or having major excavations done on certain properties.

But even as early as 1914 Florence made known her penchant for inventing things. In speaking once about her love for automobiling, Florence said that she had created a primitive turn signal, a part unknown on cars at that time. "I have invented an 'auto signaling arm,' which, when placed in the back of the fender, can be raised or lowered by electrical push buttons, thus indicating the intention of the driver," she told an interviewer for *Green Book Magazine*. "The one indicated 'stop' works automatically whenever the footbrake is pressed."[3] Several years later she was said to be the president of her mother's company, Bridgwood Manufacturing, which made an "electrical storm windshield cleaner" invented by Lotta.[4]

Lotta herself held patents for an amazing variety of inventions. Besides the windshield wiper system she created and patented in 1917, Lotta also invented an application that kept glass from fogging. This idea was offered to the United States government during the World War as a way to keep binoculars useful even in inclement weather.

If any of these ideas were indeed properly patented and viable inventions, both women would have been millionaires. But as often happens with many inventions in this post–industrial revolution era, a basic idea was created by someone, then improved upon by someone else, who eventually reaped the profit. The sewing machine, typewriter, brassiere and washing machine—even the moving picture camera and projector—are examples of how the originator of the idea was eventually eliminated from the finished product. William Drew has theorized that "perhaps the world was simply not ready to concede that females had the knowledge to develop mechanical devices capable of improving automobiles." Noting Florence's and Lotta's apparently unsuccessful patenting and marketing of their windshield wiper and the fact that it would be 1923 before such a device would be standard, Drew added, "The women who had pioneered this extremely useful innovation would receive no recognition or remuneration at all."[5]

Other events did steal Florence's attention. In January 1916, as Florence was being feted as Universal's returning star, a sad and broken man died a drunkard's death, in his case usually politely called "tuberculosis." Florence must have known her former co-star Arthur Johnson had died and may have even gone to Philadelphia for the services. But his death probably did not hurt until later that year, when Florence realized her own hopeless solitude. Other old friends had slipped away over the years. Early Biograph co-star Florence Barker, associated with Powers in 1912, had died in early 1913. John Bunny, everyone's favorite Vitagraph personality and old friend Flora Finch's nemesis, had died in 1915. In 1917, Florence had to face the death of both Biographer Fred Mace and Florence LaBadie. Mace, who had bounced around from IMP to Keystone during his active career, died a suicide in February. LaBadie, surely one of the loveliest actresses in the 1910s, was seriously injured in an August automobile accident and died the following October. Florence's world must have seemed very dark, especially when these personal tragedies were coupled with the war casualties, then the massive numbers of deaths from influenza in late 1918 and early 1919. Out of the prominent film names that had gone "over there" to fight, only Rankin Sidney Drew, son of Vitagraph's Mr. and Mrs. Sidney Drew, was destined not to return home. From influenza, however, the film colony was not as lucky. Despite law-enforced closures of places where people could congregate, such as churches, theaters, and even studios, more people died of influenza than in the War by the time it was finally over. Actresses Louise Vale and Myrtle Gonzalez died, as did actors William Courtleigh Jr., Charles Gunn and Harold Lockwood. Even Owen, Tom, and Matt Moore's sister Mary, herself an actress, died in France from influenza while doing Red Cross volunteer work.

During the time that the United States was involved in the War, Florence became heavily involved in Red Cross work. The biggest names in the industry were all lending their names and time unsparingly to "the cause." Mary Pickford, Douglas Fairbanks, Tom Mix, Clara Kimball Young and Pearl White all became very publicly associated with war bond drives or recruiting campaigns. Films like *To Hell with the Kaiser* and *Mothers of France* were enormously popular. Players with Teutonic surnames literally changed them:

Norman Kaiser became Norman Kerry, Margarita Fischer became Margarita Fisher.

Moving Picture World covered an October 1917 "special exhibition" for the Red Cross fund at the Casino Theater in Westwood, New Jersey, where the 1909 Biograph classic *The Resurrection* was shown along with Jack Pickford's *The Dummy*. The exhibition was in honor of Florence, "the well-known moving picture star who lent her services unsparingly to the aid of the Red Cross in Westwood." *World* went so far as to quote its own 1909 review about how wonderful the short film was, adding, "Florence Lawrence, even in this little one-reel picture, has given a remarkable illustration of emotional acting." The short history of the industry's own past was becoming evident when *World* pointed out all of the now-famous and superior actors who had come from Biograph: "Arthur Johnson, gone but not forgotten ... Mary Pickford, Marion Leonard, Owen Moore, Mack Sennett, David Miles, now dead, Mrs. David Miles [Anita Hendrie], Mrs. D.W. Griffith [Linda Arvidson], Charles Ennesley [Inslee], Herbert Prior and others whose names we are familiar with." A soon-to-be-repeated phrase cropped up regarding Florence: "It is to be deplored that her talent is not being turned to account in the same fashion as that of her co-workers of that period."[6]

She would wait almost a year before the next opportunity in front of the camera came along. In October 1918, she made a two-reel short for Nestor called *The Love Craze*. Unfortunately another sidetracked footnote, *Craze* was directed by J. Winthrop Kelley and co-starred former Thanhouser leading man Harry Benham. Both Kelley's and Benham's careers were floundering at this time as was the Nestor Company, once a thriving independent and now a Universal subsidiary. Kelley, an old friend of Florence's, had directed a few films in 1916 for Bluebird, but was limited to less than one a year until 1920 when he dropped from the industry's sight. Benham did find stable ground for a short time in 1918 by co-starring with Marion Davies in *Cecelia of the Pink Roses*, her second film, but his career was basically over by this time. Nestor, founded in 1910 by David Horsley, was truly the first independent company to release films in the United States, beating out IMP by several months. Horsley home-designed his own camera and attempted to join the Trust as it was formed, but missed the opportunity and decided to release his already-made films anyway. But Horsley, not much of a visionary even after this promising start, failed to see that features were the future and continued to make one-reel shorts throughout the 1910s. Subsequently, Nestor faded away by 1919. So once again Florence's vehicle back into the industry was not a very strong one. This time even *Moving Picture World* ignored her. No subsequent roles followed.

Very surprisingly, the next documented event in Florence's life is a nonevent. In April 1919, an order of dismissal was entered in the Solters' divorce case, effectively ending the proceedings. Several events could have led up to this. One, either Harry or Florence could have refused to sign the final decree and the original 1916 filing simply expired. Two, the Solters could have reconciled. Three, the Solters could have reached an agreement that it was more advantageous to remain married but to live apart. Whatever the possibilities, there was no final judgment of divorce. A poem in Florence's files was almost certainly written by Harry, possibly during this time:

> Her eyes were blue, her lips were red,
>   They seemed to speak, and what they said.
> They spoke of love, and feelings rare,
>   If she would care and I but dare.
> Her hair is wavy gold and bright,
>   Her figure shapely, strong and slight!
> My arms aching just to hold—
>   But she might scold if I were bold.
> Her feet are small, her ankle slight,
>   The [word deleted] quite all right.
> But what's the use of saying more,
>   She's just my wife, whom I adore.

Harry bought a ticket to take a train from New York to Los Angeles in February 1920, without Florence. Florence most likely was still in Westwood, but she may have gone to San Francisco late in 1919 to do vaudeville work. Harry left February 21, possibly taking a scenic route or stopping to see friends along the route. On March 1, he was admitted to the El Paso County Hospital in El Paso, Texas, directly from the train. Most likely, he had suffered a stroke while on board; no one knew who he was when he was admitted to the hospital. His trunk had fortunately been removed from the train, and a locksmith was brought in to open it.

Harry had a fatal stroke the next morning and died at 11:30 A.M. The doctor who had the task of completing his death certificate could only complete about a quarter of the spaces. His middle name was a question mark, his age was guessed to be 40, and his marital status, birthplace and parents were unknown. Somehow his profession—a producer in motion pictures—was ascertained through his belongings. A local undertaker prepared his body for the long train ride back to Maryland, passing along a bill for his services, the coffin, the pressing of Harry's suit, and the locksmith. Harry was buried in his family's plot at the Baltimore Cemetery later that month.

The saddest part of the life of Harry Lewis Solter was how quickly his star faded into complete oblivion. The man was a talented actor and creative director who had, just two years before, directed his final film. He had directed well over 100 of Florence's films and appeared in probably another hundred with the Biograph Company. He was called a "pioneer," an early protégé of

Florence, in the early 1920s, showing off her fur stole.

D.W. Griffith. Yet the *Baltimore Sun* did not even carry an obituary. *Wid's Year Book* for 1921, which has a day-by-day account for all events in 1920, did not mention his death. Only *Moving Picture World* carried a small blurb, calling his death untimely.[7]

Florence found herself alone, a widow, and in a position she never had considered ever being in. She was very suddenly independent as well; no matter how close or apart she and Harry were, she had chafed under answering to him. Reality settled around her uncomfortably, and she braced herself for yet another comeback into the entertainment field.

Most likely she headed for California around this time, if she had not moved there already. In August 1920, she appeared for a week's engagement at the Metropolitan Theatre in San Francisco with a show called the Marcus Revue; the newspaper coverage called her "the slim little girl who whistles so delightfully." Curiously, she came across as a rather world-weary gamin. The interviewer pointed out that she was an ardent suffragist, expert driver and eclectic reader. "Men amuse me, really," she said. "They are so bombastic." After hearing a male driver grind his gears outside her hotel window, she vented frustration at his ignorance. "I never can understand why people treat their cars like that," she said. "A car to me is something that is almost human, something that responds to kindness and understanding and care, just as people do." Florence was carefully posed in her hotel room during this interview, current fiction and untranslated French works ("I keep digging away at my French; it gets so rusty when you don't use it") scattered about.

At this juncture of Florence's publicity career, she was careful to mention both her accident and Mary Pickford in almost every interview. In this one, the interviewer said Florence "smiled over the days when she used to pack her shoes with paper to appear taller than Mary Pickford." This drew the informed reader back to the days when both actresses were practically ingenues, so similar in every way (including height). The descriptions of the horrible accident aroused what sympathy remained untouched after comparisons to the now-wildly popular Pickford. "And now, through sheer will power, [Florence] is starting all over again, determined to return to the life she loves."[8] No mention was made of the recent loss of her husband, which made her return not only to a labor of love but of necessity.

Sadnesses were intensified in September 1920, when fellow players Robert Harron and Olive Thomas died within a week of one another. Little Bobby Harron had been a Biographer from the old days, staying close to Griffith throughout his career. The bullet, some say fired accidentally, others on purpose, ended a horrible five years for the Harron family. His brother Charles died in an automobile accident in 1915, and his sister Mary died in the influenza epidemic in 1918. Only his brother Jack remained to carry on the family's legacy of acting. Olive Thomas, married to Mary Pickford's brother Jack, also died a mysterious death, self-poisoned accidentally or on purpose. The eeriness of these two deaths, of two very prominent and popular stars at the height of their fame cloaked the film community like a shroud. An awareness of how others viewed the film industry began to arise; the problem continued as the insiders did not like what they saw when they peered into the mirror.

Soon after the Marcus Revue engagement closed, Florence accepted a position with a dramatic company to play at the Mason Opera House in Los Angeles. More than likely this was one stop on a West Coast tour. *Moving Picture World* stated that even though Florence was not the star of the play, her name and face were quickly recognized by old friends in the audience.[9] *Photoplay* reported that Florence had been hired to be the "head of a dramatic school" in California, but had been "waylaid" by producers anxious for her acting services rather than instruction.[10]

St. Louis money again tempted Florence, and this time Florence eagerly jumped for it. H.C. Schaper, referred to several times as a wealthy and well-known St. Louis financier, put up the money to start Producers Pictures Corporation. Former Christie Company production manager George Kern was named general manager and director general, and Pathé's St. Louis exchange manager E.W. Dustin was named business manager. William Keefe was the manager of production as well as publicity. *World* reported that Kern learned of Florence's appearance at the Mason and her availability for film work and approached her immediately.

Kern and company may not have had Laemmle's flair for exploiting a star, but they did have a few tricks up their sleeve on Florence's behalf. Press releases were sent to Hollywood newspapers announcing Florence's "arrival" in Los Angeles from San Francisco, claiming that her train would be met by former Biograph co-stars Mae Marsh, Mary Pickford, Henry Walthall, Blanche Sweet and Mack Sennett among others, such as city officials, forming a welcoming committee at Union Station.[11] Interestingly, Florence was never in films with Marsh or Sweet, but the old names must have sounded good to the press agent.

Production soon began on a film called *The Unfoldment*, based on a story written by Kern. Murdock MacQuarrie was brought in to help Kern with directing the six-reel film. Florence was to portray newspaper reporter Katherine Nevin, assigned to make a propaganda film for her employer to show him in a positive light. She instead makes a picture (a movie within a movie) called *The Unfoldment*, which showed people as they really were, involved now in a contorted plot of love and scandal. Religious overtones surrounded the end of the story, intended to be inspirational.

The cast was a very good one. Barbara Bedford, a splendid actress two years into a long film career, portrays Katherine's friend Martha, and Raymond Cannon, a future scenario writer, played Jack, Katherine's brother and Martha's love interest. Katherine's lover is "Mac," played by the strong actor William Conklin, whose career stretched from 1913 until the coming of sound and included roles in *Joan the Woman* and *Sex*. Heavies were played by MacQuarrie, Charles French and Albert Prisco.

The publicity for Florence's yet-another comeback was less subtle than in the past, although it was very good. William Keefe arranged a meeting between Florence and her name-alike, Florence Lawrence, a very popular and successful critic for the *Los Angeles Examiner*. The resulting article was hilarious. The newspaper critic complained that people were constantly telling her that she did not photograph well, and the "Biograph beauty" told her about how people were always letting her have it for not giving them better coverage for pictures. The reporter pointed out that "this doesn't settle the question of how the two Florence Lawrences, both in Los Angeles, are going to keep their mail, telegrams, and worst of all, their bills straight ... Imagine, for instance, the horror of the newspaper woman when she gets a bill for a $2000 sable wrap—while meantime she's wearing a last year's coat decidedly passé as to linings and collar." The two women did agree that they liked to cook spaghetti, but other than that, "actually the two are as divergent as the poles." Florence the actress again managed to mention briefly both Mary Pickford and her accident in the article.[12]

Little Mary and the accident were a major focus in a May 1921 article for *Photoplay* by Adela Rogers St. Johns, a noted and respected writer and columnist. St. Johns handled Florence with a great deal of sympathetic tact, even though apparently St. Johns did not believe Florence capable of handling a career in the film world of 1921. In many ways, St. Johns was right. Florence did not fit into the Hollywood scene. She tired easily. Her motivation, while made easier by a love of acting, was the need for income. "I cannot tell you why she struck me instantly as being such a sad little figure," St. Johns wrote. "But when I first saw her, I felt my heart stop and sink a little as it did then I first saw the vacant places in the ranks of the returned, marching regiments of Yankees." Another comparison that St. Johns drew was to Sarah Bernhardt. "She has in her blue eyes the same look I saw in Sarah Bernhardt's the last time she came to America—that look of brave, spiritual struggle against overwhelming odds, the look of a woman who knows what it is to fight a losing fight."

Instead of being comfortably ensconced in a private dressing room as she had for so many past interviews, this time Florence was in a "shabby little room" in a "small hotel on a side street in Los Angeles ... [with] its drab wallpaper and its ugly furniture." St. Johns gave Florence's history in motion pictures and, with all this background, said she had expected to meet a "rather worldly woman ... a woman perhaps a bit passé, but assured, self-confident and triumphant." Instead she found Florence to be young, fluffy and sweet, yet haunted by disappointments and doubts. "If the old, oft-repeated theory is true that one must have lived, suffered, in order to act—then Florence Lawrence returns to the screen with a boundless treasury." This interview is one of the very few places that Harry Solter's death is mentioned as affecting her. That, combined with years of medical expenses, was forcing her back into acting. "It's a big citadel I'm attacking," she told St. Johns. "I think it is harder to 'come back' than to 'arrive.'"

Florence and her mother Lotta Lawrence in California in the early 1920s. Florence's love for all things millinery may have been honestly inherited. Photograph courtesy of Wisconsin Center for Film and Theater Research.

James Kirkwood, who for years worked under Florence's Victor banner, had nothing but praise for her. "If she's as good now as she was ten years ago you can discount the 'advance in motion picture art' and bet she'll give some of the newcomers a run for their money. She's a great artist." At least Kirkwood was willing to talk to or about her. St. Johns reported that Florence was not only "forgotten by the gateman," but by producers and actors as well ("people who *should* have remembered," St. Johns wrote bitterly). But an old stage carpenter did. Florence evidently had helped him while he was unemployed, and he thought very highly of her. "She was the best of 'em all ... She could make folks love her, she could."[13]

While Florence was busy piecing together a noble endeavor of "coming back" once again, the very industry that she was trying to integrate herself into was coming apart around her. Several groups of Hollywood workers had gone on strike in the summer to protest a pay cut, causing a slowdown in production across the industry. In September 1921, a young actress named

Virginia Rappe died after a night of partying, and days later famous film comedian Roscoe "Fatty" Arbuckle was arrested for her murder. Hollywood went berserk, followed quickly by the rest of America. The funny fat man, flushed with the excesses of the rich, was seen as typical of the Hollywood sort by Americans, whose frame of mind had just voted in Prohibition the year before. Arbuckle's movies were pulled from theaters; although he was acquitted the next April, the damage was done—not just to Arbuckle, but to Hollywood as well.

If Hollywood had been making mediocre movies during this time, much severer sanctions and boycotts may have come about considering the negative publicity. But 1921 was a beautiful year for films, with releases such as *The Three Musketeers*, *A Sailor-Made Man*, *Tol'able David*, *Little Lord Fauntleroy*, *The Four Horsemen of the Apocalypse*, *The Kid* and *Orphans of the Storm*. Of all the stars of these films, only Mary Pickford came from the pre–1910 split-reel and single-reel tradition that Florence had done so well in. Others, such as Charlie Chaplin and Harold Lloyd, had cut their teeth on the short films in the early to mid–1910s, the era in which Florence had peaked professionally. Fortunately, even Florence recognized this. "They used to say I 'grew up with the industry.' But it has outgrown me now," she told *Photoplay*. "It is like coming back to your old home to find it changed, and all your family and neighbors moved away." Still, she hoped to succeed somehow in such a crazy industry. "Screen acting is like swimming. If you once know how you never forget."[14]

One boost that Florence desperately needed was to her personal life. On May 7, 1921, she ran into a former soldier, Charles Bryne Woodring, who she had met in New York just after the war. Impulsively, the two were married five days later, May 12, by the San Francisco Justice of the Peace, Frank Deasy. In true film star fashion, they tried to keep the marriage a secret, but word leaked out by the end of June.

Little is known about Woodring. His father Andrew was from Philadelphia, and his mother, also a Florence, was from Atlanta. Charles had served in the 115th Engineers during the war, receiving the Croix de Guerre for bravery. Upon his return to civilian life, he became an automobile salesman, based out of Denver.

Florence fibbed several times on her marriage certificate. She claimed that she was 29 (closer to 34), that this was her first marriage (second), that she was single (as opposed to widowed), that she was born in Buffalo (really Hamilton), and that her father's name was George Lawrence (really Bridgwood).[15] The inaccuracies, in her own handwriting, give rise to the question of how honest she was with Woodring at any point during their marriage. According to the newspapers, the Woodrings settled on Dorland Street in San Francisco, which is also where her brother George resided, based on entries in local city directories.

Florence Lawrence, upon her "arrival" in Hollywood, in 1921. Producers Pictures, her new employer, tried to play up her arrival by train from San Francisco by meeting her at the station with various dignitaries. Photograph courtesy of Wisconsin Center for Film and Theater Research.

The Unfoldment had no doubt been long finished by this time. Producers Pictures Corporation intended to produce Florence Lawrence Super Productions as soon as this first film was released. But the release was held up until January 1, 1922. The ongoing conflicts between states rights distributors may have had something to do with it. Independent producers such as Producers Pictures had to grant the rights to their films to territorial (usually a state) distributors. This clashed with the national distributing system the larger manufacturers had established. Each state distributor had to organize the exhibitors in his territory, keeping track of film orders and agreements with each independent producing group. Producers Pictures chose to release its films through Associated Exhibitors Incorporated, who distributed their films through Pathé Distributors. The same group handled the Harold Lloyd films made by Hal Roach.

However, the newly created Producers Pictures was having a difficult time getting its films even reviewed by staple journals such as *Moving Picture World* or *Variety*. *Moving Picture World* recognized the power that a review could have in its selection, though it claimed that it strived to be fair to the "little guy"—"Our reviews will be constructive—not destructive ... The investments of the producer, distributor and exhibitors will at all times be considered"—but it was even worse than destructive for the film to be completely ignored.[16] *The Unfoldment* also was very late in being listed by Associated Distributors as available, a delay that caused it to be passed over as a selection by states rights distributors. After little to no free publicity in the form of reviews was forthcoming, Associated Exhibitors bought *The Unfoldment* a full page advertisement in *World* at the end of January which contained the statement "Now Ready" but did not mention Florence Lawrence as its star.[17] *Moving Picture World* came as close as it ever would to commenting on the film on January 28 when it declared in a very short article about Florence that "Miss Lawrence is said to have done a remarkable piece of work."[18]

The Unfoldment was doomed anyway. Even if the film had received half of the publicity that Universal's *Foolish Wives* did during January of 1922, all film news took a back burner after February 1, 1922, when someone shot the prominent and talented director William Desmond Taylor. Scandal haunted Hollywood yet again.

Chapter Eleven

THE QUIET YEARS

> *We have had no preparation, no education, no technique, no history or traditions, no precedent ... We have had to learn by growth and mistakes only, groping our way into a pathless new country.*
>
> —Hobart Bosworth

All of Hollywood tiptoed for weeks around the murder of William Desmond Taylor. Daily newspapers printed every hope, idea, confession, innuendo and rumor connected with it. *Moving Picture World*'s editor-in-chief, Arthur James, vented the frustration that everyone in the film colony must have been feeling:

> Our troubles have grown to proportions that none save a great vitality could withstand. The Arbuckle case was laid, not at the doors of individuals but at the door of the industry, and the public, with its thoughtlessness turned to account by a sensational press, pictured our business as a ceaseless series of orgies and private riots, in which we swam in vats of bootleg liquor at every sundown and contrived new debaucheries to greet each dawn.
>
> The Taylor tragedy was not the murder of an individual but, if the newspapers are to be credited, an out-cropping of the wild, hectic, dissolute, drug crazed seething that is the secret but usual life we all of us live day by day and night by night in the disheveled, disordered phantasmagoria that beggars fiction and challenges the abysses of human imagination.
>
> ...Our way back into the sunshine of clean public opinion must be slower and still a surer progress. We have the truth, we have decency, we have an overwhelming preponderance of right living upon our side.[1]

This time, Hollywood did not have the same quality films to fall back upon as proof of their good deeds. Recently released films, such as *Foolish*

Wives and *The Sheik*, may have been spectacular but they were immoral in the eyes of many socially conscious Americans. Matters were not helped when almost a hundred people were killed in a movie theater just days before Taylor's murder as snow collapsed a roof in Washington, D.C. Motion pictures and Hollywood were quickly becoming the worst things imaginable to many people.

No wonder Florence Lawrence felt out of place. Scandals and murders were not what she expected to deal with in the industry—no one did. Even if *The Unfoldment* had done well—and by general, modern accounts it was not a bad film—she may not have wanted to stay in the tainted industry. She had made a small point, important to herself, and now she could get on with her newly married life.

The Woodrings moved into a nice apartment on Argyle Street in Los Angeles, where they contemplated their future. She ultimately relaxed into a carefree year in which no motion picture could interfere, basically dropping from sight. "I want to be happy," she said in 1921, "and bring happiness to others."[2] The time had come for Florence's only audience to be Charles Woodring.

The year 1922 passed as a blur as the scandals unfolded and gradually died away. Will Hays was brought in as the new movie "czar" to attempt internal censorships, reinforcing the "morality clause" that most major manufacturers had inserted in players' contracts the year before. The industry was still thwarting efforts for federal or state control of what could be shown and what could not. Terry Ramsaye, writing a history of film up through 1925, declared that Hays had done the job: "Since the coming of Hays, the sensations of the motion picture world have not been sensational." Ramsaye points out the Hays office provided an outlet for disgruntled moviegoers to protest indecency. Other changes that rapidly came about were the standardization of contracts and the setting of a "courteous" example before America and the world. "The motion picture industry is now well out of its infancy and the Hays office is teaching it to wear long pants," Ramsaye concluded.[3] Although the Taylor murder was never solved, the public showed its dissatisfaction with those who had been close to him.[4] Mary Miles Minter lost the career she had worked for starting as a child, and Mabel Normand suffered double rejection by having been friends with both Taylor and Arbuckle. Her career soon ended as well.

Hollywood bent again to a morality crusade at the death of Wallace Reid in January 1923. This time, the actual cause of death was not hushed over as it was with Arthur Johnson. Reid, named the top actor of 1920 by Quigley, had died of alcohol and drug dependence, the facts of which no one denied. Between the trial of Arbuckle and the deaths of Taylor and Reid, Hollywood needed to clean up its image. And these were only the best publicized of the scandals. In days when divorce was taboo, Mary Pickford divorced Owen Moore and married Douglas Fairbanks too quickly to prevent rumors

Florence posing with one shoe on, one shoe off, mid–1920s. Florence loved hats and high-heeled shoes, always wanting to add height to her small frame.

from flying. Other divorces were publicly endured: Charlie Chaplin and Mildred Harris Chaplin, Alice Joyce and Tom Moore (both remarried within the year), Pearl White and Wallace McCutcheon, Rudolph Valentino and Jean Acker, and Roscoe Arbuckle and Minta Durfee, among many others. One modern historian has looked carefully at the effect that the "star scandals" had upon the development of the star system. "The cinema lost a degree of control over star discourse as newspaper writers, reformers and politicians entered into a debate over the nature of the film star's identity," Richard de Cordova wrote in his book *Picture Personalities*. "The star became the site of struggle between reformers and the industry, a subject of social controversy."[5] Coupled with the nationwide rise in divorces and the natural curiosity that comes about with public figures, negative publicity was bound to start emerging. When deaths began to occur, the effects snowballed.

In response to this atmosphere, Florence seems to have proceeded in her career very carefully at this point. She may have done some vaudeville or short touring parts during 1922 and 1923; if so, she did not leave a personal record of them. Her next foray into films came in late 1923, when she accepted a small role in *The Satin Girl*, a six-reel feature produced by Ben Wilson and directed by Arthur Rosson. Florence was Sylvia, basically a character role as a friend of the heroine. The cast was a mix of unknowns and medium-known players, the easiest recognized probably being Norman Kerry. Wilson was a well-rounded player-writer-director whose career stretched back to 1913 with Edison. Rosson had been making films for six years, having the distinction of directing Mildred Harris Chaplin in 1920's *Polly of the Storm Country*.

Florence returned to Ben Wilson in early 1924 to make one more film, *Gambling Wives*. This time old friend Dell Henderson from Biograph days was the director. Henderson had developed quite a solid reputation as a director after an equally successful career in front of the camera. *Moving Picture World* was always fond of pointing out connections between players, especially of the Biograph Company, this time claiming that D.W. Griffith had "personally trained Henderson in the art of motion picture direction."[6] Florence and Henderson working together would make a nice gesture on Henderson's part if he had had a hand in her hiring, but since she had done a film for Wilson not six months before, this seems unlikely.

Florence was again cast as a friend of the heroine, but this time in an ensemble that contained rather well-known names. Marjorie Daw, a former child star associated with Geraldine Farrar, had a decent career by 1922. She eased herself out of the industry just as sound approached. Edward Earle, another Edison product from the mid-1910s, was a very popular player, even having been crowned King of the Movies (with Billie Burke as the Queen) in a 1922 contest. The role of the husband-stealing vamp was taken by Hedda Hopper during the acting portion of her Hollywood career. Other supporting players were Betty Francisco, Ward Crane and Lee Moran.

Her days as a star were surely over, but one modern biographer claims that Florence lobbied hard for the leading role in Paramount's new screen version of *Peter Pan*. She was 38 years old (she claimed 31); Paramount would have been extremely kind to let her even do a screen test, if this were true. The character of Peter Pan requires a boyish young player capable of extremely athletic romps. Betty Bronson, half Florence's age, won the role and made *Peter Pan* into one of the top ten films of 1924. Florence may not have really understood the differences between acting when she was a star and the present-day workings of the studios. "Acting is every bit as good in the early moving pictures of fifteen years ago as it is today," she said in early 1926. "Improvements have come in the spaciousness of setting and in mechanical improvements such as lighting."[7]

She did make a drastic personal decision in the middle of 1924 that she hoped would help change her career luck—she "bobbed" her nose. The *Los Angeles Examiner* reported the procedure with remarkable tongue-in-cheek aplomb: "Miss Lawrence was rather tired of the nose she has had thus far in life. It seemed to her to have entirely too much of a hump in it."[8] *Photoplay* pointed out that this operation seemed to be a trend among actresses such as Victoria Forde and Helen Ferguson. The rationale behind Florence's surgery was apparent: "There are many in Hollywood who join us in hoping the nose operation will help this game young woman in her fight for recognition."[9]

Another incident helped her cause even more. In one of the most comprehensive articles about "lost" players done until that time, *Photoplay*'s Frederick James Smith tracked down Florence and a number of other forgotten faces from the earliest days of the screen. "Unwept, unhonored—and unfilmed. So these idols of yesteryear go on their lonely way, watching the coming of new favorites, and wondering."[10] Amazingly, the first of these types of articles had been published as early as 1916, a mere six years after players' names began to be released. And equally amazingly, there were a lot of players listed as "stars of yesterday."[11]

The fates of Florence Turner, Lottie Briscoe, Dorothy Bernard, Gene Gauntier, Helen Holmes, Cleo Madison and many others paralleled Florence's own pathetic, fluttering career. Florence Turner, the Vitagraph Girl, frankly begged for roles. "I want so to work! It is all so tragic because my work has been my very life." Lottie Briscoe, who took over Florence's roles at Lubin with Arthur Johnson, never recovered from his death and an illness of her own. Dorothy Bernard, Biograph's little girl, retired in 1922 for good from films. "I left the screen because the films demand extreme youth and I had none of that precious commodity left," she said. "There is no room in filmdom for a woman over twenty-five, unless you have a rare streak of genius and even then it's a fight." Gene Gauntier, the Kalem Girl, was completely content to be off the screen, because in 1915 she recognized that the trends were changing too fast for her. "I was glad to get out while I could still retain some pleasant memories of the good old days." Helen Holmes, after a number of successful serials, was one of the few who still quietly and regularly worked in films. Cleo Madison admitted to having a nervous breakdown several years earlier, but was now back playing "mother roles." Smith tracked down dozens of other names, mostly now lost to even film buffs, and updated their lives for the readers.

Smith was particularly incredulous that Florence Lawrence was so far out of the loop. His letter to her, slightly misaddressed, was returned to him during the process of writing the article. "Less than ten years ago Miss Lawrence ranked beside Mary Pickford and Mary Fuller as one of the premiere favorites of the films. In those days a letter merely bearing her name would have been delivered." He lamented with her that, at age 31, she should be still at the top of her career. Florence, too, knew how to make her point. "Pictures put me out; it is right that they should bring me back," she said firmly. "I am not asking for stardom. I will get there on my merits if I am given half a chance."

For the first time, Florence told the story of how she and Harry Solter were fired from Biograph, then blacklisted by the Trust.[12] Her story was, and still is today, in direct contrast to the story that Terry Ramsaye told in his multi-part series "The Romantic History of the Motion Picture," which ran in *Photoplay* during 1923, 1924 and 1925. In December 1923, he reported that Harry Solter had been "taken over by Imp at the same time that this aggressive independent took away 'The Biograph Girl,' Florence Lawrence," also referring to Florence's hiring by Laemmle as a "raiding of Biograph."[13] Ramsaye's version of the rise of the independents was published in book form in 1925 as *A Million and One Nights*, a more substantial record than a mere article in a fan magazine. Florence's role in Laemmle's success was embellished to the point of making a good story even more dramatic, more exciting.

But in contrast to the reality for Florence in 1924, she was forgotten by the very industry she felt she had helped create. "It is hard to feel that you have given the best of your life to motion pictures—and that they have no place for you," she said. Florence Turner felt much the same way, and she seemed to have been in much more desperate straits than Florence. "The public's memory for time is very short," the Vitagraph Girl said. "People, not having seen me for seventeen years on the films, rate it as twenty-five, quite forgetting dates and also that there were no pictures that long ago." Turner's plight caught the attention of Marion Davies, who brought her back from England where her company had gone bankrupt during the War. Davies also gave Turner a role in her production *Janice Meredith*.[14]

No one charitably kicked roles toward Florence Lawrence. She may not have wanted that anyway. She told another interviewer that she resented being called an "old-timer," though she always pointed out her years of experience as a film actress. "If you were only ten years old when you started in the films, and then you work for ten years in the movies, you are credited with being forty years old." Florence herself was shaving a lot of years off her age: For her to be the 31 she claimed in 1924, she would have had to have been 14 when she started making films in 1907. But Florence had routinely taken years off her age, ever since she was cast as a 16-year-old girl in *Daniel Boone* at the age of 20.

Since only scattered film parts were coming her way, she turned back to the theater as her means of self-expression. She toured with a group called "Coast-to-Coast Vaudeville," featuring herself and four other acts probably during November 1925. At its conclusion, she then put together a short sketch, or "playlet" as it was billed, called "Diamond Cut Diamond" and began touring at medium-sized arenas in California by the end of 1925 through spring of 1926. She also toured with a revival of "The Blue Flame" in 1926. A surviving contract from her March 1926 appearance with "Diamond" at the American Theatre in San Jose, California, shows that Florence Lawrence and Company was paid $200 for four days' worth of appearances, Wednesday through Saturday. The details of this contract reflect the newly found morality rage Americans were undergoing. The artist, by signing the contract, agreed to remove any part of the act that the manager deemed objectionable and agreed not to appear on stage drunk or under the influence of drugs, among other things. Interestingly, the small print also prohibits any work on the radio during the contracted times.[15]

A newspaper commenting on Florence's vaudeville career in 1926 stated that "Hollywood is continually pressing her to cancel her theatrical tourns [sic] to give her whole time to film character parts." Florence countered this idea by stating that she wanted to work on stage to make sure she still had the ability, even suggesting that she was willing to work anonymously; "I just wanted to see if I had it in me to make another stage reputation."[16] Desperation may have played a part in her determination; only a few years before, she had written in a note, "Sometimes I think I would like to go back to the stage but I don't believe I could stand the adverse criticism if there should be any."[17]

Florence found another new interest to keep her busy when she was not touring or making brief appearances in films. Some time during the 1920s, she and Woodring opened Hollywood Cosmetics, a store that sold Florence's own line of beauty aids and treatments, located at 821 Fairfax Avenue in Hollywood. The lids for her concoctions bore a likeness similar to Florence's profile, and she placed photos of herself in the windows of the shop. The store managed to stay afloat for several years, probably not with booming business because American women were still not used to wearing makeup. Actresses, on the other hand, needed makeup suited for harsh, artificial lights. Florence no doubt understood what was needed for these conditions and probably knew some secrets of her own, and she may have tried to cater to the filmmaking population with a limited degree of fulfillment. She was not the only one in town with this idea. Max Factor had moved to Los Angeles from St. Louis in 1908 and very quietly and successfully set up shop, far away from the dueling cosmetic giants of New York, Elizabeth Arden and Helena Rubenstein. Factor created special makeups for players with formulas so revolutionary and flattering that the Academy of Motion Picture Arts and Sciences presented him with an award for his contribution to beauty in films. He continued to adapt his makeup for brighter lights and eventually for color films. Also in the slowly emerging cosmetics business was an old firm called the California Perfume Company, later known as Avon, which sold their floral scented products door-to-door.[18] Florence's Hollywood Cosmetics never had much hope of serious contention in this field.

The camera still beckoned, and small film roles continued to come her way. She had a bit part in the 1926 film *The Johnstown Flood*, which started the career of Hollywood's soon-to-be newest sweetheart Janet Gaynor, and also starred a former stuntman and movie cowboy, George O'Brien. Later in the year, she played two character parts in *The Greater Glory* (also known as *The Viennese Melody*).

Florence's work in *The Greater Glory* put her in contact with some of the industry's most-respected names. Anna Q. Nilsson had been brought over from Sweden to work with the Kalem Company in the mid–1910s and had steadily worked her way to being one of the best actresses in America. She and Florence had a short dramatic scene together in the film. In her other character, Florence did a comedy bit with Jean Hersholt. Hersholt was not only a great actor, but a great person. Even an actress as self-centered as Lina Basquette recognized his uniqueness: "He was a brilliant artist of the old school who approached film-making as a dedicated architect approaches a blueprint, building histrionic performances that shine with integrity."[19] Hersholt has been given much of the credit for the foundation of the Motion Picture Home in Woodland Hills, California.

Florence may have had a small part in Colleen Moore's 1926 film *Twinkletoes*, but after this, the roles completely dried up. She once again turned her attentions to her personal life and the cosmetics store that she and Woodring were trying to run. At some time during the 1920s, Florence's mother came to live in California as well. Evidently her businesses in the east had soured or gone bankrupt. Besides the mining and real estate business that she had been running for most of the decade, Lotta also had tried her hand at family moving picture manufacturing. She claimed ten years experience in the motion picture business on her lengthy advertising letterhead, with copy scrolling the bottom declaring, "What would the nation give to see George Washington and family in their home life, as well as other notable activities of his life in motion pictures" and "The Bride can show her wedding festivities to her grandchildren years hence." This idea, unique for the 1910s, promised to take excellent and entertaining moving pictures, then provide the customer with a projector so easy to run that a child of 12 could do so. The company would then file the negatives away in steel vaults for safety, readily available for copying at the customer's request. Unfortunately, this company seems to have done nothing. Years would elapse before home movies would become affordable for the average family.

Lotta and Florence did not seem to have the business judgment that other performers did from this period (for example, Mary Pickford and her mother Charlotte Smith). Gerald McDonald, in a 1953 *Films in Review* article entitled "Origin of the Star System," attributed Florence's lack of business sense to her career downfall, while Mary Pickford's savvy helped her rise over the rest of the field.[20] Given Florence's fragile mental state at the height of her popularity, her career moves were not bad, but it certainly would have been advantageous to have stayed with one company or at least negotiated more favorable contracts for herself. Instead, she was saddled with an already-established director-husband, and she often was at a disadvantage for having broken a contract before or having left abruptly.

Lotta's luck seems to have been little better. Her work in excavation and sales businesses seemingly vanished, although she beat the stereotypical odds by staying in such a field for as long as she did. Since she had indeed patented the windshield wiper in 1917, she either signed away the rights early on or did not enforce the idea ownership when wipers became available on cars in the mid–1920s. Her anti-fogging device for binocular lenses does not seem to have gone anywhere. The home movie idea was before its time. Neither mother nor daughter seemed to be able to stay married, either.

Florence quite often used her business address on Fairfax Avenue as a personal address during the 1920s; perhaps she and Woodring were living apart. In 1928, she posed for a whimsical series of photos outside her shop, showing off a blunt-edged haircut and a modest lab coat to project a professional appearance. The business must have been prospering, for Florence and Woodring would not have had the money to just let it operate at a loss.

The next year, 1929, turned out to be a grievous one for Florence. Her mother died suddenly on August 20, two days after her sixty-ninth birthday. Without much warning, Florence had lost her best friend and confidante. Lotta died in such obscurity that even *Variety* ignored the veteran stage performer's death. Florence had her mother's body cremated at the Hollywood Crematory and the ashes interred in the Friendship Community Niche at the Hollywood Memorial Cemetery.

Before the end of the year, Florence found that she had lost her other confidant, too. According to divorce papers filed the following year, Florence and Charles Woodring separated on December 12, 1929. They had had no children, according to the divorce-desertion complaint, and they had previously entered into a settlement to divide the community property (most likely Hollywood Cosmetics, since they had not purchased a house). Florence brought the divorce suit on Woodring, alleging that he had left her less than four months after her mother had died.[21] An interlocutory judgment of divorce was granted on February 11, 1931, and the divorce was finalized on February 20, 1932. Florence was free once again, but this time more alone than she cared to be.

She must have undergone a form of metamorphosis during these years. She began to find more, albeit small, film roles. She settled her mother's

Florence posed for an attractive series of photographs in 1928 outside her shop, Hollywood Cosmetics. Her stylish blonde haircut is surprisingly modern. Hollywood Cosmetics closed in 1931. Photograph courtesy of Wisconsin Center for Film and Theater Research.

estate, possibly beginning a suit to claim royalties on the windshield wiper, using the newly found copy of the patent granted to her mother August 6, 1918. "If Miss Lawrence's claims are allowed and her demands of royalties granted, she will come into millions of dollars," one newspaper rhapsodized.[22] Nothing ever came of this suit; manufacturers must have proven that the inventions they were using had come from earlier patents. Lotta's invention was not quite like the wiper used today. Her patent had a roller system that could apparently clean both sides of the glass on any vehicle that had a windscreen ("automobiles, trolley cars, locomotives and the like"). A track was set upon the top of the windshield, and a motorized carriage with wipers extending down either side of the glass attached to the track. The carriage hummed back and forth, wiping the glass as it went.[23] The device was very unusual, especially for 1917, and might have been successful given the right marketing.

In 1932, Florence also donated a large amount of her personal papers to the Los Angeles County Museum of History, Science and Art (now known as the Natural History Museum of Los Angeles County). This museum was, and is, busy collecting Hollywood memorabilia of all kinds, including papers, photographs and personal items. Florence turned over meticulously amassed clippings and letters from 1904 to 1930, plus poems, scripts, calling cards and blank letterhead. The trove filled three boxes, full of information pertinent to film history and Florence's life story. Since Florence did the gathering and donating herself, she must have carefully screened what went into this veritable time capsule. For instance, not all of Harry's numbered "suicide" letters from 1912 are present. There is no mail between Florence and Woodring included. Today her memorabilia is located in the Seaver Center for Western History Research, part of the Museum, along with material and items from Charlie Chaplin, Marion Davies, Florence Turner and many others.

Around this time, Florence also donated many other photographs and personal papers to collector Daniel Blum. Florence must have been close to him, for she signed one of the photos, "To my more than Brother Dan Blum." On a copy of her sheet music given to him, she jotted, "This was when I was very good." Blum took Florence's collection along with hundreds of others to create several books very important to the entertainment history world: *A Pictorial History of the Silent Screen*, *A Pictorial History of the Talkies* and *A Pictorial History of the American Theater, 1900–1951*. Blum's collection makes up the cornerstone of the film archives at the Wisconsin Center for Film and Theater Research in Madison, Wisconsin.

Florence made one last marital attempt in late 1933 when she married a man named Henry Bolton. Of him, little is known save his November 27, 1933, to February 6, 1934, marriage to Florence. The two eloped to Yuma, Arizona, a popular trysting spot for Hollywood couples where the waiting period was nonexistent and the town open for such liaisons. Yuma was extremely busy during the 1930s and 1940s as former silent stars and the up-and-coming celebrities all dashed across the border for weddings that lasted, on average, two years. Constance Bennett, John Barrymore, Billie Dove, Richard Dix, Mary Astor (twice) and Janet Gaynor were among the silent stars who were married there, and Claudette Colbert, Errol Flynn, Bette Davis, Loretta Young and Jean Harlow were talkies stars who made their way to this "marriage mecca."

Bolton evidently was an alcoholic with a nasty temper and big mouth. Florence, having sensitive feelings anyway, was embarrassed several times by his behavior. Bolton bragged to Florence's friends that he ruled the roost, and if Florence tried to interfere he would knock her around. They were living in an apartment on Cahuenga Boulevard just outside the gates of Laemmle's Hollywood fortress, Universal City. Florence found herself in a dreadful situation in an even worse location. Her husband was a rude and insensitive clod, and she was living in the shadows of what could have been her greatest triumph, a fact Bolton probably did not overlook either.

The cad became a brute quickly. On February 6, 1934, Bolton came home drunk, and at 2 A.M. dragged a sleeping Florence from bed and beat her mercilessly. Florence claimed in her divorce statement that her "head was severely bruised and lacerated, leaving a considerable sized lump, her lips cut, her eyes blackened, and her face, in general, rendered black and blue." Her injuries were severe enough that she had fainting spells for days after; the humiliation, she maintained, was as painful as the unprovoked beating. Florence immediately packed up and left, serving Bolton with divorce papers the next month. She asked that her maiden name be restored "for professional reasons."[24] The divorce was quickly made official.

Florence emerged from all of the personal turmoil of the previous five years a broken woman. She had nothing left—her career was over, her personal life in shambles, her health precarious. She tried to take a deep breath and carry on, but each step was painful and it did not seem worthwhile to even face each coming day.

But acting somehow called out to her again, and she discovered the small living that could be made—playing small and tiny roles in the big movies Hollywood was making now. And, amazingly, now she might even be able to speak lines in these roles.

Chapter Twelve

HER LAST PART

They've great respect for the dead in Hollywood, but none for the living.
—Errol Flynn

How the moving pictures changed in the last part of the 1920s and early 1930s is practically irrelevant to the life of Florence Lawrence. She, like so many in Hollywood, could only watch from the sidelines as stunning changes came about, most obviously the melding of voice to film. She watched the little flickering film industry that she had helped to form move past the overture and enter the first act with a loud frenzied burst of excitement.

The silent film nearly perfected itself as an art form as the 1920s moved on. Film subjects toyed with morality, comedy, sanity. A feature without a single subtitle was touted as the perfect film. The movie-watching public fell in love with a fresh-faced starlet yearly, still wondering if the temperament on the screen reflected a real person or if it was all still make-believe.

Florence knew better. But even as avid a filmgoer as she was, she still must have winced at the absolute pain reflected in the face of Renée Falconetti in *La Passion de Jeanne d'Arc* or wondered if the future really looked like *Metropolis*. Or had the Great War really looked like *Wings*? And then the Warner Brothers dropped sound into this nearly perfect scene, forcing just about everyone, from the theater owner who faced expensive rewiring to the lowliest prop man who now could not drop anything during a take, to start over from scratch. Horror stories of players running screaming from the sound testing room were not uncommon, and good careers promised to vanish overnight, especially for the foreign stars whose accented voices did not record well. Regional American voices could sound odd on tape, too, as did some men who did not sound as masculine as they should. Studios set up elocution classes to train actors and actresses.

Still, movies boomed. In 1930, a year after the Depression began, average weekly attendance at the movie theaters was 90 million. Almost 600 films are released. The easy salability of the double feature merely increased studio output.[1] Lots of movies were needed.

And within the glittering town called Hollywood there was, of course, the poorer side where independent film manufacturers thrived on rented studios, common settings and a vast, low-paid labor force. This was Poverty Row, tucked away around Gower Street off Sunset Boulevard. Since many films made there were Westerns, the area was also called Gower Gulch. Films here were made hurriedly and cheaply, then sold to states rights markets, again usually cheaply. If production costs were low enough and the marketing done correctly, the film could make a profit. Dozens of little companies sprang up, churning out quickie movie after quickie movie. Lina Basquette ended up on Poverty Row after being blacklisted by Hollywood's big studios. She was told to bring her own horse, and she groused later that he was paid more than she was, plus got free lunch. She called working there a "professional demise."[2]

Most other performers did not feel this sting. Like Florence, they were merely glad for the work. Hope was in the very dirt they worked on. As Michael Pitts pointed out in his book *Poverty Row Studios, 1929–1940*, the Poverty Row work force was an incredibly diverse and interesting group. "It is often said that those who worked on Poverty Row were either on their way up or on their way down," Pitts said. "One can watch the evolution of a future star or acclaimed director, writer or photographer or see a has-been making another valiant attempt at a comeback."[3]

Former Bluebird general manager M.H. Hoffman began Allied Pictures Corporation in 1931, snagging former silent cowboy star Hoot Gibson while Gibson was on the outs with Universal. Gibson, who was still in high demand as a screen cowboy into the sound era, eventually made 11 films for Allied before becoming entangled in a Laemmle lawsuit.[4] The third of these was called *The Hard Hombre*, a humorous Western about a peaceful man who is mistaken for a desperate criminal. Florence somehow won a cameo speaking-role as the real Hard Hombre's jilted girlfriend, usually called Sister since she shows up to exact her revenge with her brother, played by Tiny Sandford. Besides the usual bunch of cowboys and Gibson, Lina Basquette and Mathilda Comont were featured.

Florence makes a good impression in the film, slender and pretty, sporting a feather boa to make her look slightly well-to-do. Her voice is clear and unaccented. She did not get to ride a horse in the film, but did drive a team from a buggy. She appeared more petite than she really was against the huge figure of Sandford, who later became better known as a foil for Laurel and Hardy. Lastly, although Florence was 45 years old, she did not look it. Sister was supposed to be Sandford's little sister; in reality he was six years her junior.

Otto Brower directed *The Hard Hombre*, which was released at the end of September 1931. In this era of independent studios, he evidently was free to move about, for only a month later another film he directed, *Pleasure,* was released by a different Poverty Row company, Artclass Pictures. Florence was credited by some to be in this production, too. Lina Basquette appears in this film as well, as do Carmel Myers and Conway Tearle.

The independent market overloaded itself during the early years of the Great Depression by making too many films aimed for audiences who scarcely had even nickels to spare. Florence's next credit came at Paramount: *Sinners in the Sun.* Florence was buried in masses of extras, but she may have been surprised to see at least one familiar face in that crowd—Florence Turner. Writer Chester Bahn of the *Syracuse Herald* found the two women and singled out their stories.

> Included in the 725 bit players and extras more or less ... are Florence Lawrence and Florence Turner. So unimportant to the story are the characters they enact that the two are denied cast identification. Neither do you find their names mentioned in the press sheet thoughtfully prepared and provided by the Paramount Publix publicity department ... Yet in the screen's pioneer days—long before the discovery of Hollywood—the Misses Lawrence and Turner, the former as "The Biograph Girl" and the latter as "The Vitagraph Girl," were full-fledged stars. There was not a nickelodeon operator, newly come from the women's wear trade, who did not count himself thrice blessed when he was privileged to present their pictures ... Once great stars ... today, "extra women for character roles"; theirs is the tragedy that is Hollywood.[5]

The Florences probably were not able to even meet Cary Grant or Carole Lombard, the film's stars.

An extra's work was never easy. The thousands of people who poured into Hollywood every year, hoping to "make it big," used extra and bit roles as their entry into films. Since the mid–1920s, the Hollywood Chamber of Commerce tried to curb the dead-ended flow of hopefuls, especially young people who were told back in their hometowns that "they ought to be in pictures." The Chamber's advice was consistent—bring enough money to last a year, and, girls, bring your mother. The casting couch was not a myth.

Florence, and so many other silent film former stars like Florence Turner, fought desperately for every part, bit or extra, that came along. To have been forgotten so completely must have been more painful as the years went on. But if she looked around her, she would have realized that of all the pioneers like herself still trying to make movies, Mary Pickford was the only one who was still a star. And Mary was, and always had been, in a class of her own. Even Griffith, the master, was fading fast, becoming dated. All of the other 1910-era players were out of the business, doing bits, or dead.

Hollywood and current filmmaking must have constantly amazed her.

The early 1930s ushered in the studio system, where big-name players were placed under contract for certain lengths of time with film quotas to fill. In some ways, sound did not improve these early movies. Often dialogue was just added because it could be. Screen performers were thrust into the role of song-and-dance vaudevillian as filmed "revue" shows were popping up.

A few roles did creep Florence's way. Mary Pickford was probably responsible for at least one, a minor part in Mary's last film, *Secrets*. Mary made a version of the film in 1930, only to completely scrap it and start anew three years later. As extras, she hired many of the old silent stars who had worked with her long ago: King Baggot, Paul Panzer, Elsie Janis and Florence, among others. Mary considered *Secrets* to be "credible," but blamed the Depression on its miserable box office receipts. *Secrets*, Mary remembered, was released on the day that President Roosevelt declared a bank holiday: "Very few people were spending money on entertainment in the weeks that followed."[6]

As Mary decided to quit the industry, Florence found herself busier than she had been in several years. She was credited on wire reports as having a small role in a W.C. Fields-Baby LeRoy picture called *The Old-Fashioned Way* (1934).[7] Her one-time director Dell Henderson also may have had a role in this picture. The next year, at least one publicity shot has Florence in another W.C. Fields film, *The Man on the Flying Trapeze*, although she was not listed in the credits.

The year 1936 also proved to be a busy one. In April, Metro-Goldwyn-Mayer (commonly called "Metro" around Hollywood) announced that the company would be placing at least a dozen of the screen's first stars on their payrolls as extras, giving them preference in character roles. The old familiar names and faces, mostly middle-aged, lined up for press release photographs. For many, Florence included, this was the first contract they had had in years. Florence was joined at Metro by old friends King Baggot and Flora Finch. Other players from the 1910s and early 1920s employed at Metro were Naomi Childers, Mahlon Hamilton, Helene Chadwick and Jules Cowes.

For several of these older players, Metro's generosity turned out to be the spark they needed to continue their failing careers. Childers received several named roles in films into the 1940s, as did Hamilton. For the rest, this contract was the end of their attempts of breaking back into films. Chadwick, who had such a busy career in the 1920s, virtually vanished after 1936. Finch, once John Bunny's haughty little sidekick in the early 1910s and later a popular character actress in the 1920s, also disappeared after 1936. Both Chadwick and Finch died in 1940.

Metro's charitable gesture toward these players is questionable at best. Metro's head, Louis B. Mayer, was indisputably not known for his kindness; one biographer claimed that Mayer rebelled against the very thought of philanthropy, but acknowledged at the same time that he did not object to having his name in the serious, not gossip, press. "Mayer was looking for a much

Twelve—Her Last Part

A studio shot of Florence taken around 1933. Florence's weary expression tells much about her career and life at this time. Photograph courtesy of Wisconsin Center of Film and Theater Research.

more dignified kind of publicity; one that emphasized his patriotism, his civic-mindedness and his work for the political party of his choice, the G.O.P."[8] Perhaps his hiring of these old stars was a nod toward his own advancing age (Mayer had just turned 50 himself). More probably he just wanted to have the studio's name under such a positive photograph.

Also in 1936, J. Stuart Blackton, readily identified as one of the top pioneers of the industry, organized a group of the first film celebrities called Associated Cinema Stars. While the social aspect of the group was the primary purpose, Blackton and others wanted to expose many of these out-of-work pioneers to employment possibilities. The *Motion Picture Herald* formally stated, "An all-over purpose is the eradication of the imaginary but often severely drawn dividing line between box office generations, to the end that a competent player may not be penalized for past drawing power." Over 100 former film faces (including Florence's) were there. The inaugural meeting was at the Los Angeles Biltmore Hotel, often the site of the new Academy Awards dinners, at the end of August 1936. Organizers intended for the event to become an annual happening. Even D.W. Griffith became a member of the group, joining Clara Kimball Young, Maurice Costello, Agnes Ayers, Ethel Clayton and Dorothy Davenport (better known as Mrs. Wallace Reid). Even though the Association was short-lived, Florence must have enjoyed the gatherings and reminisces, especially when a show of early films was presented.[9]

Memories were all she would have of some of her old friends. Many were dead by 1936, most in obscurity, forgotten even by their peers. Florence's leading men had not fared well over the years. Arthur Johnson had died in 1916. Vitagraph co-star William Shea died shortly after that, in 1918, when Florence was struggling with her shadows. John Cumpson died even before Johnson, in 1913. *The Unfoldment* co-star William Conklin had a fatal stroke in 1935. Only Owen and Matt Moore still struggled on, although Owen would die a year after she did. Matt had a long career in films, appearing in small character roles in almost a hundred movies through 1958, two years before his death.

Her rivals for popularity from the 1910s were also fading away. Clara Kimball Young had her last minor role in the early 1940s, after more than a decade of film obscurity. Mabel Normand died in 1930 of tuberculosis, her career stunted eight years before by association with the murdered William Desmond Taylor. Florence Turner, like Florence, struggled in the 1930s for bits and finally died, exhausted, in 1946 at the Motion Picture Home in Woodland Hills. Mae Murray, whose career started with Lasky in the mid–1910s, found herself bankrupt and homeless by 1936. William Farnum, another acting brother of Dustin and Marshall, declared bankruptcy in the 1930s, as did director Marshall Neilan and former Biograph actress Blanche Sweet. It would not be until 1942 that the Motion Picture Relief Fund would dedicate its Country Home, where some of these destitute former players could safely and finally retire.

Florence also worked in a small part in a Paramount film called *Hollywood Boulevard* in 1936. The all-star and all-former-star cast gave many players their most interesting work during the 1930s. Harry Myers, Mae Marsh, Maurice Costello, Ruth Clifford and William Farnum all had small roles. Florence was not so lucky; her part ended up on the cutting room floor, along with Louise Brooks, Rosemary Theby and Harold Lloyd.

In late 1937, the *Los Angeles Times* briefly summarized the careers of a few "old-timers" still working in pictures. "Edwin August, leading man—bits ... Mrs. Thomas Jefferson, actress—wardrobe department ... Betty Blythe, star vamp—bits ... Barbara Bedford, leading lady—bits ... Helene Costello, leading lady—bits ... Agnes Ayers, star—bits ... Florence Lawrence, leading lady—bits."[10] Florence was not the only film star to fall far; in fact, others seem to have fallen farther, faster.

At one point while she was working for Metro, possibly in the middle of 1937, Florence developed a painful condition that could have probably been diagnosed as agnogenic myeloid metaplasia or myelofibrosis, a rare disease where bone marrow is gradually replaced by collagen fibers. She was treated by a Dr. Lester Laurian, who described her ailment in 1938 as "a bone disease which produces anemia and depression."[11] She had also complained of terrible bone pain. While all of her symptoms do not precisely match myelofibrosis, this disease does seem to be the closest. Myelofibrosis does not cause anemia, but it does cause bone pain, and depression often occurs at the hopelessness of the disease. However, if the myelofibrosis is complicated by a deficiency of vitamin B-12, which can cause both anemia and neuropsychiatric problems, the symptoms all would match. The symptoms of myelofibrosis, as understood today, include fluid and pain in the abdomen, joint and bone pain, and skin eruptions. No cure was known then, but the disease could be controlled for a number of years.

In the mid–1930s, Florence moved to a small West Hollywood

neighborhood on Westborne Avenue, off Melrose Avenue, and only a dozen blocks from her old Hollywood Cosmetics store. The house she lived in may have been a duplex or a multi-bedroom home, for at least two other people lived there, a Metro employee named Bob and his sister. The three seem to have been good friends. A young woman named Marian Menzer lived next door. Florence apparently had built up a comfortable cocoon of friends once again.

Metro must have kept her busy, for the studio was having steadily building years during this time. In 1937, the studio released around 65 films; in 1938, over 90. Florence's activities were not documented, nor were the extra roles credited. Metro did boast of having "all the stars in heaven" on their rosters in the mid–1930s. Clark Gable, Jeanette MacDonald, Spencer Tracy, Mickey Rooney, the Marx Brothers, Greer Garson, Hedy Lamarr and Judy Garland all were under Mayer's thumb at some point during the decade. Several of them chafed at the system that the studios had unconsciously created; Florence would have loved to be under such pressure.

Instead, Florence gradually settled into a depression, with her health completely gone. Film work she could get was uncredited, an act of charity. She still wrote poetry, getting better at it as years went on. One poem, "Despair," found in her papers given to the Natural History Museum, must have been written in the early 1930s. Her continued misery is achingly apparent:

> Tired of living, I'm weary, I long to lie down and die.
> To find for the sad heart and dreary, The end of the
>   Pilgrimage nigh.
> Weary, so weary of wishing, For things that were mine
>   by right,
> They took them away and gave me, A world of blackness
>   and night.
>
> Weary and tired of waiting, Waiting for sympathy sweet,
> I'm tired of wishing for friendship, but its all so fairy
>   and fleet!
> I long for the end of my sorrows, I'm tired of the
>   blinding day.
> My feet seem to falter and stumble, Along the rough
>   rocky way.
>
> Exhausted! Tired of drifting, Down the dark stream
>   of life.
> Tired of breasting the billows, the Billows of toil
>   and strife.
> Wishing and waiting so sadly, For love that is best of all,
> When you find it: its just a mere shadow dear, and
>   nothing is left but the wall.[12]

On Wednesday, December 28, 1938, Florence seems to have given up. She was scheduled to report to work at 1:00 P.M. for a small role in an upcoming film, but canceled by calling the Metro casting office that morning, claiming illness.

What happened next is unclear. Neighbor Marian Menzer heard her scream some time during the day. One newspaper article claimed Florence ran to Marian's next-door house, crying out that she had poisoned herself. Another said she called Marian on the telephone, telling her to call a doctor. Other articles say that Marian found Florence writhing and screaming on the floor of her own home. Marian called an ambulance, which took Florence to the Beverly Hills Emergency Hospital. Florence Lawrence was pronounced dead soon after arriving at 2:45 P.M., one hour after consuming a mixture of cough syrup and ant paste. The coroner's office was immediately called for an autopsy, and her body was sent to the county morgue at 4:30 P.M. Wilma Booker of the Motion Picture Relief Fund called Pierce Brothers Mortuary Company to handle the services.

Deputies Zahn and Cook from the Hollywood station of the Los Angeles Sheriff's Department investigated the scene at Florence's house, where they found a suicide note addressed to Bob, the studio worker who lived in Florence's house. The note read: "Call Dr. Wilson. I am tired. Hope this works. Good-by, my darlings. They can't cure me so let it go at that. Lovingly, Florence. P.S. You've all been swell guys. Everything is yours." In several newspaper articles, Dr. Wilson reads as Dr. Nelson, and the word "darlings" is singular. This note was the only possession that the coroner's office listed as her property; it was turned over to her brother George, who was still living in San Francisco. The coroner's register lists the probable cause of her suicide as "ill health."

Florence's death certificate, true to form, mixes fact with Florence's own brand of fiction. Her birth date is wrong, giving her three extra years. The coroner's register generously says that she was 44 years old. But most of the Hollywood newspapers and the Associated Press wire obituary correctly say that she was 52. Most of the personal information found on her official death certificate was repeated on a standardized death form used by Pierce Brothers Mortuary. In addition to the age discrepancies, her father's name was listed as George on one and Charles on the other. Poor Harry Solter was thrown further into permanent obscurity by omission (Woodring and Bolton are listed as Florence's surviving husbands) or misspelling (Salter once again, or in one case Slotter). One amazing and correct fact does stand out—Florence had been an actress in moving pictures for 31 years.

The funeral home that handled her services was Pierce Brothers Mortuary, now known as Pierce Brothers Cunningham and O'Connor Mortuary, located on West Washington Boulevard in Los Angeles. In their records of her service, the directors noted that an unknown man, probably Bob, who evidently knew Florence well, told them, after viewing her in her coffin, that she looked very nice; a woman with him, possibly his sister, said she looked fine. Florence was dressed in her own clothes that friends had brought in.[13]

The funeral was held on Friday, December 30, at 3:00 P.M. at the Pierce Brothers Chapel. There is no record of who attended. The Motion Picture Relief Fund handled most of the service, from buying the casket to selecting the minister. The Rev. Neal Dodd, the so-called "Padre of Hollywood," conducted Florence's service at their behest. He selected "Crossing the Bar" and "When Our Heads Are Bowed with Woe" as the music to be played.

She was buried at the Hollywood Memorial Cemetery on Santa Monica Boulevard in Los Angeles, alongside hundreds of other movie stars, some famous, some forgotten. Her grave, also purchased by the Motion Picture Relief Fund, was a single plot, number 300 in section 2-West. The location is not very good, within 100 yards of Santa Monica Boulevard. Grass barely covers the ground around her grave. Hollywood Memorial Cemetery has been the site of controversy in the mid–1990s, starting with severe financial problems; it sold for scarcely $250,000 at a 1997 auction. With so many famous celebrities buried there (Douglas Fairbanks, Rudolph Valentino, and Marion Davies, plus approximately 80,000 other people), the topic raised concerns and consternation not only in Los Angeles but across the nation.

But Florence's grave has not been completely neglected. Though it was unmarked for many years, a prominent British actor, knowing only about her sad life but wishing to remain anonymous, bought a simple bronze marker for her in 1991. It reads, "Florence Lawrence, The Biograph Girl, The First Movie Star, 1890–1938." Over the years, a few caregivers have graced the site with rock arrangements and small plants. A large urn, full of a plant with purple flowers, sits nearby. Cellophane-wrapped roses are occasionally left. Perhaps these visitors know Florence's favorite flowers were roses.

The year 1938 saw the end of more than a few fading stars from the early years of movies. Players such as Pauline Frederick, Myrtle Stedman, Warner Oland, Conway Tearle and Pearl White all died during the year. Silent film directors Melville Brown, Oscar Apfel, Arthur Hotaling and John Blyston also died in 1938. Thanhouser actor Richard Cummings and Florence's former co-star Harry Myers both died three days before Florence did, causing the Hollywood *Citizen-News* to proclaim upon Florence's death: "Filmdom's Grim Cycle Runs Course," referring to the eerie coincidence of three famous people dying close together. The fact that Florence chose to kill herself was taken in casual Hollywood fashion as well; the same article in the *Citizen-News* announced, "Florence Lawrence Uses Poison Cocktail for Final Worldly Gesture," and dramatically ended the piece with the sentence, "Florence Lawrence had played her last part."[14] Suicide was becoming an accepted exit for those who seemed to have no future in Hollywood. Ross Alexander, Marie Walcamp, Karl Dane, Max Linder, Lou Tellegen, Peg Entwistle, Tom Forman,

A recent gift from an unnamed, sympathetic friend, Florence's grave marker reads, "Florence Lawrence, The Biograph Girl, The First Movie Star, 1890–1938." Florence would have loved the altered birth date. Photograph by Annette M. D'Agostino.

Art Acord and Claude Gillingwater had all taken their own lives in the 1920s or 1930s. Even in the early films that Florence had made 30 years before, suicide was shown as a great means of escape. In Biograph's *The Way of Man*, Florence's scarred character successfully used a faked suicide to start her life over and allow others to get on with their lives. In real life, Harry Solter had threatened to commit suicide when marital times were difficult, effectively getting Florence's attention.

There were no glowing editorials or commentaries about Florence Lawrence after her death. At most, the basic wire story of her suicide ran in the nationwide metropolitan newspapers the day after it occurred, and *Variety* and *Newsweek* both ran small notices within a week. Even her hometown of Hamilton only ran a tiny photo with a brief cutline. Florence was remembered in these stories as once being a star of great importance, having been the original "Biograph" and "Imp" girls, as well as "Baby Flo, the Child Wonder." She was also remembered for having acted in the early days with Mary Pickford, Maurice Costello and Clara Kimball Young, even though she had made only a handful of films with Pickford and Costello and none with Young. These most famous names were used in 1938 because they were the only ones that the eldest in the talkies public could remember; forgotten were the dozens of shorts made with long-dead stars such as Arthur Johnson and John Cumpson.

One interviewer tracked down King Baggot for his response to her death. "No matter what happens," he said sadly, "just stay in there and pitch." He fondly recalled their days together at IMP, adding, "If you're in there pitching all the time, any day may start the New Year you've been waiting for." He knew Florence's New Year had never started. He was still waiting for his.

The article providing the most commentary of her death, including a very recent photograph, was the cover story on the Hollywood *Citizen-News*, which called her career "tragic," playing up the 1915 fire where she was supposed to have saved Matt Moore from death. "The suicide of Miss Lawrence brought to a close a long struggle against ill health and ended another Hollywood story of fame which turned into near-obscurity ... Ill health prevented her from working frequently and her savings from the days of stardom were swept away." Her ill health was attributed to both lingering injuries from the fire and "an ailment caused by insufficient marrow in the bones."[15]

Florence's death did catch at least one film historian by surprise. Edward Wagenknecht in *The Movies in the Age of Innocence* said, "She was the last kind of person one would have thought a promising subject for suicide." He added a wistful endnote to his remembrances of Florence: "Only a few days before her death she sent a photograph to a collector who had requested it. 'I only wish,' she wrote, 'that the producers thought as highly of me as you do.'"[16]

Chapter Thirteen[1]

FLORENCE WHO?

If I had my life to live over, I think I'd be in clover—
If I slipped on a peel, I'd fall head over heel,
  Into the Waters of DOVER!
ALL OVER!

—Florence Lawrence

For the most part, Florence has been forgotten by not only Hollywood, but American and women's history. Although she is usually cited as the first movie star, film histories tend to repeat the spectacular, inaccurate Ramsaye story as told in his 1925 book *A Million and One Nights*. Books published since then, even through the 1990s, speak of Laemmle's raid of the Biograph studios, ignoring the fact that three or four months passed between Florence's employment by the two studios, and ignoring her statements to the contrary. Tom Gunning, author of *D.W. Griffith and the Origins of the American Narrative Film*, points out that the very title of Ramsaye's book shows Ramsaye's "entertaining" interpretation of early film history. "Ramsaye tweaked stories to make them more dramatic, and he did this with his account of Lawrence," Gunning says. However, he adds that given Ramsaye's proximity to the era and his association with the industry, readers of his work should be thankful for his endeavor; "His book was close enough to the period to provide a strong sense of what it was like." But what writers have done after Ramsaye is a different story. Film historians are perpetuating Ramsaye's myth by not doing their own research and accepting his work as fact. But Gunning also points out this is sometimes due to a diminished sense of the importance of the early cinema and the general unavailability of primary resources.[2]

This lack of sources includes not only magazines and trade journals, but also the films themselves. Florence's work with the Biograph Company is well documented and surprisingly well-preserved at the Library of Congress. However, copies are not distributed freely, restricting would-be viewers to on-site research only. Florence's other work is sparsely saved, and sometimes what is languishing in an archive does not reflect the actress at her best. Also, short films such as Florence made have not been completely catalogued or given the priority that features have been given over the years. And today, the showings of silent films are relegated to a few specialty theaters and late-night showings on a couple of cable channels. What is shown are the better-known features by the stars who came after Florence: Charlie Chaplin, Buster Keaton, Clara Bow, Janet Gaynor and Mary Pickford.

"Little Mary" also contributes to Florence's neglect. "I think that the 'craze' for Mary Pickford which directly followed Florence's, and admittedly lasted longer, stole much of Florence's thunder, making Mary Pickford the first female remembered,"[3] said Annette D'Agostino, author of two invaluable *Moving Picture World* indices. Film historian Charles Musser agrees: "In some ways her story was eclipsed by Mary Pickford."[4]

The reason for this stretches back to the personalities of the two women. Mary Pickford, while also a superior artist, would not work unless the contract was completely in her favor. Florence lacked the negotiating skills and leverage that Mary possessed. But even now, Pickford has lost her luster. "Barely remembered now in the passing of time and fashion, Pickford was once, simply, the most powerful person in Hollywood" ran the summary of Pickford in the *Entertainment Weekly, the 100 Greatest Movie Stars of All Time*.[5] In the late 1970s, Ken Wlaschin said that the stereotyping of Mary's characters has led to her lack of popularity to modern film buffs. "Her myth as the girl-woman Little Mary, America's (and the World's) sweetheart, has not endured," he said in his book *The Illustrated History of the World's Greatest Movie Stars*. "Perhaps her star will shine brightly again—fashions change, even among film historians—but for the moment she is definitely in eclipse."[6]

And while Mary's lack of popularity is explained away in these two listings, Florence's appeal is more subtle. In *Entertainment Weekly*, writer and critic Ty Burr asks the reader, "Let us now have a moment of silence in memory of Florence Lawrence. Don't know who she is? That's okay—most audiences in 1909 didn't know her name either."[7] Burr, in his brief summary of her career, does not fall into the Ramsaye trap. His salute to the first star in a modern, national magazine has helped to bring Florence to the surface of today's mainstream. Wlaschin, in his thumbnail sketch of Florence and her career in his book, tells the Ramsaye story, expounding that "Florence Lawrence was the first movie star to become famous by name, and the star system began with her in 1910." He adds, truthfully, too, "Today she is virtually unknown, except to film historians, despite her importance."[8] Film writer and archivist John Cocchi agrees: "Her place in film history appears secure, although overshadowed by other early stars as Pickford, Marsh and the Gishes."[9]

Anthony Slide, a great film historian who has revived the art of film research and writing, feels that the timing of Florence's career is instrumental in her lost story. "Her career as a star ended before the notion of a 'star' was fully realized."[10] Richard de Cordova, after attempting to reconstruct Florence's career steps in his book *Picture Personalities*, noted that not only Florence suffered after those years. "Even without the accident it seems that Lawrence was destined, by the middle teens, to fade into relative obscurity like other early stars, such as Florence Turner and Mary Fuller," he said. "After only a few years these stars already seemed like part of a bygone era."[11]

But would Florence have made an impact if her health and luck had allowed her to create a successful feature career? Many of the early actresses to make features—Helen Gardner, Anita Stewart, Margarita Fischer—are similarly forgotten. But Florence seems to have had a unique ability to touch her audience, even in the days when productions were hurried and technology limited. D'Agostino sees Florence as a very special actress in those days. "Florence Lawrence was the first film actor or actress to deeply ingratiate herself with the moviegoer, beyond the ordinary 'good performer,'" she says. "She hit a chord with her audience, and so touched them with her artistry that—for *some* reason—they *had* to know who that 'Biograph Girl' was, by name. They felt that they knew her."[12] Gunning, who also has studied Florence's career, feels the same way. "The early fan letters that she received as well as trade paper commentary shows that early audiences saw her as someone they would like to met, someone they felt comfortable with." He elaborates by trying to see the persona that the audience saw: "Lawrence on the screen projected an image that people could both admire (she was active, pretty, athletic and humourous), and also feel at home and familiar with."[13]

Florence was such a natural that she made audiences see themselves on screen or let the audience share in her emotions as she portrayed them for the camera. Cocchi feels that "her spirit and ability to adapt to any role" made her special to these early audiences.[14] Joseph Eckhardt, biographer of Siegmund Lubin, thinks that she conveyed herself through film like few others. "In spite of using the histrionic gestures typical of the stage, Florence Lawrence was nevertheless believable enough to attract the attention and sympathies of her early movie audiences," he says. "The kinds of roles she played and the believability of her playing were certainly the sources of some of her appeal."[15] Musser explains that her appeal also came across on a purely basic level: "She played ordinary women, combining qualities of toughness and vulnerability."[16]

Carlos Bustamante, Professor of Audiovisual Design at the University of Arts Berlin, enjoys watching the early silent short films to see the development of the art in progress. "I am still amazed by the early films and the solutions directors, actors and technicians found for narrative problems." This admiration crosses over to Florence as well: "Florence Lawrence's acting, her ability to develop several emotional levels seemingly simultaneously, thrills me more than watching a well-edited chase ... Her timing, the quick-changing expressive control of her body, head and hand movements, the alternating degrees of tension and relaxation, gracefulness and woodenness are a joy to watch and to follow."[17]

Although histrionic acting is terribly dating in films, Florence's use of it seems rather natural. When she puts her hand to her cheek and shakes her head, the viewer thinks that is what she would do whether she was on film or in her own living room. She talked with her hands and conveyed complex emotions with even slight positioning or action.

Gene Vazzana, player researcher and editor of the newsletter *Silent Film Monthly*, compared her stardom to the only other known at that time — theatrical. "She was identifiable and publicized as a star, gaining the fame of stage actresses, but more accessible all across the country."[18] Vaudeville too had its own star system, and of course vaudeville can be seen as regular entertainment for middle to lower working classes in those days. Advertising in vaudeville was extremely common even in the smallest of venues, so when motion pictures began doing the same sort of advertising, the entertainment-minded public was ready for it.

Florence Lawrence, the actress, is remembered primarily through the roles she played. She certainly did portray an amazing variety of parts, probably even for the standards of that day. The Jones series, directed by D.W. Griffith, is named by several film historians as her most unforgettable. Slide calls the Jones comedies "arguably the first series films, with characters familiar to all members of the audience."[19] D'Agostino, after reading the "wonderful" reviews for Mr. and Mrs. Jones films while researching her book *An Index to Short and Feature Film Reviews in Moving Picture World*, says that those films attracted her attention immediately. "I found myself listing this series as one that, given half the chance, I'd love to see in full."[20] Gunning likes the Jones series as well, but also enjoys seeing *After Many Years*, *Song of the Shirt*, and *The Salvation Army Lass*, all Biograph dramas.[21]

Other historians also list Florence's very first film and one of her last films as their favorites. Musser thinks *Daniel Boone* is a special film, and Cocchi sees *The Hard Hombre* as his favorite. Musser cited Florence's memoirs of making *Daniel Boone* in his article "Preclassical American Cinema" for revealing the important "co-directing" concept in the very earliest of narrative film.[22] Cocchi thinks Florence's appearance in *The Hard Hombre* made that film different. "Her brief but intense role made an impact in an ordinary oater [Western]."[23]

But another part of the neglect of Florence Lawrence is a neglect of the film industry in general from its beginning through 1915, when *The Birth of a Nation* was released. Sadly, most of the general public has never seen a silent short film, and most rarely even consider that films were made before 1920. And even among writers of film histories, there is a tendency to generalize the silent era into one period of study. Film writer and researcher Philip Leibfried feels that the silent era from 1895 to 1915 has greatly been neglected from the standpoint of the players. "This is the least documented era of film history, at least as far as the performers are concerned."[24] Even more specifically, the years 1910 to 1915 need additional study, according to Slide. "The period 1910–1915 is so important because it saw the creation of the feature film, the basis of all cinema since then."[25] Cocchi cites the importance of the same years but for slightly different reasons. "[The years] 1910–1915 should be fully detailed, as this was the time when film really became an art, with publicized players and appealing stories, rather than just scenics."[26] Gunning has much the same feelings: "It was a period of rapid transition in our history, and few places display these transitions as vividly as the film industry."[27]

Straightforward film histories, encompassing silents through the present, are generally not kind to the early film personalities. Most are lumped together, regardless of style or director or year, into "those who worked for Griffith" and those who did not. The lucky ones who are listed—and a list is all they will get—generally worked for Griffith. Florence may get a brief nod as Laemmle's stooge in the St. Louis caper, which is usually shown as the origin of the star system. Even those important early women directors, Alice Guy Blanche and Lois Weber, rate only cursory mention.

In the relatively few histories of women on the screen, the pages are understandably more gracious. Ethan Mordden studied his subject well and ignored Ramsaye, telling Florence's story as Florence would have liked, truthful and funny (although she probably would have resented the chapter-long comparison with Theda Bara). After summarizing Florence's trip to St. Louis, Mordden said, "Not only was a star born, but the whole star business, for other independents saw what it did for Lawrence and followed Laemmle's lead. They were smart. While maintaining a star system was vastly more expensive than employing an anonymous labor pool, films without stars proved unworkable. The Trust studios resisted it ... and died."[28]

Women have always had a rough relationship with the screen. The old career-versus-family monster shakes its tsk-ing head. Linda Arvidson recalled that while single women and married career actress were certainly welcome at the Biograph, "wives of the good actors were not popular around the studio," even when women were needed in scenes.[29] The pages of movie magazines were full of the forgotten actresses who married and vanished from the screen, for these were the days when a woman's place was firmly in the home. Family and career were simply seen as incompatible.

Another backlash women had to deal with, more so than men, was the aging factor. Griffith himself demanded young actresses. He righteously claimed that untraining a well-seasoned stage player for films simply took too long: "I pick out young people and teach them in less time than it would take me to alter the methods of people from the boards." The "truth-telling camera" does not lie, he added, gently trying to explain why he surrounded himself with youth and beauty. But as Gene Gauntier gleefully pointed out, Griffith also liked his leading women to be blonde, another strike against many women, herself included.[30] Florence tried to compensate for this by routinely taking years off her age, for her fair skin and blonde hair photographed satisfactorily, well past her late twenties and into her early thirties. Her saucy, hoydenish screen attitude no doubt also helped keep her "image" young.

Being a woman in film also had other problems, some not apparent until years later. William Drew, author of *Speaking of Silents: First Ladies of the Screen*, wonders where all of the women's films have gone. "That so many fine films and outstanding performances by ... [notable silent film] actresses has been lost is appalling enough," Drew said in his 1996 article "Damsels In Distress: Strong Silent Women Held Hostage in Film Archives." "But this void in cinema history is compounded by the inexcusable failure of archives to make the surviving films of these actresses available to the public through video copies."[31] Some women, even those lucky and savvy enough to retain control of their films, still could only watch helplessly as their copies of the nitrate-based films turned into red dust, some in the archives they had been given to. Florence never owned the rights to any of her films; when films were constantly being made and seemingly practically disposable, such foresight was lacking for most players.

Florence's four years at IMP, Lubin and Victor are represented in less than a dozen film scraps in scattered vaults around the world. So beyond Florence's work at Biograph, much of her other work is completely lost, causing critics and historians alike to speculate as to just how far Florence was able to perfect her craft past 1909. How bad was *Elusive Isabel*? How good was *The Unfoldment*? What kind of a director was Harry Solter? How much was he influenced by Griffith? These questions will probably go unanswered. The films are hopelessly and irreplaceably gone, not even lucky enough to be locked up "safely" somewhere.

And while women in film history feel neglected, women in history have been neglected, period, even more so. This is an old story, of course, not even worth a weary protestation here. But women such as Florence are also ignored even in women's history books. A simple survey of diverse, mainstream women's studies, such as *Woman's Almanac* or *The Women's Chronology*, practically ignores everyone but the very biggest of film names, usually not with a great deal of accuracy, but with good intentions. Another non-textual treatment of women's history, *A History of Women in America*, not only ignores women's role in early film, but also ignores women in most other arts as well. In the same vein, Florence's devotion to the women's suffrage movement does not appear in any of the cause's contemporary magazines, such as *Woman Voter*.

An even more personal blow to Florence was that many of the early film folks did not leave much in the form of written or personal records. Those who did achieve enough success (Mary Pickford, Mack Sennett, Billy Bitzer, D.W. Griffith, etc.) to rate writing an autobiography, fail to mention Florence beyond the appellation of "The Biograph Girl." Several of these former film stars, writing in the 1920s, did remember her with more detail then, still cautious no doubt because Florence's star was so dim then. Mary Pickford, writing in the *Ladies' Home Journal* in 1924, saw Florence only as a stepping stone to her own success. In the Biograph dressing room, there were only two vanities for the "stars" to use when dressing. Mary had been eyeing those tables "from the first day." "When Florence Lawrence left the company, I got that coveted dressing table."[32] She did not mention her at all in her later autobiography, *Sunshine and Shadow*. Linda Arvidson was understandably more thoughtful toward her former friend, although her work is often tainted with petty jealousy and slightly vengeful attitudes toward certain stars. "The movies were as the breath of life to her," Arvidson said of Florence. "She never minded work." Arvidson thought highly of Florence's versatility and her enthusiasm. But Arvidson also related what she remembered were Mack Sennett's thoughts about Florence: "He never approved whole-heartedly of anything we did ... Florence Lawrence didn't suit him either—'She talks baby-talk.' And to Sennett 'baby-talk' was the limit!"[33] Sennett himself only seemed to vaguely remember that Florence was "The Biograph Girl" and the first screen star, but thought that "it was not until Mary Pickford's enormous success that players on the screen began to be identified."[34] Gene Gauntier remembered Florence only as a fellow player at Biograph and remembered that Marion Leonard was "The Biograph Girl," and Billy Bitzer merely recalled her work in the "Jones" comedies. The frightening thought of being forgotten not only by the industry seems to have begun much earlier with Florence being forgotten by her friends and fellow screen companions.

But what does all this mean? Florence Lawrence was the first player, male or female, to use her name to advertise not only a single motion picture but also the production company she worked for. The company, in turn, was able to place more films into theaters because the public wanted to see the films that she was in.

Is this worthy of any attention? Modern Americans probably have not thought of America without Hollywood, a truly unique and very American feature that transcends the actual city of Los Angeles. The name Hollywood conjures up the image of fur boas, white limousines, camera flashes, haute couture. What would America be without Hollywood? The "rich and famous" catchphrase is a deeply rooted part of the American psyche, and no other place in the world captures the imagination of "film-making" as does Hollywood. Modern television and film personalities are simply big news and have been for many years. Ordinary events in their lives fill inches of column space in newspapers and magazines, and now on the Internet. Stars' marriages and divorces unwillingly become headlines, "behind the scenes" is part of standard American vocabulary, and today's players realize that becoming a public figure comes with this particular brand of fame. They grant interviews or issue press releases in an attempt to curb the flow of information, but a speeding ticket on public record finds it way into the news as well.

So what does Florence Lawrence, a one-time star and forgotten actress, have to do with this? She simply kicked open the door. The use of her name in IMP advertisements, after building her reputation as a great actress in the Biograph films, helped to keep IMP afloat. When IMP did well, the other independents did better. And when the independent film manufacturers were strong enough to withstand legal battles against the Trust, the Trust began to crumble. The film industry, also an infant art form, as was film, thus began. Florence was not personally responsible for this, however. Neither was Carl Laemmle. The combination of good timing, receptive atmosphere and the growing positive public reactions to film in general all created a favorable environment for the star system to be formed. Florence just happened to be the first one to step from the train.

Florence only benefited from IMP's defiance for a short while. Thousands of other stars have followed her gradually upward path that peaked, crested and declined. But she made a good living while it lasted. She enjoyed herself. She was thrillingly alive before the camera. She set an example for other actresses to follow, and she inspired countless others who just were able to see her films. She only wanted to please her public.

But tastes change, and what is in favor one day is not the next. Florence learned the hard way that her services were no longer needed. She resisted accepting the fact that she was not wanted. She did not live without films well, and she chose not to live in the world created around her. Her death, shocking and sad, still almost comes as a surprise that she held on as long as she did. And her death did not cause any great outcry, other than slight stabs at pity for the silent film actor whose medium had vanished. Her death was just another ending of another once happy career gone sad.

Florence Lawrence deserves her place in history. And with a stamp of her little foot and a swoon with her wrist against her forehead, she catches her audience's attention. Once engaged, she smiles and waves, then blows a kiss goodbye.

Filmography

Florence Lawrence made several hundred films, many at a time when the actors, actresses and directors were barely credited for their work. Therefore, identifying Florence Lawrence films is a challenge at best. Being able to identify her in a short paper-based print or deteriorating nitrate stock can be nearly impossible, even in films where she has been given credit in other sources.

All of the films below have been verified in at least one contemporary source (such as magazines of the era or Florence's own notes and letters) or two modern sources (books, magazines, etc.).

Each film has a set of abbreviations that give additional background:

PC: production company
R: release date
D: director
C: cameraman
S: script/writer

A: additional actors
L: film length (1000 feet was one reel, or about 12 minutes)
W: where the film was shot
P: plot summary

An asterisk (*) marks a lead or prominent role; the character name is given if known. A question mark (?) indicates doubt.

1907

Daniel Boone, or Pioneer Days in America* [Boone's daughter]
PC: Edison; R: probably March; D: Edwin S. Porter, Wallace McCutcheon; A: Lotta Lawrence, Susanne Willis, Mr. and Mrs. William Craven; L: 1000 feet; W: Bronx Park; P: Daniel Boone is captured by Native Americans when he tries to rescue his abducted daughter.

The Boy, the Bust and the Bath
PC: Vitagraph; R: probably August; L: 425 feet; P: A girl is the object of peeking affection in a boarding house.

The Shaughraun* [Moya]
PC: Vitagraph; R: probably December; D/C: J. Stuart Blackton, Albert E. Smith; S: based on Dion Boucicault's play; A: William Shea; L: 700 feet; W: Central Park, New York City; P: An Irishman tries to avenge an arrest.

The Despatch Bearer*
PC: Vitagraph; R: probably December; D/C: J. Stuart Blackton, Albert E. Smith; L: 725 feet; P: A woman replaces her injured beau on a spy mission.

1908

Francesca da Rimini, or The Two Brothers [?]
PC: Vitagraph; R: probably February; D: J. Stuart Blackton or William Ranous; A: Maurice Costello; L: 1000 feet; P: A tragic love story where Francesca married Lanciotto but loves his brother Paolo.

Macbeth, Shakespeare's Sublime Tragedy [?]
PC: Vitagraph; R: probably April; D: William Ranous; L: 835 feet; P: Shakespeare's Scottish history of Macbeth usurping the throne by murdering his predecessor.

Romeo and Juliet, a Romantic Story of the Ancient Feud Between the Italian Houses of Montague and Capulet [?]
[Florence Lawrence is attributed to this film in every modern filmography, most notably in Blum's *A Pictorial History of the Silent Screen*; however, she stated in 1914 that Florence Turner played the lead.]
PC: Vitagraph; R: June; D: J. Stuart Blackton or William Ranous; A: Paul Panzer, Harry Solter; L: 915 feet; W: Central Park, New York City; P: Shakespeare's tragedy where two feuding houses are secretly united with the marriage of their children.

Lady Jane's Flight, a 17th Century Romance [?]
PC: Vitagraph; R: July; D: J. Stuart Blackton; L: 583 feet; P: A period romance of an eloping couple, trying to escape her father's wrath.

The Viking's Daughter, the Story of the Ancient Norseman [Theckla?]
PC: Vitagraph; R: probably July; D: J. Stuart Blackton; L: 447 feet; P: A Saxon prisoner rescues his Viking captor's daughter, resulting in his freedom and their marriage.

Salome, or The Dance of the Seven Veils [?]
PC: Vitagraph; R: August; D: J. Stuart Blackton; A: Maurice Costello; L: 710 feet; P: An adaptation of the Biblical story of John the Baptist's death, when Herod is enchanted by Salome's dance and grants her one grisly wish—John the Baptist's head.

Richard III, A Shakespearean Tragedy [?]
PC: Vitagraph; R: September; D: J. Stuart Blackton and William Ranous; A: William Ranous, Florence Turner, Julia Swayne Gordon, Florence Auer, Thomas Ince, Maurice Costello, Paul Panzer, Harry Solter; L: 990 feet; P: Shakespeare's historical drama that tells the fate of the two princes in the Tower at hands of the future Richard III.

Antony and Cleopatra, a Love Story of the Noblest Roman and the Most Beautiful Egyptian [?]
PC: Vitagraph; R: November 3; D: J. Stuart Blackton or Charles Kent; A: William Ranous, Maurice Costello, Paul Panzer, Earle Williams; L: 995 feet; P: Shakespeare's tragedy of the ill-fated love affair between the Roman and the Egyptian.

Julius Caesar, an Historical Tragedy [?]
PC: Vitagraph; R: December 1; D: William Ranous or J. Stuart Blackton; A: William Ranous, William Shea, Paul Panzer, Earle Williams, Maurice Costello; L: 980 feet; P: Shakespeare's historical tragedy of the rise and fall of Caesar, done in 15 scenes.

The Dancer and the King, a Romantic Story of Spain [?]
PC: Vitagraph; R: December 19; D: J. Stuart Blackton; A: Maurice Costello; L: 650 feet; P: A dancer enchants a lecherous king but rebuffs his advances, resulting in his vengeful anger.

[Biograph films made during last half of the year]

The Bandit's Waterloo
PC: Biograph; R: August 4; D/S: D.W. Griffith; C: Arthur Marvin; A: Marion Leonard, Harry Solter, Arthur Johnson; L: 839 feet; P: A Spanish tale of a maiden who unwittingly attracts the attentions of an outlaw.

The Calamitous Elopement [?]
PC: Biograph; *R:* August 7; *D/S:* D.W. Griffith; *C:* Billy Bitzer; *A:* Linda Arvidson, John Cumpson, Tony O'Sullivan, D.W. Griffith, Harry Solter, George Gebhardt; *L:* 738 feet [Florence was probably not in this, even though credited as such in many places.]; *P:* Papa dislikes his daughter's suitor, so the couple elopes, pursued by Papa and a bungling burglar.

Balked at the Altar
PC: Biograph; *R:* August 25; *D/S:* D.W. Griffith; *C:* Arthur Marvin; *A:* Mabel Stoughton, Harry Solter, Mack Sennett, Linda Arvidson, D.W. Griffith, Arthur Johnson; *L:* 703 feet; *W:* Fort Lee, New Jersey; *P:* A wedding tale that involves the congregation chasing the groom throughout the countryside.

Betrayed by a Handprint* [Myrtle Vane]
PC: Biograph; R; September 1; *D/S:* D.W. Griffith; *C:* Billy Bitzer, Arthur Marvin; *A:* Kate Bruce, Harry Solter, Linda Arvidson; *L:* 833 feet; *P:* A society lady turns thief after losing at cards, but is caught when she leaves a palm print at the scene of the crime.

The Girl and the Outlaw* [Nellie Carson]
PC: Biograph; *R:* September 8; *D/S:* D.W. Griffith; *C:* Arthur Marvin; *A:* Dorothy West, Wilfred Lucas, Charles Inslee; *L:* 835 feet; *W:* Fort Lee, New Jersey; *P:* A western tragedy of a young woman falling in love with the wrong man, paying for her mistake with her life.

Behind the Scenes: Where All Is Not Gold That Glitters* [Mrs. Bailey]
PC: Biograph; *R:* September 11; *D/S:* D.W. Griffith; *C:* Arthur Marvin; *A:* Kate Bruce, George Nicholls, Gladys Egan; *L:* 530 feet; *P:* An actress reluctantly leaves her sick child in order to work at the theater, only to find the child dead at her return.

The Red Girl
PC: Biograph; *R:* September 15; *D:* D.W. Griffith; *C:* Arthur Marvin; *S:* D.W. Griffith, E.V. Stanner Taylor; *A:* Linda Arvidson, Mack Sennett, Harry Solter, Clara T. Bracey, Arthur Johnson, Charles Inslee, Tony O'Sullivan, Marion Sunshine; *L:* 1014 feet; *P:* A western story involving the friendship of two women, united in driving off an ardent suitor.

The Heart of O Yama* [O Yama Sum]
PC: Biograph; *R:* September 18; *D/S:* D.W. Griffith, from *Madame Butterfly* or *Tosca*; *C:* Arthur Marvin; *A:* Harry Solter, D.W. Griffith; *L:* 881 feet; *P:* A Japanese princess is dragged to the altar to marry a man she despises; her hatred drives her to kill him and herself.

Where the Breakers Roar
PC: Biograph; *R:* September 22; *D:* D.W. Griffith; *C:* Billy Bitzer, Arthur Marvin; *S:* D.W. Griffith, E.V. Stanner Taylor; *A:* Linda Arvidson, Arthur Johnson, Mack Sennett, Guy Hedlund, Charles Inslee, Harry Solter, Marion Leonard; *L:* 566 feet; *W:* Central Park, New York City[?]; *P:* A seaside romance is interrupted by an escaped lunatic, who kidnaps the maiden and tries to flee in a rowboat.

The Smoked Husband* [Mrs. Bibbs]
PC: Biograph; *R:* September 25; *D:* D.W. Griffith; *A:* John Cumpson, Kate Toncray, Linda Arvidson, Arthur Johnson, Alfred Paget, Mack Sennett, Robert Harron; *L:* 470 feet; *W:* West 12th Street, New York City; *P:* Technically the first Jones comedy, where the husband is caught in the fireplace while trying to spy on his wife.

The Stolen Jewels* [Mrs. Jenkins]
PC: Biograph; *R:* September 29; *D/S:* D.W. Griffith; *C:* Billy Bitzer; *A:* John Cumpson, Harry Solter, Gladys Egan, Charles Inslee; *L:* 630 feet; *W:* New York Curb Exchange, New York City; *P:* A family is driven to poverty after Baby misplaces Mama's diamonds.

The Devil
PC: Biograph; *R:* October 2; *D/S:* D.W. Griffith; *C:* Billy Bitzer; *A:* Jeanie MacPherson, D.W. Griffith, Frank Gebhardt, Harry Solter; *L:* 570 feet; *P:* A tragic tale of temptation—a husband and wife are taunted by the Devil.

The Zulu's Heart
PC: Biograph; *R:* October 6; *D/S:* D.W. Griffith; *C:* Billy Bitzer; *A:* Mack Sennett, Alfred Paget, John Cumpson, Arthur Johnson; *L:* 776

feet; *W:* Cliffside, New Jersey; *P:* An African tribesman, overwhelmed by the death of his own daughter, goes to great lengths to protect the child of his enemy.

Father Gets in the Game
PC: Biograph; *R:* October 10; *D/S:* D.W. Griffith; *C:* Billy Bitzer; *A:* Mack Sennett, Linda Arvidson, Charles Gorman, Jeanie MacPherson, Marion Leonard, Harry Solter; *L:* 604 feet; *W:* Central Park, New York City; *P:* Father adopts a reckless, devil-may-care attitude after he perceives his own old-fashioned demeanor.

*The Barbarian, Ingomar**
[Parenthia]
PC: Biograph; *R:* October 13; *D/S:* D.W. Griffith, based on Ernest Thompson Seton novel; *C:* Billy Bitzer; *A:* Arthur Johnson, Charles Inslee, Linda Arvidson, Harry Solter, Wilfred Lucas; *L:* 806 feet; *W:* Cos Cob, Connecticut; *P:* A brave Greek girl goes to rescue her father, who has been captured by a band of barbarians.

The Vaquero's Vow
PC: Biograph; *R:* October 16; *D/S:* D.W. Griffith; *C:* Billy Bitzer; *A:* Linda Arvidson, Wilfred Lucas, Gladys Egan, Mack Sennett, Charles Inslee, Harry Solter, Jeanie MacPherson, Frank Evans; *L:* 805 feet; *P:* A Mexican love story where a luckless woman disdains a poor suitor for a dashing but mercenary musician.

*The Planter's Wife** [Nellie]
PC: Biograph; *R:* October 20; *D/S:* D.W. Griffith; *C:* Billy Bitzer; *A:* Linda Arvidson, Arthur Johnson, Charles Inslee; *L:* 865 feet; *W:* Little Falls, New Jersey; *P:* Wife's tomboy sister prevents her from leaving her husband.

*Romance of a Jewess**
[Ruth Simonson]
PC: Biograph; *R:* October 23; *D:* D.W. Griffith; *A:* Guy Hedlund, Mack Sennett, Alfred Paget, John Cumpson, Gladys Egan; *L:* 964 feet; *P:* A young Jewess marries against her father's wishes. They reunite only as she dies.

*The Call of the Wild**
[Gladys Penrose]
PC: Biograph; *R:* October 27; *D/S:* D.W. Griffith, based on Jack London novel; *C:* Arthur Marvin; *A:* Charles Inslee, Charles Gorman, Mack Sennett; *L:* 988 feet; *W:* Fort Lee and Coytesville, New Jersey; *P:* A well-educated Native American returns to the wilderness after being rebuffed by his sweetheart.

*Concealing the Burglar**
[Mrs. Brown]
PC: Biograph; *R:* October 30; *D/S:* D.W. Griffith; *A:* Linda Arvidson, Mack Sennett, Arthur Johnson; *L:* 663 feet; *P:* Mrs. Brown is forced to either hide a burglar or he will pretend he is her paramour; she ends up shooting him.

*After Many Years** [Mrs. Davis]
PC: Biograph; *R:* November 3; *D:* D.W. Griffith; *C:* Billy Bitzer, Arthur Marvin; *S:* Frank Woods, based on Alfred, Lord Tennyson's poem "Enoch Arden"; *A:* Charles Inslee, Herbert Prior, Linda Arvidson, Gladys Egan; *L:* 1033 feet; *P:* A husband and wife are separated by a shipwreck, finally reuniting after the returning husband thinks she has remarried.

The Pirate's Gold
PC: Biograph; *R:* November 10; *D:* D.W. Griffith; *C:* Billy Bitzer, Arthur Marvin; *S:* D.W. Griffith, E.V. Stanner Taylor; *A:* Linda Arvidson, Tony O'Sullivan, Harry Solter; *L:* 966 feet; *P:* Gold is hidden within the bricks of a fireplace by a dying pirate, exposed years later by a bullet fired by a would-be suicide.

*Taming of the Shrew** [Katharina]
PC: Biograph; *R:* November 10; *D:* D.W. Griffith; *C:* Billy Bitzer, Arthur Marvin; *S:* D.W. Griffith, Harry Solter, based on Shakespeare; *A:* Arthur Johnson, Wilfred Lucas, Linda Arvidson, Harry Solter; *L:* 1048 feet; *W:* Fort Lee and Coytesville, New Jersey; *P:* Shakespeare's story of Kate, her waspish tongue and her (im)patient husband Petruchio.

*The Song of the Shirt**
[the seamstress]
PC: Biograph; *R:* November 17; *D:* D.W. Griffith; *S:* D.W. Griffith, Frank Woods, based on Thomas Hood's poem; *A:* Linda Arvidson, Harry Solter, Mack Sennett, Alfred Paget; *L:* 638 feet; *P:* An impoverished seamstress must leave her dying sister to work. The rich and the poor are shown in stark contrast.

The Ingrate
PC: Biograph; R: November 20; D/S: D. W. Griffith; C: Billy Bitzer, Arthur Marvin; A: Arthur Johnson, Herbert Yost; L: 893 feet; W: Cos Cob, Connecticut; P: An ungrateful guest forces himself upon his host's wife and sets a trap for the husband.

A Woman's Way
PC: Biograph; R: November 24; D/S: D.W. Griffith; A: David Miles, Dorothy Bernard, Arthur Johnson, Harry Solter, L: 676 feet; W: Coytesville and Little Falls, New Jersey; P: A carefree girl chooses to save her brutal fiancé from her would-be rescuers.

The Clubman and the Tramp
PC: Biograph; R: November 27; D:S: D.W. Griffith; C: Billy Bitzer; A: Jeanie MacPherson, Linda Arvidson, Mack Sennett, John Cumpson; L: 994 feet; W: West 12th Street, New York City; P: A capricious gentleman finds himself in trouble after a tramp successfully impersonates him.

The Valet's Wife
PC: Biograph; R: December 1; D/S: D.W. Griffith; C: Billy Bitzer, Arthur Marvin; A: Robert Harron, Guy Hedlund, Mack Sennett, Owen Moore, Arthur Johnson, Harry Solter, Mabel Stoughton; L: 508 feet; P: A bachelor invents a family to receive an increase in his allowance; a hastily procured wife and child prove disastrous.

Money Mad
PC: Biograph; R: December 4; D/S: D.W. Griffith; C: Billy Bitzer; A: Charles Inslee, Arthur Johnson, Mack Sennett, Harry Solter; L: 684 feet; P: The life of a sum of gold, from its first owner (who it was stolen from) to its last (who knocked over a candle in her haste to count it).

The Feud and the Turkey
[Nellie Caulfield]
PC: Biograph; R: December 11; D/S: D.W. Griffith; C: Arthur Marvin, Billy Bitzer; A: Linda Arvidson, Violet Mersereau, Mack Sennett, Clara T. Bracey, Herbert Miles, Eddie Dillon; L: 904 feet; W: Shadyside, New Jersey; P: The Hatfields and the McCoys meet Romeo and Juliet—two families feud but are happily reunited by the birth of a grandchild.

The Reckoning
PC: Biograph; R: December 15; D: D.W. Griffith; C: Billy Bitzer; S: Frank Woods, D.W. Griffith, based on Dwight Cummings' story; A: Mack Sennett, Harry Solter, Eddie Dillon; L: 462 feet; W: Hoboken, New Jersey; P: A husband must confront his wife and her lover.

The Test of Friendship*
[Jeannie Coleman]
PC: Biograph; R: December 15; D/S: D.W. Griffith; C: Billy Bitzer; A: Arthur Johnson, Marion Leonard, Jeanie MacPherson, Mack Sennett, Harry Solter, Violet Mersereau; L: 775 feet; W: Hoboken, New Jersey; P: A millionaire seeks to discover how others live, working in a factory. His friendship with a factory girl turns into love when she unconsciously sacrifices all she has for him.

An Awful Moment
[Mrs. Mowbray]
PC: Biograph; R: December 18; D/S: D.W. Griffith; C: Arthur Marvin; L: Linda Arvidson, Marion Leonard, Kate Bruce, Gladys Egan, Mack Sennett, Charles Gorman, Florence Barker, Dorothy West; L: 737 feet; P: A vengeful woman sets a trap for a gun to fire on a judge's wife when he opens the door.

The Christmas Burglars
PC: Biograph; R: December 22; D/S: D.W. Griffith; C: Billy Bitzer; A: Arthur Johnson, Gladys Egan, Adele DeGarde, Mack Sennett; L: 679 feet; W: 8th Avenue at 14th Street, New York City; P: An impoverished woman accidentally drops her child's pitiful note to Santa. A miserly pawnbroker finds it and does all in his power to make their Christmas happy.

Mr. Jones at the Ball* [Mrs. Jones]
PC: Biograph; R: December 25; D/S: D.W. Griffith; C: Billy Bitzer; S: D.W. Griffith; A: John Cumpson, Jeanie MacPherson, Mack Sennett; L: 503 feet; P: Mr. Jones makes an unscheduled appearance at a dance minus his ripped pants.

The Helping Hand
PC: Biograph; R: December 29; D/S: D.W. Griffith; C: Arthur Marvin; A: Flora Finch,

George Gebhardt, Linda Arvidson, Robert Harron, Arthur Johnson, Dorothy Sunshine, Mack Sennett, Harry Solter, Herbert Miles; *L:* 841 feet; *P:* A romance set in a busy office.

1909

One Touch of Nature [Mrs. Murray]
PC: Biograph; *R:* January 1; *D:* D.W. Griffith; *C:* Arthur Marvin; *S:* E.V. Stanner Taylor; *A:* Arthur Johnson, Gladys Egan, Adele DeGarde, Kate Bruce; *L:* 725 feet; *P:* A policeman gives refuge to an orphan after his own child dies and his wife goes mad.

Mrs. Jones Entertains* [Mrs. Jones]
PC: Biograph; *R:* January 7; *D/S:* D.W. Griffith; *C:* Billy Bitzer; *A:* John Cumpson, Jeanie MacPherson, Linda Arvidson, Mack Sennett; *L:* 550 feet. [Incorrectly listed in several modern sources as *Miss Jones Entertains.*]; *P:* Mr. Jones impersonates a waiter for his wife's temperance club meeting, topping off their meal with rum-laced coffee.

The Criminal Hypnotist
PC: Biograph; *R:* January 9; *D/S:* D.W. Griffith; *C:* Billy Bitzer; *A:* Owen Moore, Marion Leonard, Arthur Johnson, Mack Sennett, Harry Solter; *L:* 626 feet; *P:* A gullible but good girl is hypnotized by a dishonest professor so she will rob her father's desk.

The Honor of Thieves* [Rachel Einstein]
PC: Biograph; *R:* January 11; *D/S:* D.W. Griffith; *C:* Billy Bitzer; *A:* Owen Moore, Harry Solter, Mack Sennett, Frank Powell; *L:* 681 feet; *W:* Hudson Street, New York City; *P:* A trusting girl falls victim to a thief who wants to rob her father's store. She frees herself and corners the thief with a gun.

The Sacrifice
PC: Biograph; *R:* January 14; *D/S:* D.W. Griffith, based on O. Henry's story "The Gift of the Magi"; *C:* Billy Bitzer; *A:* Mack Sennett, Arthur Johnson, Marion Leonard, Harry Solter, Owen Moore; *L:* 438 feet; *P:* Mrs. Hardluck sells her hair for a watchfob and Mr. Hardluck sells his watch for a comb.

Those Boys!
PC: Biograph; *R:* January 18; *D/S:* D.W. Griffith; *C:* Billy Bitzer, Arthur Marvin; *A:* Linda Arvidson, Clara T. Bracey; *L:* 342 feet; *P:* Two boys find a gun and are about to shoot a target that would have resulted in the death of a sister, when their mother finds them.

Mr. Jones Has a Card Party* [Mrs. Jones]
PC: Biograph; *R:* January 21; *D/S:* D.W. Griffith; *C:* Billy Bitzer; *A:* John Cumpson, Arthur Johnson, Mack Sennett, Flora Finch, Jeanie MacPherson; *L:* 583 feet; *W:* Grand Central Station, New York City; *P:* Mrs. Jones misses the train to a temperance meeting and returns home to find her husband in the midst of a party.

The Fascinating Mrs. Francis
PC: Biograph; *R:* January 21; *D/S:* D.W. Griffith; *C:* Billy Bitzer; *A:* Mack Sennett, Linda Arvidson, Marion Leonard, Charles West, John Cumpson; *L:* 417 feet; *P:* An actress pretends to be of loose morals to dissuade a persistent young suitor.

Those Awful Hats
PC: Biograph; *R:* January 25; *D/S:* D.W. Griffith; *C:* Billy Bitzer; *A:* Flora Finch, Linda Arvidson, Mack Sennett, John Cumpson, Arthur Johnson, Robert Harron; *L:* 185 feet; *P:* A theater installs a large claw to physically remove an offendingly large hat and its wearer.

The Girls and Daddy
PC: Biograph; *R:* February 1; *D/S:* D.W. Griffith; *C:* Billy Bitzer; *A:* Robert Harron, Dorothy Bernard, Charles Gorman, Mack Sennett, Arthur Johnson, Kate Bruce, Florence Barker, Gladys Egan, D.W. Griffith, Charles Inslee, Wilfred Lucas, Dorothy West, Clara T. Bracey, Harry Solter; *L:* 901 feet; *W:* Fort Lee, New Jersey. [This cast list is impossibly long for this simple story; if Florence is not the oldest daughter, she is not in it.] *P:* Two girls receive money from their grandmother, attracting the attention of two thieves. One thief has a change of heart, helping capture the second.

The Brahma Diamond
PC: Biograph; *R:* February 4; *D/S:* D.W. Griffith; *C:* Billy Bitzer; *A:* Eddie Dillon, Owen Moore, Arthur Johnson; *L:* 1036 feet;

P: A tourist in India steals a diamond to help offset his mounting debts, leaving a girl and her lover to pay for its loss.

A Wreath in Time* [Mrs. Goodhusband]
PC: Biograph; *R:* February 8; *D/S:* D.W. Griffith; *C:* Billy Bitzer; *A:* Mack Sennett, Harry Solter, Arthur Johnson, Jeanie MacPherson, Marion Leonard; *L:* 558 feet; *W:* 8th Avenue at 14th Street, New York City; *P:* A misreported train wreck that supposedly kills her husband sends Mrs. Goodhusband to buy a funeral wreath. He returns home drunk and in trouble.

The Curtain Pole
PC: Biograph; *R:* February 15; *D/S:* D.W. Griffith; *C:* Billy Bitzer; *A:* Linda Arvidson, Mack Sennett, Jeanie MacPherson, Arthur Johnson, Clara T. Bracey, Harry Solter; *L:* 765 feet; *W:* Fort Lee, New Jersey; *P:* A soused Frenchman attempts to get a very long curtain pole back to his host's house, with disastrous results.

His Ward's Love
PC: Biograph; *R:* February 15; *D/S:* D.W. Griffith; *C:* Billy Bitzer; *A:* Arthur Johnson, Owen Moore; *L:* 235 feet; *P:* A minister thinks his young ward loves a young man in town, but she actually loves her guardian.

The Joneses Have Amateur Theatricals* [Mrs. Jones]
C: Biograph; *R:* February 18; *D/S:* D.W. Griffith; *C:* Billy Bitzer; *A:* John Cumpson, Clara T. Bracey, Harry Solter, Marion Leonard, Mack Sennett, Owen Moore; *L:* 400 feet; *P:* Mr. and Mrs. Jones have a misunderstanding when Mr. Jones playacts a scene with Mrs. Trouble during a meeting of the amateur drama club.

The Golden Louis
PC: Biograph; *R:* February 22; *D/S:* D.W. Griffith; *C:* Arthur Marvin; *A:* Arthur Johnson, Kate Bruce, Gladys Egan, Owen Moore, Mack Sennett, Marion Leonard, Wilfred Lucas, Adele DeGarde; *L:* 474 Feet; *W:* Bleecker Street, New York City; *P:* A good-intentioned French knight borrows back a gold coin he has tossed into a beggar child's basket; in turn he wins more money for her, but it is too late.

The Politician's Love Story
PC: Biograph; *R:* February 22; *D/S:* D.W. Griffith; *C:* Billy Bitzer, Arthur Marvin; *A:* Mack Sennett, Alfred Paget, Marion Leonard, Linda Arvidson, Florence LaBadie, Frank Powell, Kathlyn Williams, Lee Dougherty; *L:* 526 feet; *W:* Central Park, New York City; *P:* A politician is offended by a series of cartoons in the newspaper; his attempt to angrily confront the artist is thwarted when he meets her.

At the Altar
PC: Biograph; *R:* February 25; *D/S:* D.W. Griffith; *A:* Linda Arvidson, John Cumpson, Mack Sennett, Marion Leonard, Kate Bruce, James Kirkwood, Charles Gorman, Charles Hill Mailes, Frank Gebhardt, Harry Solter, D.W. Griffith, Clara T. Bracey, Robert Harron, Arthur Johnson, Dorothy West, Herbert Yost; *L:* 972 feet; *W*; Edgewater, New Jersey; *P:* A spurned suitor plants a gun to fire upon the bride at the altar. Just in time the police learn of the trap and rush in to stop the "accident."

His Wife's Mother* [Mrs. Jones]
PC: Biograph; *R:* March 1; *D/S:* D.W. Griffith; *C:* Arthur Marvin; *A:* John Cumpson, Mack Sennett, Arthur Johnson, Mrs. Herbert Miles, Charles Inslee, Flora Finch; *L:* 523 feet; *W:* Bleecker Street, New York City; *P:* Mr. Jones sets up his mother-in-law to get drunk, again inciting the wrath of Mrs. Jones—this time against her mother.

The Prussian Spy* [Lady Florence]
PC: Biograph; *R:* March 1; *D:* D.W. Griffith; *C:* Billy Bitzer; *A:* Marion Leonard, Arthur Johnson, Owen Moore, Mack Sennett; *L:* 465 feet; *P:* Lady Florence rejects the advances of a French count, preferring a young soldier. He is hidden in a closet while the count searches for him, dying there when shots are fired at it by the count's men.

A Fool's Revenge
PC: Biograph; *R:* March 4; *D/S:* D.W. Griffith, from Victor Hugo's story "Le Roi s'amuse" and the Verdi opera *Rigoletto*; *C:* Billy Bitzer; *A:* Marion Leonard, Owen Moore, Linda Arvidson, Vivien Prescott, John Cumpson, Fred Mace, Mack Sennett; *L:* 1000 feet; *P:* The fool's daughter attracts a melancholy duke, creating a pure and holy love. She sacrifices herself from her father's plot.

The Roue's Heart
PC: Biograph; *R:* March 8; *D/S:* D.W. Griffith; *C:* Billy Bitzer; *A:* Marion Leonard, Herbert Yost, John Cumpson, Gladys Egan, Owen Moore, Harry Solter, Adele DeGarde; *L:* 755 feet; *P:* A playboy falls in love with a sculptress who feels their positions and conditions are too contrasted ever to allow them to be happy.

The Wooden Leg* [Claire]
PC: Biograph; *R:* March 8; *D:* D.W. Griffith; *C:* Billy Bitzer, Arthur Marvin; *A:* Arthur Johnson; *L:* 240 feet; *P:* Papa's choice for a suitor leaves hastily when he thinks the girl has a wooden leg.

The Salvation Army Lass* [Mary Wilson]
PC: Biograph; *R:* March 11; *D/S:* D.W. Griffith; *C:* Billy Bitzer, Arthur Marvin; *A:* Marion Leonard, Florence LaBadie, Florence Barker, John Cumpson, Harry Solter, Arthur Johnson, Dell Henderson, Mack Sennett, Owen Moore, Eddie Dillon, Linda Arvidson; *L:* 926 feet; *W:* Fort Lee, New Jersey; *P:* A wayward girl, running from the clutches of thieves, finds help in the Salvation Army, setting an example even for her felonious boyfriend.

I Did It, Mamma [Mamma]
PC: Biograph; *R:* March 15; *D:* D.W. Griffith; *A:* Gladys Egan, Arthur Johnson, Adele DeGarde; *L:* 372 feet; *P:* Mamma jumps to the conclusion that one child ate all the tarts while another finally contritely admits guilt.

The Lure of the Gown* [Veronica]
PC: Biograph; *R:* March 15; *D/S:* D.W. Griffith; *C:* Billy Bitzer, Arthur Marvin; *A:* Marion Leonard, Vivien Prescott, Owen Moore, Mack Sennett, Edwin August, Charles Inslee, Arthur Johnson; *L:* 547 feet; *W:* Fort Lee, New Jersey; *P:* After a beautiful dress turns the head of her fickle boyfriend, a street singer dons a similar gown to impress him and a multitude of others at a ball.

And a Little Child Shall Lead Them
PC: Biograph; *R:* March 22; *D/S:* D.W. Griffith; *C:* Billy Bitzer; *A:* Arthur Johnson, Marion Leonard, Adele DeGarde, Johnny Tansey; *L:* 340 feet; *P:* The toy of a dear departed child brings a separated family back together.

The Deception* [Mabel Colton]
PC: Biograph; *R:* March 22; *D/S:* D.W. Griffith; *A:* Herbert Yost, Mack Sennett, Arthur Johnson, Dorothy West, Linda Arvidson, Mary Pickford; *L:* 653 feet; *P:* The wife of a struggling artist tells him she is working as a piano teacher, but is actually toiling in a laundry.

Jones and His New Neighbors* [Mrs. Jones]
PC: Biograph; *R:* March 29; *D/S:* D.W. Griffith; *C:* Billy Bitzer; *A:* John Cumpson, Flora Finch, Mack Sennett, Gladys Egan; *L:* 454 feet; *W:* Perry Street, New York City; *P:* Mr. Jones accidentally enters the wrong flat—they all look alike—making quite an impression on his neighbors.

The Medicine Bottle [Mrs. Parker]
PC: Biograph; *R:* March 29; *D/S:* D.W. Griffith; *C:* Billy Bitzer; *A:* Gladys Egan, Marion Leonard, Linda Arvidson, Jeanie MacPherson, Adele DeGarde, Clara T. Bracey, Owen Moore, Dorothy West; *L:* 472 feet; *P:* A suspenseful story of poison, almost accidentally administered as medicine.

A Drunkard's Reformation
PC: Biograph; *R:* April 1; *D/S:* D.W. Griffith, incorporating Emile Zola's "L'Assommoir"; *C:* Billy Bitzer; *A:* Linda Arvidson, Arthur Johnson, Adele DeGarde, Mack Sennett, Marion Leonard, Herbert Yost, Owen Moore, David Miles; *L:* 983 feet; *P:* An alcoholic husband and father is transformed after attending a play depicting the evils of drink.

The Road to the Heart
PC: Biograph; *R:* April 5; *D/S:* D.W. Griffith; *C:* Arthur Marvin; *A:* David Miles, Mack Sennett, John Cumpson, Clara T. Bracey, James Kirkwood, Anita Hendrie; *L:* 618 feet; *P:* In a fit of discontent, a Mexican cowboy tosses out his daughter and son-in-law, followed by his wife. His inability to cook drives him to their new home.

Trying to Get Arrested
PC: Biograph; *R:* April 5; *D:* D.W. Griffith; *C:* Billy Bitzer, Arthur Marvin; *S:* D.W. Griffith, Mack Sennett, based on O. Henry's story; *A:* Owen Moore, Arthur Johnson, John

Cumpson, Kate Bruce, Mack Sennett, Jeanie MacPherson; *L:* 344 feet; *W:* Palisades, New Jersey; *P:* A tramp commits crime after crime, trying to get a warm bed in jail.

Schneider's Anti-Noise Crusade [Lena]
PC: Biograph; *R:* April 8; *D/S:* D.W. Griffith; *C:* Billy Bitzer, Arthur Marvin *A:* John Cumpson, Owen Moore, Arthur Johnson, Clara T. Bracey; Mack Sennett, Flora Finch; *L:* 556 feet; *P:* When burglars enter his home, Schneider helps them remove all offending noise-makers from the premises.

The Winning Coat
PC: Biograph; *R:* April 12; *D/S:* D.W. Griffith; *C:* Billy Bitzer; *A:* Owen Moore, Harry Solter; *L:* 767 feet; *P:* Plans to abduct the Queen are hastily stuffed into a coat pocket, which is subsequently won by a banished courtier who breaks up the kidnapping attempt.

Confidence* [Nellie Burton]
PC: Biograph; *R:* April 15; *D:* D.W. Griffith; *C:* Billy Bitzer, Arthur Marvin; *A:* John Cumpson, Kate Bruce, Linda Arvidson, Arthur Johnson, Owen Moore, Jeanie MacPherson, Charles Inslee; *L:* 973 feet; *P:* An old boyfriend blackmails a surgeon's wife with old love letters. When the surgeon finds out, he merely tosses them unread into the fire.

Lady Helen's Escapade* [Lady Helen]
PC: Biograph; *R:* April 19; *D:* D.W. Griffith; *C:* Billy Bitzer; *S:* E.V. Stanner Taylor; *A:* Dorothy Bernard, Vivien Prescott, Mack Sennett, Dorothy West, Arthur Johnson, John Cumpson, Jeanie MacPherson, Owen Moore, Herbert Miles; *L:* 765 feet; *W:* Fort Lee, New Jersey; *P:* For a lark, a wealthy woman awkwardly hires herself out as a cook. During her adventure, she falls in love with a poor musician.

A Troublesome Satchel
PC: Biograph; *R:* April 19; *D:* D.W. Griffith; *C:* Arthur Marvin, Billy Bitzer; *A:* John Cumpson, Mack Sennett, Arthur Johnson, Harry Solter, W. Chrystie Miller, Clara T. Bracey; *L:* 212 feet; *W:* Fort Lee, New Jersey; *P:* Even thieves return this honest man's satchel of burglar's tools bought by mistake.

The Drive for a Life* [Mignon]
PC: Biograph; *R:* April 22; *D:* D.W. Griffith; *C:* Billy Bitzer, Arthur Marvin; *A:* Arthur Johnson, Marion Leonard, Mary Pickford[?], Robert Harron, Clara T. Bracey; *L:* 940 feet; *W:* Fort Lee, New Jersey; *P:* Spurned lover sends poisoned candy to his new fiancée.

'Tis an Ill Wind That Blows No Good* [Mary Flinn]
PC: Biograph; *R:* April 29; *D/S:* D.W. Griffith; *C:* Billy Bitzer, Arthur Marvin; *A:* Mack Sennett, Arthur Johnson, Tony O'Sullivan, Clara T. Bracey, Herbert Prior, Sidney Olcott; *L:* 876 feet; *P:* A man with a good right punch becomes a policeman on the spot after a topsy-turvy chase ends with the arrest of a wanted criminal.

The Eavesdropper
PC: Biograph; *R:* May 3; *D/S:* D.W. Griffith; *C:* Billy Bitzer, Arthur Marvin; *A:* Linda Arvidson, David Miles, Clara T. Bracey; Herbert Miles, Marion Leonard, Harry Solter; *L:* 644 feet; *P:* A wealthy rancher overhears a parting conversation between lovers and does all he can to keep them together.

The Note in the Shoe* [Ella Berling]
PC: Biograph; *R:* May 6; *D/S:* D.W. Griffith; *A:* Marion Leonard, Owen Moore, Arthur Johnson, Tony O'Sullivan, John Cumpson, Mack Sennett; *L:* 711 feet; *P:* A factory shoe packer is fired after hiding a pen pal note in the lining of a shoe. The factory owner later marries her.

Jones and the Lady Book Agent [Mrs. Jones]
PC: Biograph; *R:* May 10; *D/S:* D.W. Griffith; *C:* Billy Bitzer; *A:* John Cumpson, Flora Finch, Mack Sennett, Robert Harron, Linda Arvidson; *L:* 589 feet; *P:* Mr. and Mrs. Jones have a disagreement based on a set-up by an angered lady book seller.

A Baby's Shoe
PC: Biograph; *R:* May 13; *D/S:* D.W. Griffith; *C:* Billy Bitzer, Arthur Marvin; *A:* Owen Moore, Kate Bruce, W. Chrystie Miller, Arthur Johnson, Kate Toncray, Mack Sennett, Linda Arvidson, Harry Solter, Clara T.

Bracey, George Nicholls; *L:* 999 feet; *W:* Central Park, New York City; *P:* Two children separated at birth are almost married before the story comes out. He goes on to be a priest, she a nun.

The Jilt
PC: Biograph; *R:* May 17; *D/S:* D.W. Griffith; *C:* Billy Bitzer, Arthur Marvin; *A:* Arthur Johnson, Owen Moore, Tony O'Sullivan, Marion Leonard, Mack Sennett, George Nicholls; *L:* 977 feet; *W:* Riverside Drive, New York City; *P:* A woman who jilted her fiancé finds herself jilted when her new fiancé finds out what she did.

The Resurrection* [Katyusha]
PC: Biograph; *R:* May 20; *D:* D.W. Griffith; *C:* Billy Bitzer, Arthur Marvin; *S:* Frank E. Woods, from Leo Tolstoy's novel; *A:* Arthur Johnson, Clara T. Bracey, Owen Moore, Linda Arvidson, John Cumpson, Mack Sennett, Marion Leonard; *L:* 999 feet; *P:* A Russian peasant girl rises above the petty strifes of the world when she is abandoned by her rich lover.

Eloping with Auntie* [Margie]
PC: Biograph; *R:* May 24; *D/S:* D.W. Griffith; *C:* Billy Bitzer, Arthur Marvin; *A:* Mack Sennett, Arthur Johnson, Clara T. Bracey; *L:* 614 feet; *P:* The suitor that Dad disliked dresses up as her auntie to fool Dad into giving him the money that he intended to use to send his daughter to Europe.

Two Memories
PC: Biograph; *R:* May 24; *D/S:* D.W. Griffith; *C:* Billy Bitzer; *A:* Marion Leonard, Owen Moore, Mary Pickford, Lottie Pickford, Arthur Johnson, Mack Sennett, Clara T. Bracey, Robert Harron; *L:* 318 feet; *P:* A foolish quarrel separates young lovers with tragic results: She becomes a lifeless society woman, he dies a broken man.

Eradicating Aunty
PC: Biograph; *R:* May 31; *D/S:* D.W. Griffith; *C:* Billy Bitzer, Arthur Marvin; *A:* Owen Moore, Arthur Johnson, Florence Auer, Stephanie Longfellow; *L:* 545 feet; *W:* Fort Lee, New Jersey; *P:* A meddling aunt is sent packing by her husband's clowning friend.

What Drink Did
PC: Biograph; *R:* June 2; *D/S:* D.W. Griffith; *C:* Billy Bitzer; *A:* Arthur Johnson, Gladys Egan, Adele DeGarde, David Miles, Mack Sennett, Tony O'Sullivan, Harry Solter, George Nicholls, Flora Finch; *L:* 913 feet; *W:* Fort Lee, New Jersey; *P:* A child dies when she runs in front of a bullet meant for her father, causing him to be sober for life.

Her First Biscuits [Mrs. Jones]
PC: Biograph; *R:* June 17; *D/S:* D.W. Griffith; *C:* Billy Bitzer; *A:* Mary Pickford, John Cumpson, Marion Leonard, Arthur Johnson, Mack Sennett, Tony O'Sullivan, Charles Inslee, Harry Myers, Linda Arvidson, Flora Finch, Owen Moore, Harry Solter, Charles Craig, Guy Hedlund, George Nicholls, Marion Sunshine; *L:* 514 feet; *P:* Mrs. Jones' biscuits are like lead, much to the dismay of the hungry people who have found their way into her kitchen.

The Peachbasket Hat* [Mrs. Jones]
PC: Biograph; *R:* June 24; *D/S:* D.W. Griffith; *C:* Billy Bitzer, Arthur Marvin; *A:* Mary Pickford, John Cumpson, Jeanie MacPherson, Linda Arvidson, Charles West, Gene Gauntier, Owen Moore, Marion Leonard, Anita Hendrie, Mrs. Herbert Miles, Clara T. Bracey; *L:* 666 feet; *W:* Fort Lee, New Jersey; *P:* Mrs. Jones buys a dreadful hat and loses the baby. Mr. Jones hates the hat but finds the baby.

The Way of Man* [Mabel Jarrett]
PC: Biograph; *R:* June 28; *D/S:* D.W. Griffith; *C:* Billy Bitzer, Arthur Marvin; *A:* Mary Pickford, Arthur Johnson, Gladys Egan, Kate Bruce, Mack Sennett, James Kirkwood, Charles West; *L:* 986 feet; *W:* Edgewater, New Jersey; *P:* An exploding lamp mars the lovely features of a man's fiancée, causing him to involuntarily recoil at her appearance. She gently leads his love in a new direction, then disappears.

The Necklace
PC: Biograph; *R:* July 1; *D:* D.W. Griffith; *C:* Billy Bitzer, Arthur Marvin; *S:* Frank E. Woods, based on Guy de Maupassant story; *A:* Rose King, Charles Inslee, Mack Sennett, Billy Quirk, Mary Pickford, Arthur Johnson, James Kirkwood, Owen Moore, Lottie Pickford, Frank Powell, Caroline Harris, Stephanie Longfellow; L; 969 feet; *P:* A stolen necklace,

borrowed from a friend, sets a downward path for a young couple—debt, poverty, and death.

The Country Doctor
PC: Biograph; *R:* July 6; *D/S:* D.W. Griffith; *C:* Billy Bitzer; *A:* Frank Powell, Mary Pickford, Linda Arvidson, Kate Bruce, Gladys Egan, Adele DeGarde, Stephanie Longfellow; *L:* 942 feet; *W:* Greenwich, Connecticut; *P:* A doctor makes the awful decision to care for another dying child when his own child at home is dying, too.

The Cardinal's Conspiracy
PC: Biograph; *R:* July 12; *D:* D.W. Griffith, Frank Powell; *C:* Billy Bitzer; *A:* Frank Powell, Linda Arvidson, Edwin August, Mack Sennett, Mary Pickford, Harry Solter, Owen Moore, Kate Bruce, Thomas Ince; *L:* 995 feet; *W:* Greenwich, Connecticut; *P:* A cardinal schemes to bring a flighty princess and her intended husband-prince together.

Jealousy and the Man
PC: Biograph; *R:* July 22; *D/S:* D.W. Griffith; *C:* Billy Bitzer; *A:* James Kirkwood, Tony O'Sullivan; *L:* 418 feet; *W:* Fort Lee, New Jersey; *P:* A man sees his wife pass his best friend a note and assumes the worst. Tables are turned when he learns she was arranging a surprise party for him.

Sweet and Twenty
PC: Biograph; *R:* July 22; *D:* D.W. Griffith; *C:* Billy Bitzer; *A:* Mary Pickford, James Kirkwood, Billy Quirk; *L:* 572 feet; *W:* Greenwich, Connecticut; *P:* A wooing boy accidentally kisses his girl's sister and has to start all over to win her affections.

The Slave* [Nerada]
PC: Biograph; *R:* July 29; *D/S:* D.W. Griffith; *C:* Billy Bitzer; *A:* James Kirkwood, Harry Solter, Mary Pickford, William J. Butler, Owen Moore, Henry B. Walthall, Mack Sennett, Kate Bruce, Arthur Johnson, Gladys Egan, Marion Sunshine; *L:* 998 feet; *P:* A young Roman wife and mother sells herself at the slave market so her husband and child can survive. A former suitor unwittingly purchases her, then sets her free.

The Mended Lute* [Rising Moon]
PC: Biograph; *R:* August 5; *D:* D.W. Griffith; *C:* Billy Bitzer; *S:* E.V. Stanner Taylor; *A:* James Kirkwood, Owen Moore, Mack Sennett, Arthur Johnson, James Youngdeer, Red Wing, Billy Quirk; *L:* 996 feet; *W:* Cuddebackville, New York; *P:* A Native American love story where a husband catches his wife with her former lover. He later releases them when he admires the other man's stamina and bravery.

Jones' Burglar* [Mrs. Jones]
PC: Biograph; *R:* August 9; *D/S:* D.W. Griffith; *C:* Billy Bitzer; *A:* John Cumpson, Arthur Johnson, Frank Powell, Harry Solter, Owen Moore, William J. Butler, Tony O'Sullivan, Mack Sennett; *L:* 338 feet; *W:* Coytesville, New Jersey; *P:* Mr. Jones gets to play the hero when a cowardly burglar interrupts his stealthy late-night return home.

Mrs. Jones' Lover, or I Want My Hat* [Mrs. Jones]
PC: Biograph; *R:* August 19; *D/S:* D.W. Griffith; *C:* Billy Bitzer; *A:* John Cumpson, Dorothy Bernard, Tony O'Sullivan, Mack Sennett; *L:* 467 feet; *P:* Mr. Jones wants an explanation for a fresh bunch of roses and a man's hat at his house. Mrs. Jones, peevishly annoyed at his jealousy, declines to answer.

Love's Stratagem*
PC: Independent Motion Pictures (IMP); *R:* November 1; *D:* Harry Solter [?]; *A:* William Ranous; *L:* 954 feet; *P:* "Love story … Has Romeo and Juliet backed off the boards and gasping for wind." [*MPW*, 30 October 1910, p. 615]

The Forest Ranger's Daughter* [title character]
PC: IMP; *R:* November 15; *D:* Harry Solter [?]; *L:* 700 feet; *P:* An independent daughter goes about catching her spouse by hoodwinking Papa, only until Papa catches on and brings a minister.

Her Generous Way*
PC: IMP; *R:* November 29; *D:* Harry Solter [?]; *L:* 970 feet; *P:* A wife innocently inspires suspicion by generously giving away some money given to her for a hat.

Lest We Forget*
PC: IMP; *R:* December 20; *D:* Harry Solter [?]; *L:* 920 feet; *P:* A rich little girl helps a

poor little girl by making their Christmas happy and enjoyable.

The Awakening of Bess* [Bess]
PC: IMP; *R:* December 27; *D:* Harry Solter[?], William Ranous[?]; *A:* King Baggot; *L:* 985 feet; *P:* "It's a love story, not mushy but powerful and convincing." [*MPW*, 25 December 1909, p. 906]

1910

The Winning Punch*
PC: IMP; *R:* January 3; *D:* Harry Solter; *A:* King Baggot; *L:* 957 feet; *P:* A boxing match nets $1000 and the girl, whose affections were wavering between the winner—a college boy—and a greedy count.

The Right of Love*
PC: IMP; *R:* January 10; *D:* Harry Solter; *A:* King Baggot; 975 feet; *P:* Two girls fall for the same boy.

The Tide of Fortune*
PC: IMP; *R:* January 17; *D:* Harry Solter; *L:* 975 feet; *P:* A black-sheep son returns home with a fortune only to find his once-prosperous family's situation reversed.

Justice in the Far North*
PC: IMP; *R:* February 7; *D:* Harry Solter; *L:* 950 feet; *P:* A suffering wife shoots her abusive husband, who comes around to appreciate her.

The Blind Man's Tact*
[Reviewed in *Moving Picture World* as *The Blind Man's Act*.] *PC:* IMP; *R:* February 14; *D:* Harry Solter; *L:* 650 feet; *P:* A man with bandages from eye surgery discerns a burglar in his house by peeping from under the bandages.

Jane and the Stranger* [Jane]
PC: IMP; *R:* February 21; *D:* Harry Solter; *A:* King Baggot; *L:* 900 feet; *P:* Jane thinks she has witnessed a murder and the man is arrested; Jane then learns the truth and saves him from hanging.

The Governor's Pardon*
PC: IMP; *R:* February 28; *D:* Harry Solter; *L:* 980 feet; *P:* An honest man trades places with a convict so the convict can see his dying wife, but he is killed on his way back to prison. The governor must step in to assure the right man is released from prison.

Mother Love*
PC: IMP; *R:* March 7; *D:* Harry Solter; *L:* 989 feet; *P:* A mother loses her sanity when she loses her child. Her husband brings home a newly-adopted child, which restores her health.

The Broken Oath*
[Listed as *The Broken Bath* in IMP advertisement; also mistakenly called *The Broken Path*] *PC:* IMP; *R:* March 14; *D:* Harry Solter; *L:* 950 feet; *P:* A girl saves her sweetheart several times from the dealings of a deceitful gang that he has fallen in with.

His Sick Friend*
PC: IMP; *R:* March 21; *D:* Harry Solter; *L:* 700 feet; *P:* When she discovers that her husband is playing poker instead of visiting a "sick friend," his wife make it appear she has had a visitor. When the husband returns he actually finds a man hiding beneath the table, very much to the wife's surprise.

The Stage Note*
PC: IMP; *R:* March 28; *D:* Harry Solter; *L:* 700 feet; *P:* A clever girl inventively uses a stage prop to attract help when burglars enter her house.

Transfusion*
PC: IMP; *R:* March 28; *D:* Harry Solter; *L:* 960 feet; *P:* After an accident, a young girl desperately needs a blood transfusion to save her life. A young blacksmith agrees to be the donor and wins her heart, too.

The Miser's Daughter* [title character]
PC: IMP; *R:* April 4; *D:* Harry Solter; *A:* King Baggot; 1910 *L:* 980 feet; *P:* A girl pulls a fast switch on the fiancé handpicked by her father.

Filmography

His Second Wife*
PC: IMP; R: April 7; D: Harry Solter; A: King Baggot; L: 970 feet; P: Dramatic love triangle between two women and a man.

The Rosary*
PC: IMP; R: April 11; D: Harry Solter; L: 950 feet; P: A love story between two art students.

The Maelstrom*
PC: IMP; R: April 21; D: Harry Solter; L: 960 feet; P: A girl marries a man she hardly knows or understands. At a crisis, the two suddenly realize what they mean to each other.

The New Shawl*
PC: IMP; R: April 28; D: Harry Solter; L: 990 feet; P: A dramatic comedy of a husband's jealousy when he finds his wife's shawl in a suspicious place.

Two Men*
PC: IMP; R: May 2; D: Harry Solter; L: 985 feet; P: An orphaned girl raised by a miner in the wilderness finds love with a tenderfoot even though the miner loves her, too.

The Doctor's Perfidy*
PC: IMP; R: May 16; D: Harry Solter; L: 985 feet; P: A young doctor jealously tries to harm a patient. The patient survives and is reunited with his old sweetheart, a nurse.

The Eternal Triangle*
PC: IMP; R: May 23; D: Harry Solter; A: King Baggot, Harry Solter; L: 950 feet; P: A wife is tempted to cheat on her older, doting husband with a dashing young count. When the count mortally injures the husband in a fight, the wife chooses to join him in death.

A Reno Romance*
PC: IMP; R: May 30; D: Harry Solter; L: 990 feet; P: A couple goes to Reno to be divorced but changes their mind at the last moment.

The Nichols on a Vacation* [Miss Nichols]
PC: IMP; R: June 6; D: Harry Solter; A: John Cumpson; L: 990 feet; P: Mr. Nichols arranges an ill-planned rendezvous at the same restaurant his wife and daughter are dining at. When Mr. Nichols is caught, he abandons his date, who picks up with the daughter's beau.

A Self-Made Hero*
PC: IMP; R: June 23; D: Harry Solter; P: A man desperately tries to win over his sweetheart's dad through various impossible situations.

A Game for Two*
PC: IMP; R: June 30; D: Harry Solter; A: Owen Moore, King Baggot; L: 970 feet; P: A wife tries to drive away her husband's friend by flirting with him; trouble arises when the friend flirts back.

The Call of the Circus*
PC: IMP; R: July 7; D: Harry Solter; L: 950 feet; P: A circus girl must decide to stay under the big top or marry the minister who loves her.

Old Heads and Young Hearts*
PC: IMP; R: July 11; D: Harry Solter; L: 998 feet; P: Two fathers have a hard time reconciling themselves to their children's wedding.

The Mistake*
PC: IMP; R: July 21; D: Harry Solter; L: 1000 feet; P: A husband learns from his mistake after he wrongly accuses his wife of infidelity.

Bear Ye One Another's Burdens*
PC: IMP; R: July 28; D: Harry Solter; A: King Baggot; L: 975 feet; P: When an infirm husband learns of the dire circumstances his wife must endure, he makes every effort to bring himself back to health.

The Irony of Fate*
PC: IMP; R: July 30; D: Harry Solter; A: King Baggot, Owen Moore; L: 995 feet; P: A rejected suitor rebuffs the woman he loves even though she is available after her husband's death.

Once Upon a Time*
PC: IMP; R: August 8; D: Harry Solter; L: 984 feet; P: A woman is forced to reevaluate the quiet man in her life when she finds he could be her knight in shining armor.

Among the Roses*
PC: IMP; R; August 15; *D:* Harry Solter; *L:* 990 feet; *P:* A woman innocently stealing roses catches the attention of the owner of the garden, who falls in love with her.

The Senator's Double* [?]
PC: IMP; *R:* August 18; *D:* Harry Solter; *L:* 995 feet; *P:* A senator falls victim to morphine addiction, having a look-alike man substitute for him to give a speech.

The Taming of Jane* [Jane]
PC: IMP; *R:* August 22; *D:* Harry Solter; *L:* 960 feet; *P:* A fickle tomboy believes she has accidentally killed her annoying suitor. She gives him another chance by marrying him.

The Widow* [title character]
PC: IMP; *R:* August 29; *D:* Harry Solter; *L:* 1000 feet; *P:* Two hapless but interested men pursue a disinterested widow with comic results.

Debt*
PC: IMP; *R:* September 22; *D:* Harry Solter; *P:* A happily-ever-after story that brings an extravagant wife back after her husband makes a fortune.

The Right Girl* [?]
PC: IMP; *D:* Harry Solter

Pressed Roses*
PC: IMP; *R:* September 26; *D:* Harry Solter; *L:* 990 feet; *P:* A note attached to roses and instructions attached to a pair of pants creates a comical misunderstanding between sweethearts.

All the World's a Stage*
PC: IMP; *R:* October 3; *D:* Harry Solter; *P:* A jealous husband misinterprets the excellent performance that his actress wife is doing with his best friend.

The Count of Montebello*
PC: IMP; *R:* October 24; *D:* Harry Solter; *A:* Owen Moore, King Baggot, William R. Daly; *L:* 994 feet; *P:* Gerald and Percy inherit a fortune and spend all of it in pursuit of a young heiress.

1911

His Bogus Uncle*
PC: Lubin; *R:* January 30; *D:* Harry Solter; *L:* 1000 feet; *P:* A scheming suitor ends up losing a girl to a rival even after he receives an inheritance.

Age Versus Youth*
PC: Lubin; *R:* February 2; *D:* Harry Solter; *L:* 1000 feet; *P:* A brash young man inherits a business, only to lose it when the older folks he fired open a rival firm. He also learns a lesson in love from the daughter of his enemy.

A Show Girl's Stratagem*
PC: Lubin; *R:* February 13; *D:* Harry Solter; *A:* Harry Myers; *L:* 1000 feet; *P:* A sympathetic showgirl assumes the guilt for her cousin who is cheating on her husband.

The Test*
PC: Lubin; *R:* February 20; *D:* Harry Solter; *A:* Harry Myers; *L:* 1000 feet; *P:* A girl must choose between two boys; the test reflects how each one would help the poor.

Nan's Diplomacy*
PC: Lubin; *R:* February 27; *D:* Harry Solter; *A:* Harry Myers; *L:* 1000 feet; *P:* Nan acts like she is insane when a former sweetheart appears in her husband's life. Strangely her affliction is lessened when the rival is out of the house.

His Friend, the Burglar*
PC: Lubin; *R:* March 9; *D:* Harry Solter; *A:* Arthur Johnson; *L:* 1000 feet; *P:* A husband uses a ruse to sneak back into his house after a gentlemen's night out.

Vanity and Its Cure*
PC: Lubin; *R:* March 9; *D:* Harry Solter; *A:* Harry Myers; *L:* 1000 feet; *P:* A silly and extravagant wife must learn to curb her wild ways before her husband will retrieve her from her mother's home, where she been working to pay board.

The Actress and the Singer*
PC: Lubin; *R:* March 13; *D:* Harry Solter; *A:* Arthur Johnson; *L:* 1000 feet; *P:* A prima donna falls in love with the voice of a singer

on a tape and offers him a role in her upcoming production.

Her Artistic Temperament*
PC: Lubin; R: March 20; D: Harry Solter; A: Arthur Johnson; L: 1000 feet; P: A girl from the country tries big city life with disastrous results, although her letters tell a much brighter story.

Her Child's Honor*
PC: Lubin; R: March 27; D: Harry Solter; A: Arthur Johnson; L: 1000 feet; P: A mother unknowingly commits bigamy when her first husband, who was supposed to be dead, comes back into her life. She makes the ultimate sacrifice in order to preserve her innocent child's legitimacy.

The Wife's Awakening*
PC: Lubin; R: April 3; D: Harry Solter; A: Harry Myers, Arthur Johnson; L: 1000 feet; P: An older husband feels his wife's interest in a young former suitor is worth sacrificing his own happiness for; he leaves so they can be together. He is stunned to learn six months later that his wife has not divorced him, but increased the family.

Opportunity and the Man*
PC: Lubin; R: April 10; D: Harry Solter; A: Arthur Johnson; L: 1000 feet; P: One man squanders a fortune, another takes $5 to create a fortune, eventually getting another man's house and sweetheart.

The Two Fathers* [daughter]
PC: Lubin; R: April 17; D: Harry Solter; A: Harry Myers, Arthur Johnson; L: 1000 feet; P: An impoverished father is forced to give up his daughter for adoption. After she is grown and pursued by suitors, she finds she has two fathers who care for her greatly.

The Hoyden*
PC: Lubin; R; April 24; D: Harry Solter; A: Arthur Johnson, Ethel Elder; L: 1000 feet; P: A young tomboy is hastily married to a soldier who immediately returns to overseas duty. When he returns, he does not recognize the lovely woman his hoyden wife has become.

The Sheriff and the Man*
PC: Lubin; R: April 27; D: Harry Solter; A: Arthur Johnson; L: 1000 feet; P: A righteous Western lawman must decide if he should allow a criminal, his old friend, to escape.

A Fascinating Bachelor*
PC: Lubin; R: May 1; D: Harry Solter; A: Arthur Johnson; L: 1000 feet; P: A nurse is only doing her duty when she attends to her patient, ignoring all those around her, including a love-sick bachelor.

That Awful Brother*
PC: Lubin; R: May 8; D: Harry Solter; A: Arthur Johnson; L: 1000 feet; P: A wayward brother puts his family through the wringer in a series of misadventures that culminate with him being mistaken for a burglar in his own house.

Her Humble Ministry*
PC: Lubin; R: May 18; D: Harry Solter; A: Spottiswoode Aiken, Ethel Elder, Arthur Johnson; L: 1000 feet; P: A reformed woman shows a petty thief the right path by her good example and Biblical teachings.

A Good Turn*
PC: Lubin; R: May 25; D: Harry Solter; A: Jack Standing, Arthur Johnson; L: 1000 feet; P: A woman's sweetheart is prevented from killing himself by two burglars who are afraid they will be accused of murder if he pulls the trigger.

The State Line*
PC: Lubin; R: May 29; D: Harry Solter; A: Harry Myers; L: 1000 feet; P: A kindhearted criminal saves the life of a child—the sheriff's daughter—and is allowed to make it across the state line to avoid jail. He righteously returns to warn the town of an impending flood, risking rearrest.

A Game of Deception*
PC: Lubin; R: June 1; D: Harry Solter; A: Arthur Johnson; L: 1000 feet; P: A minister's son and an actress are engaged and misunderstandings abound.

The Professor's Ward*
PC: Lubin; R: June 8; D: Harry Solter; A: Arthur Johnson; L: 1000 feet; P: An orphaned young woman falls in love with her guardian,

rejecting the suitor that the guardian assumed she would be happy with.

Duke de Ribbon Counter*
PC: Lubin; *R:* June 15; *D:* Harry Solter; *A:* Arthur Johnson; *L:* 1000 feet; *P:* An heiress, a businessman and a ne'er-do-well play romantic tag.

Higgenses Versus Judsons*
PC: Lubin; *R:* June 22; *D:* Harry Solter; *A:* Arthur Johnson, Harry Myers, Edna Payne; *L:* 1000 feet; *P:* A typical "Kentucky" feud where the sons and daughters on opposing sides fall in love, dismantling their fathers' guns to prevent further bloodshed.

The Little Rebel*
PC: Lubin; *R:* July 1; *D:* Harry Solter; *A:* Arthur Johnson; *L:* 1000 feet; *P:* A Civil War spy story where a girl and an officer stand on opposite sides of the conflict. After the war is over, they realize they are on the same side.

Always a Way*
PC: Lubin; *R:* July 8; *D:* Harry Solter; *A:* Arthur Johnson; *L:* 1000 feet; *P:* A minister is talked into performing a ceremony for two "Native Americans"—only to learn that the couple is actually his sister and the beau he despised.

The Snare of Society*
PC: Lubin; *R:* July 10; *D:* Harry Solter; *A:* Arthur Johnson; *L:* 1000 feet; *P:* A society woman loses at cards and is forced to turn over a ring from her husband. Her husband is confused by its loss and lack of explanation until she regains her ring and dignity by winning at cards.

During Cherry Time*
PC: Lubin; *R:* July 27; *D:* Harry Solter; *A:* Arthur Johnson; *L:* 1000 feet; *P:* When an outgoing actress accidentally spoils a budding romance, she teaches the young girl how to flirt and dress to win back her beau.

The Gypsy*
PC: Lubin; *R:* August 3; *D:* Harry Solter; *A:* Arthur Johnson; *L:* 1000 feet; *P:* A lively gypsy refuses to vacate a wealthy young man's land where her tribe is camped, which fascinates him rather than angers him. After they marry they suffer the usual pains of two dissimilar people getting to know one another.

Her Two Sons*
PC: Lubin; *R:* August 7; *D:* Harry Solter; *A:* Arthur Johnson, Albert McGovern, Harry Myers; *L:* 1000 feet; *P:* One son is a minister, the other a cad, and they both love the same girl. She impulsively marries the fickle one but he shallowly rejects her soon after.

Through Jealous Eyes*
PC: Lubin; *R:* August 17; *D:* Harry Solter; *A:* Arthur Johnson, Julia Stuart; *L:* 1000 feet; *P:* A jealous mother mistakes the affections shown on her future daughter-in-law by her husband.

A Rebellious Blossom*
PC: Lubin; *R:* August 21; *D:* Harry Solter; *A:* Arthur Johnson; *L:* 1000 feet; *P:* A widow threatens her rebellious daughter that she will remarry if the girl does not behave at school.

Romance of Pond Cove*
PC: Lubin; *R:* August 31; *D:* Harry Solter; *A:* Arthur Johnson; *L:* 1000 feet; *P:* A young man loses his wealth and his shallow fiancée, only to be consoled by her younger sister.

The Story of Rosie's Rose*
PC: Lubin; *R:* September 7; *D:* Harry Solter; *A:* Arthur Johnson, Edna Payne; *L:* 1000 feet; *W:* Maine; *P:* Two brothers vie for the hand of a girl who has symbolically given a rose to each of them.

The Life Saver*
PC: Lubin; *R:* September 21; *D:* Harry Solter; *A:* Arthur Johnson, Harry Myers; *L:* 1000 feet; *W:* Maine; *P:* At a seaside lifesaving station, a romance is kindled between a local girl and a lifeguard. It is later threatened by the arrival of tourists.

The Matchmaker*
PC: Lubin; *R:* September 25; *D:* Harry Solter; *A:* Arthur Johnson, Albert McGovern; *L:* 1000 feet; *P:* Several romances blossom after a young governess catches the eye of an aristocrat.

*The Slavey's Affinity**
PC: Lubin; *R:* October 11; *D:* Harry Solter; *A:* Arthur Johnson; *L:* 1000 feet; *P:* A maid loves her employer with a simple and honest love, sacrificing her happiness to insure his.

*The Maniac**
PC: Lubin; *R:* October 16; *D:* Harry Solter; *A:* Arthur Johnson; *L:* 1000 feet; *P:* A society girl just about to be married must come to grips with the fact that her father is not dead, but has been in jail. The snag is that an escaped mental patient has assumed the identity of her truly dead father.

*A Rural Conquerer**
PC: Lubin; *R:* October 26; *D:* Harry Solter; *A:* Arthur Johnson; *L:* 1000 feet; *P:* A discouraged beau learns a few tricks by observation and doubles his efforts to gain the affections of his girl.

*One on Reno**
PC: Lubin; *R:* November 3; *D:* Harry Solter; *A:* Arthur Johnson; *L:* 1000 feet; *P:* A sophisticated comedy of an outgoing wife's boredom with her husband's bookish ways. She thinks of getting a divorce in Reno but finds her husband suddenly attentive.

*Aunt Jane's Legacy**
PC: Lubin; *R:* November 6; *D:* Harry Solter; *A:* Arthur Johnson; *L:* 1000 feet; *P:* Aunt Jane rejected her niece's beau in favor of one of her nephews; when the nephews begin to bicker, the beau triumphantly breaks up the battle.

*His Chorus Girl Wife**
[title character]
PC: Lubin; *R:* November 13; *D:* Harry Solter; *A:* Arthur Johnson; *L:* 1000 feet; *P:* A young man marries a woman found to be unacceptable by his parents and he suffers the inevitable withdrawal of funds. Gradually a reconciliation is brought about.

*A Blind Deception**
PC: Lubin; *R:* November 23; *D:* Harry Solter; *A:* Arthur Johnson, Charles Brandt; *L:* 1000 feet; *P:* A young man pretends to be blind in order to keep a young woman in attendance. She discovers his lie and leaves angrily; a horrible accident occurs and he truly becomes blind, winning her sympathy.

*A Head for Business**
PC: Lubin; *R:* December 4; *D:* Harry Solter; *A:* Arthur Johnson; *L:* 1000 feet; *P:* A smart young lady shows her skill for business when she uses her beau's money to purchase a piece of land much needed by his brother.

*A Girlish Impulse**
PC: Lubin; *R:* December 11; *D:* Harry Solter; *A:* Arthur Johnson; *L:* 1000 feet; *P:* A hastily written letter is used in a blackmail scheme by a scorned suitor.

*Art Versus Music**
PC: Lubin; *R:* December 20; *D:* Harry Solter; *A:* Arthur Johnson; *L:* 1000 feet; *P:* A pianist's music makes a painter unable to work. Even more distractions ensue when they fall in love.

1912

*The Surgeon's Heroism**
PC: Lubin; *R:* January 8; *D:* Harry Solter; *A:* Arthur Johnson; *L:* 1000 feet; *P:* A surgeon risks his life to finish surgery on a patient when a fire breaks out in the hospital.

*A Village Romance**
PC: Lubin; *R:* January; *D:* Harry Solter; *A:* Arthur Johnson; *L:* 1000 feet.

*In Swift Water**
[Florence Armstrong]
PC: Victor; *R:* July 12; *D:* Harry Solter; *A:* Owen Moore, Gladden James; *L:* 1000 feet; *W:* Cuddebackville, New York; *P:* A foolish suitor gains favor in a girl's eyes when he pretends to have saved her life. When the truth is told, she rejects him for the real hero.

*The Players** [Flo Lakewood]
PC: Victor; *R:* July 19; *D:* Harry Solter; *A:* Owen Moore, John McCullough; *L:* 1000 feet; *P:* Two actors, trying to soak up local color for an upcoming play, fall in love with the other's character.

Not Like Other Girls* [Flo]
PC: Victor; R: July 26; D: Harry Solter; A: Owen Moore; L: 2000 feet[?]; P: A young seminary girl fools around with love until she realizes her beau and his father are serious.

Taking a Chance* [Mrs. Flo Mills]
PC: Victor; R: August 2; D: Harry Solter; A: Owen Moore; L: 1000 feet; P: A confusing little love story where a matchmaking wife brings suspicion upon herself by trying to reunite a couple.

The Mill Buyers* [Flo]
PC: Victor; R: August 9; D: Harry Solter; A: Owen Moore; L: 1000 feet; P: Her mother does not like him but the honest suitor wins the hand of the girl when he returns a lost pocketbook.

The Chance Shot*
[Also listed as *A Chance Shot.*] PC: Victor; R: August 16; D: Harry Solter; A: Owen Moore; L: 1000 feet; P: A stray bullet accidentally kills a blackmailer who was holding a secret from a wife's past over her.

Her Cousin Fred* [Flo Ballard]
PC: Victor; R: August 23; D: Harry Solter; A: Fred Malcolm, Victory Bateman, Edwin Morris, Owen Moore; L: 1000 feet; P: Fred is set on being a matchmaker for his cousin Flo and his friend George. After nearly killing one another a few times, they hit it off well.

The Winning Punch*
PC: Victor; R: August 30; D: Harry Solter; A: Owen Moore; L: 1000 feet; P: A country suitor is jealous of a rival for his girl's hand; this culminates in a fight.

After All* [Margie]
PC: Victor; R: September 6; D: Harry Solter; A: Owen Moore; L: 1000 feet; P: Orin, a spurned suitor, threatens to kill Rob, the man Margie loves, if she does not leave Rob for Orin.

All for Love*
PC: Victor; R: September 13; D: Harry Solter; A: Owen Moore; L: 1000 feet; P: unavailable.

Flo's Discipline* [Flo]
PC: Victor; R: September 20; D: Harry Solter [?]; A: Owen Moore; L: 1000 feet; P: When the principal returns from a conference, she finds her boarding school boys have taken over the school. She soon sets matters straight.

The Advent of Jane*
[Dr. Jane Bixby]
PC: Victor; R: September 27; D: Harry Solter; A: Owen Moore; L: 1000 feet; P: Jane, a new doctor in a rural town, solves the mystery of a moonshiner's still after a series of misunderstandings with the townsfolk.

Tangled Relations*
PC: Victor; R: October 4; D: Harry Solter; A: Owen Moore, Victory Bateman, M.B. Maher, Matt Moore, Lillian Langdon, Pauline Curley, Norman Taurog; L: 1000 feet; P: unavailable.

Betty's Nightmare* [Betty]
PC: Victor; R: October 11; D: Harry Solter; A: Owen Moore; L: 1000 feet; P: A cook on a farm yearns to be an actress. Her daydreams turn into nightmares and she seeks comfort in the arms of the hired hand.

The Angel of the Studio*
PC: Victor; R: October 25; D: Harry Solter; A: Owen Moore; L: 1000 feet; P: A "goosie" girl endeavors to make herself attractive to an artist, but he only sees the artificial beauty of a model.

The Redemption of Riverton*
[June Martin]
PC: Victor; R: November 1; D: Harry Solter; A: Owen Moore; L: 1000 feet; P: When a minister tries to clean up Riverton, he finds an unexpected ally in the barkeeper's granddaughter.

Sisters*
PC: Victor; R: November 8; D: Harry Solter; A: Owen Moore; L: 1000 feet; P: A fireman rescues a woman he thinks is his wife. The woman dies and the fireman contemplates suicide until he learns that the dead woman was his wife's long-lost sister.

The Lady Leone* [Leone Mervyn]
PC: Victor; R: November 15; D: Harry Solter; A: Owen Moore; L: 2000 feet; P: An heiress,

under the protection of the Queen, finds herself wanted by several suitors, but falls in love with a poor knight.

1913

Suffragettes Parade in Washington
PC: Kinemacolor; R: March 3; W: Washington, D.C.

The Closed Door*
[Florence Ashleigh]
PC: Victor; R: October 3; D: Harry Solter; S: Leslie T. Peacock; A: Matt Moore[?], Frank Alexander; L: 2000 feet; P: A beloved daughter marries a man to relieve her father's financial woes, keeping the marriage in name only by means of a locked door. When financial reverses hit her husband and he leaves the house with a gun, she sends the key to that door as an inviting incentive.

The Girl O' the Woods*
[Mab Hawkins]
PC: Victor; R: October 17; D: Harry Solter; S: Charles H. Hoadley; A: Matt Moore; L: 2000 feet; P: A wild girl, raised in the woods, falls in love with an artist.

The Spender*
PC: Victor; R: October 31; D: Harry Solter; A: Matt Moore, Earle Foxe, Charles Craig, Jack Newton, Lenora Von Ottinger; L: 2000 feet; P: An actress cures a wayward young man of his extravagant spending.

His Wife's Child* [Flo]
PC: Victor; R: November 14; D: Harry Solter; A: Matt Moore, Percy D. Standing, Jane Carter, Lenora Von Ottinger, Earle Foxe, Irene Wallace; L: 2000 feet; P: A young girl survives a dreadful childhood as good as orphaned, growing up to right an old wrong.

Unto the Third Generation*
[Esther Stern]
PC: Victor; R: November 28; D: Harry Solter; A: Percy D. Standing, Jack Newton, Frank Bennett, Earle Foxe, Matt Moore, Joseph MacDonald, Lenora Von Ottinger; L: 2000 feet; P: A young Jewish woman wrestles with the dilemma of interfaith marriage.

Influence of Sympathy*
PC: Victor; R: December 5; D: Harry Solter; A: Matt Moore, Jack Stebbins, Jack Newton, Charles Craig; L: 2000 feet; P: A mother, grieving the loss of her child, finds contentment in loving a lame little orphan.

A Girl and Her Money*
[Florence Kingsley]
PC: Victor; R: December 19; D: Harry Solter; S: Leslie T. Peacock; A: Matt Moore; L: 2000 feet; P: A society girl changes places with her maid for an adventure, but when the maid dies suddenly, the girl keeps up the charade even into marriage with a poor clerk.

1914

The Coryphee* [Flo]
PC: Victor; R: January 2; D: Harry Solter; S: based loosely on the play *School for Scandal*; A: Matt Moore; L: 2000 feet; P: An actress assumes a guilty appearance to save her faithless cousin's marriage.

The Romance of the Photograph* [Flo]
PC: Victor; R: January 16; D: Harry Solter; A: Matt Moore; L: 2000 feet; P: A wayward girl gets more than trouble when she falls in love with the handsome image of a burglar in a photograph.

The False Bride*
[Florence Gould and Amy St. Clair]
[Florence played a dual role in this film.] PC: Victor; R: January 30; D: Harry Solter; S: Leslie T. Peacock; A: Matt Moore, Percy D. Standing, Joseph Singleton, Ed Morris, Jane Carter, Hazel Reid; L: 3000 feet; P: A woman of loose morals is substituted for a young bride.

The Law's Decree* [Flo]
PC: Victor; R: February 13; D: Harry Solter; A: Matt Moore; L: 2000 feet; P: A shop girl assumes the guilt of her mother and is sent to prison.

The Stepmother* [Flo]
PC: Victor; R: February 27; D: Harry Solter; A: Matt Moore; L: 2000 feet; P: A new bride tries to win the affection of her stepchild.

The Honeymooners* [Florence Blair]
PC: Victor; *R:* March 13; *D:* Harry Solter; *A:* Matt Moore, Miss Davis, Lloyd Ingraham; *L:* 2000 feet; *P:* Two couples head for Reno to swap partners, but change their minds at the last minute.

Diplomatic Flo* [Flo]
PC: Victor; *R:* March 27; *D:* Harry Solter; *S:* Don Buchanan; *A:* Matt Moore, Sam Edwards, Edward Shalot; *L:* 3000 feet; *P:* A woman adopts the guise of a spy when she uncovers an arms plot concerning a country in Central America.

The Little Mail Carrier*
PC: Victor; *R:* April 10; *D:* Harry Solter; *A:* Matt Moore; *L:* 2000 feet; *P:* A female mail carrier is injured on her route and recovers at a bachelor's lodge.

The Pawns of Destiny* [Flo]
PC: Victor; *R:* May 8; *D/S:* Harry Solter; *A:* Matt Moore, Charles Craig; L; 3000 feet; *P:* A maid risks her life for her employer, whom she adores.

The Bribe*
[Also listed as *The Bride.*] *PC:* Victor; *R:* May 22; *D:* Harry Solter; *A:* Matt Moore, Percy D. Standing; *L:* 2000 feet; *P:* A reworking of the Biograph story *The Criminal Hypnotist*. A woman is commanded under hypnosis to break into her father's safe.

The Disenchantment* [Flo]
PC: Victor; *R:* May 22; Harry Solter; *A:* Matt Moore, Percy D. Standing, Laura Oakley, Jack Newton, Bernadt Niemeyer, Betty Emerson, Charles Craig; *L:* 2000 feet; *P:* A maid throws over her beau to work for a musician she idolizes; when he fails to live up to her ideals, she takes her old boy back.

The Doctor's Testimony* [Flo Lund]
PC: Victor; *R:* June 5; *D:* Harry Solter; *A:* Matt Moore, Hector Dion; *L:* 2000 feet; *P:* A doctor commits perjury in order to win a woman whose husband could go to prison based on his testimony.

A Singular Cynic* [Flo Weldon]
PC: Victor; *R:* June 19; *D:* Harry Solter; *A:* Matt Moore; *L:* 2000 feet; *P:* When placed in a position to choose between two jealous suitors, Flo turns the tables on them by choosing a third.

Her Ragged Knight* [Flo]
PC: Victor; *R:* July 3; *D:* Harry Solter; *A:* Inez Ranous, William J. O'Neill, Jack Newton, John C. Brownell, Frank Bixby; *L:* 2000 feet; *P:* A confirmed bachelor unexpectedly receives custody of a ward, who he pawns off unseen to a spinster aunt. When they unknowingly meet, they fall in love.

The Great Universal Mystery
PC: Universal; *R:* July 10; *D:* Allan Dwan; *A:* around 30 Universal film stars participated in this short mystery; *L:* 1000 feet

The Mad Man's Ward* [Flo]
PC: Victor; *R:* July 31; *D:* Harry Solter; *A:* Matt Moore, Charles Craig, John C. Brownell, William O'Neill; *L:* 2000 feet; *P:* A hoydenish girl is brought up by a reclusive "mad man."

The Honor of the Humble* [Flo]
PC: Victor; *R:* August 14; *D:* Harry Solter; *A:* Matt Moore, William J. O'Neill; *L:* 2000 feet; *P:* A young girl finds herself in love with a count; her father does not approve.

Counterfeiters*
PC: Victor; *R:* August 28; *D:* Harry Solter; *A:* Matt Moore; *L:* 2000 feet; *P:* The counterfeiters are not making money but mischief as they disguise themselves to escape from her disapproving parents.

A Mysterious Mystery* [Miss Lawrence]
PC: Victor; *R:* September 11; *D:* Harry Solter; *A:* Matt Moore; *L:* 2000 feet; *P:* A moving picture actress is mistaken for an escaped asylum patient; the real insane girl steps into the actress' life.

The Man Who Was Never Kissed* [Florence Lloyd]
[Also listed as *The Woman Who Won*] PC: Victor; R: October 9; D: Harry Solter; A: Matt

Moore; L: 2000 feet; P: An experiment on how a couple should love one another fails when the pure and platonic gives way to kisses.

1916

Elusive Isabel* [Isabel Thorne]
PC: Universal Pictures/Bluebird; R: May 1; D: Stuart Paton; C: Eugene Gaudio; S: Raymond Schrock, from Jacques Futrelle's novel; A: Sydney Bracy, Harry Millarde, Wallace Clarke, William Welsh, Paul Panzer, Jack Newton, Sonia Marcel; L: 6000 feet; W: Washington, D.C.; P: A conspiracy to take over the world is uncovered when several Latin diplomats visit the United States.

1917

The Face on the Screen*
PC: Universal; R: January 6; D: Harry Solter; S: Leslie T. Peacock; L: 1000 feet; P: unavailable.

1918

The Love Craze*
PC: Nestor; R: October 21; D/S: Winthrop Kelley; A: Harry Benham; L: 2000 feet; P: unavailable.

1922

The Unfoldment* [Katherine Nevin]
PC: Associates Exhibitors/Producers Pictures; R: January 1; D: George Kern, Murdock MacQuarrie; A: Barbara Bedford, Charles French, William Conklin, Albert Prisco, Lydia Knott, Murdock MacQuarrie, Wade Boteler; L: 5795 feet; P: A young newspaper woman unfolds a telling series of events by making a film of occurrences in her life.

1923

The Satin Girl
PC: Grand-Asher Distribution Corporation/Ben Wilson Productions; R: November; D: Arthur H. Rosson; A: Mabel Forrest, Norman Kerry, Marc MacDermont, Clarence Burton, Kate Lester, Reed House, William H. Turner, Walter Stevens; L: 5591 feet; P: A story within a story, where a woman who thinks she has amnesia realizes that she has been reading the whole story in a book.

1924

Gambling Wives
PC: Arrow Productions/Ben Wilson Productions; R: April 3; D: Dell Henderson; A: Marjorie Daw, Dorothy Brock, Edward Earle, Lee Moran, Betty Fransisco, Joe Girard, Ward Crane, Hedda Hopper; L: 6438 feet; P: A husband realizes his wife is being lost to gambling, just as he is being courted by a mysterious woman.

1926

The Johnstown Flood
[Florence had an uncredited bit part in this film.] PC: Fox; R: February 28; D: Irving Cummings; A: George O'Brien, Janet Gaynor, Florence Gilbert, Anders Randolf, Paul Nicholson, Paul Panzer, Max Davidson, Walter Perry, Sid Jordan; L: 6357 feet. P: A town is swept away by a killer flood

The Greater Glory
[Also listed as *The Viennese Melody*] PC: First National; R: May 2; D: Curt Rehfeld; S: June Mathis, from Edith O'Shaughnessy's novel *The Viennese Melody*; A: Conway Tearle, Anna Q. Nilsson, May Allison, Jean Hersholt, Ian Keith, Nigel De Brulier; L: 9710 feet.

1931

The Hard Hombre [Sister]
PC: Allied Productions; D: Otto Brower; W: Jack Natteford; A: Hoot Gibson, Lina

Basquette, Tiny Sandford, Glenn Strange, Mathilda Comont; Rosa Gore; *L:* 65 minutes; *P:* A peaceful man is mistaken for a hardened criminal.

Homicide Squad [cabaret patron]
PC: Universal Pictures; *R:* August 1; *D:* George Melford; *S:* Henry LaCossit; *A:* Noah Beery, Mary Brian; *P:* The police use a gangster's son as his weak spot.

1932

Sinners in the Sun
[Florence had an uncredited bit part in this film.] *PC:* Paramount Pictures; *D:* Alexander Hall; Based on Mildred Cram's novel *Beachcomber*; *C:* Ray June; *A:* Cary Grant, Carole Lombard, Adrienne Ames, Alison Skipworth, Luke Cosgrove, Chester Morris; *L:* 70 minutes; *P:* A tangled love story where young lovers misunderstand one another, then marry others for the wrong reasons.

1933

Secrets
[Florence had an uncredited bit part in this film.] *PC:* Mary Pickford; *D:* Frank Borzage, Marshall Neilan; *C:* Ray June; *S:* Frances Marion *et al.* based on May Edginton's short story; *A:* Mary Pickford, Leslie Howard, Doris Lloyd, Ned Sparks, Virginia Grey, Ethel Clayton, Mona Maris, C. Aubrey Smith; *L:* 85 minutes; *P:* Mary Marlowe elopes with John Carlton, traveling west, meeting with many hardships and tragedies, ultimately triumphing for a successful marriage and life.

1934

The Old-Fashioned Way
[Florence's participation in this film has not been verified.] *PC:* Paramount Pictures; *D:* William Beaudine; *C:* Ben Reynolds; *S:* W.C. Fields *et al. A:* W.C. Fields, Baby Le Roy, Judith Allen, Joe Morrison; *L:* 66 minutes.

1935

The Man on the Flying Trapeze
[Florence's participation in this film has not been verified.] *PC:* Paramount Pictures; *D:* Clyde Bruckman; *C:* Alfred Gibbs; *S:* W.C. Fields, Jack Cunningham; *A:* W.C. Fields, Mary Brian, Kathleen Howard; *L:* 65 minutes.

1936

One Rainy Afternoon
[Florence had an uncredited bit part in this film.] *PC:* United Artists [Mary Pickford, Jesse Lasky]; *D:* Rowland V. Lee; *C:* Merritt Gerstad, J. Peverell Marley; *S:* Stephen Morehouse Avery *et al. A:* Francis Lederer, Ida Lupino, Hugh Herbert, Roland Young; *L:* 79 minutes; *P:* A man scandalously kisses the wrong woman in a dark theater.

1936–1938

Florence is beleived to have been an extra in many MGM movies.

Notes

Chapter One

1. Many books tell the story of how motion pictures were invented, some in great detail, some with bare sketches. For further information, see Terry Ramsaye's *A Million and One Nights*, the *History of the American Cinema* series and Gene Brown's *Movie Time*.
2. Florence Lawrence, "Growing Up with the Movies," Part 1, *Photoplay*, November 1914, p. 38.
3. *Ibid.*, pp. 35–36.
4. *Ibid.*, p. 36.
5. *Ibid.*
6. Mary Pickford, *Sunshine and Shadow* (Garden City, New York: Doubleday, 1955), p. 38.
7. "Ovation for Film Star at Union Station," *St. Louis Times*, 26 March 1910, p. 3.
8. "Florence Lawrence: Who and What She Is," *New York Star*, 4 April 1914, p. 21.
9. Lillian Gish (with Ann Pinchot), *The Movies, Mr. Griffith, and Me* (Englewood Cliffs, New Jersey: Prentice Hall, 1969), p. 14.
10. Lawrence, "Growing Up with the Movies," p. 37.
11. "Florence Lawrence," *Photoplay*, November 1912, p. 105.
12. Lawrence, "Growing Up with the Movies," p. 37.
13. George Lawrence, letter to Charlotte Bridgwood, 15 September 1911, Natural History Museum of Los Angeles County, Seaver Center for Western History Research, The Florence Lawrence Collection, Box 1, Folder 3.
14. *Ibid.*
15. Florence Lawrence letter, 5 October 1912, Natural History Museum of Los Angeles County, Seaver Center for Western History Research, The Florence Lawrence Collection, Box 1, Folder 2.
16. Lawrence, "Growing Up with the Movies," pp. 38–39.
17. Terry Ramsaye, *A Million and One Nights: A Modern Classic, a History of the Motion Picture Through 1925* (New York: Simon and Schuster/Touchstone, 1986, reprint of 1926 edition), p. 441.

18. "Ovation for Film Star at Union Station," p. 3.
19. Gladys Roosevelt, "Florence Lawrence, of the Victor Company," *Motion Picture Story*, October 1913, pp. 124–125.
20. John Anderson, *The American Theatre* (New York: Dial, 1938), pp. 66–67. A separate series of essays, collectively called "The Motion Picture in America," by Rene Fulop-Miller, are also published in this book.
21. James Cleaver, *Theatre Through the Ages* (New York: Hart, 1967), p. 357.
22. Lawrence, "Growing Up with the Movies," p. 40.
23. *Ibid.*, pp. 40–41.
24. See comments made by Charles Musser and Jay Leyda in *Before Hollywood: Turn-of-the-Century American Film* (New York: Hudson Hills, in association with the American Federation of Arts, 1987.), p. 58.
25. *Ibid.*, p. 41.
26. [Edison Manufacturing Company Advertisement] *Moving Picture World*, 6 April 1907, p. 74.
27. Lawrence, "Growing Up with the Movies," p. 41.
28. Florence Lawrence, "Growing Up with the Movies," Part 2, *Photoplay*, December 1914, p. 94.
29. *"The Seminary Girl," Washington Democrat*, 16 October 1907, p. unknown [clipping from Natural History Museum of Los Angeles County, Seaver Center for Western History Research, The Florence Lawrence Collection, Box 3, Folder 35].

Chapter Two

1. Florence Lawrence, "Growing Up with the Movies," Part 2, *Photoplay*, December 1914, p. 91.
2. *Ibid.*, pp. 94–95.
3. *Ibid.*, p. 94.
4. As quoted in Anthony Slide, *The Big V: A History of the Vitagraph Company* (Metuchen, New Jersey: Scarecrow, 1987), pp. 13–14. Thanks to Philip Leibfried.
5. Lawrence, Part 2, pp. 92–96.
6. "Interviews with Manufacturers—Vitagraph," *Moving Picture World*, 8 February 1908, p. 95.
7. Anthony Slide, *The American Film Industry: A Historical Dictionary* (Westport, Connecticut: Greenwood, 1986; reprint, Lake Geneva, Wisconsin: Limelight, 1990), p. 372.
8. "Vitagraph Company Lose All Their Old Reels," *Moving Picture World*, 16 July 1911, p. 149.
9. Lawrence, Part 2, p. 97.
10. Robert Hamilton Ball, *Shakespeare on Silent Film: A Strange Eventful History* (New York: Theatre Arts, 1968), p. 311.
11. *Ibid.*, p. 98.
12. *Ibid.*, p. 96.
13. *"Antony and Cleopatra"* [review], *Moving Picture World*, 14 November 1908, pp. 379–380.
14. Lawrence, Part 2, pp. 97–98.
15. Lawrence, Part 2, p. 99.
16. Ball, p. 47.
17. Florence Lawrence, "Growing Up with the Movies," Part 4, *Photoplay*, February 1915, pp. 97–98.
18. For additional information about Griffith's film career, see Eileen Bowser,

"Griffith's Film Career Before *The Adventures of Dollie*," *Film Before Griffith*, John L. Fell, editor (Berkeley: University of California Press, 1983), pp. 367–373.
  19. Lawrence, Part 4, p. 96.
  20. Will Fleming, letter to Florence Lawrence, 7 August 1904, Natural History Museum of Los Angeles County, Seaver Center for Western History Research, The Florence Lawrence Collection, Box 1 Folder 6.
  21. Gene Gauntier, "Blazing the Trail," *Woman's Home Companion*, November 1928, p. 132. [Reprinted on the Silent Film Bookshelf at http://www.cinemaweb.com/silentfilm.]
  22. Linda Arvidson, *When the Movies Were Young* (New York: Benjamin Blom, 1925, reprinted 1968), pp. 46–47.
  23. G.W. Bitzer, *Billy Bitzer: His Story* (New York: Farrar, Straus and Giroux, 1973), p. 64.
  24. Henry Stephen Gordon, "The Story of David Wark Griffith," Part IV, *Photoplay*, September 1916, p.86.
  25. Lawrence, Part 4, p. 98.
  26. Arvidson, p. 59.
  27. Eileen Bowser, *The Transformation of Cinema, 1907–1915*, Volume 2 of the History of the American Cinema series (New York: Charles Scribner's Sons, 1990). The sources for Ms. Bowser's statements are *Variety*, 26 January 1907, p. 12; *Moving Picture World*, 4 May 1907, p. 140; Joseph Medill Patterson, "The Nickelodeons: The Poor Man's Elementary Course in Drama," *Saturday Evening Post*, 23 November 1907; and *Moving Picture World*, 11 July 1908, p. 2.
  28. Gene Brown, *Movie Time: A Chronology of Hollywood and the Movie Industry from Its Beginnings to the Present* (New York: Macmillan, 1995) p. 9.
  29. "Growth of the Film Business," *The Billboard*, 15 September 1906, p. 16; and "Moving Pictures," *The Billboard*, 13 October 1906, p. 21. Excerpts from both of these articles are also reprinted in George Spratt, *Spellbound in Darkness* (Greenwich, Connecticut: New York Graphic Press Society Ltd., 1966), pp. 62–63.
  30. Robert Allen, "Motion Picture Exhibition in Manhattan, 1906–1912: Beyond the Nickelodeon," *Film Before Griffith*, John L. Fell, editor (Berkeley: University of California Press, 1983), pp. 162–175.
  31. Garth S. Jowett, "The First Motion Picture Audiences," *Film Before Griffith*, John L. Fell, editor (Berkeley: University of California Press, 1983), pp. 196–206.
  32. Joseph Medill Patterson, "The Nickelodeons, The Poor Man's Elementary Course in the Drama," *Saturday Evening Post*, 23 November 1907, p. 11.
  33. *Sears, Roebuck and Co. 1908 Catalogue No. 117* (Chicago: Gun Digest Company, 1969), p. 535.
  34. "The Nickelodeon," *Moving Picture World*, 4 May 1907, p. 140.
  35. Linda Arvidson Griffith, "Early Struggles of Motion Picture Stars," *Film Flashes, the Wit and Humor of a Nation in Pictures* (New York: Leslie-Judge, 1916), not paginated.
  36. Bitzer, p. 7.
  37. Lawrence, Part 3, p. 96.

Chapter Three

  1. Mabel Normand (with Chandler Sprague), "Film Star Tells How She Started as Tragedienne," *Los Angeles Examiner*, 2 March 1924, p. unknown. Reprinted in *Taylorology*, Issue 42, June 1996. In this same article, Mabel Normand also recalls seeing

Florence Lawrence on the set, working on a film; however, this is not possible since Florence had long since left Biograph when Mabel arrived.

2. Lillian Gish (with Ann Pinchot), *The Movies, Mr. Griffith, and Me* (Englewood Cliffs, New Jersey: Prentice Hall, 1969), pp. 73–74.

3. Mary Pickford, "My Own Story," *Ladies' Home Journal*, July 1924, p. 102.

4. Linda Arvidson Griffith, "Early Struggles of Motion Picture Stars," *Film Flashes, the Wit and Humor of a Nation in Pictures* (New York: Leslie-Judge, 1916), not paginated.

5. Gish, dedication page.

6. *Ibid.*, p. 37.

7. Gene Gauntier, "Blazing the Trail," *Woman's Home Companion*, November 1928, p. 16. [Reprinted on the Silent Film Bookshelf at http://www.cinemaweb.com/silentfilm].

8. Mabel Normand (with Chandler Sprague), "Thrice I Turned My Back on Film Career," *Los Angeles Examiner*, 24 February 1924, p. unknown. Reprinted in *Taylorology*, Issue 42, June 1996.

9. Robert Walsh, "David W. Griffith Speaks," *New York Dramatic Mirror*, 14 January 1914, p. 54.

10. Florence Lawrence, "Growing Up with the Movies," Part 3, *Photoplay*, January 1915 p. 97.

11. *Ibid.*, p. 100.

12. *Ibid.*, pp. 100–101.

13. *Ibid.*, p. 101.

14. Linda Arvidson, *When the Movies Were Young* (New York: Benjamin Blom, 1925, reprinted 1968), pp. 59–60.

15. Lawrence, Part 3, p. 102.

16. State of New Jersey Certificate and Record of Marriage, certificate No. 484; additional information in personal correspondence with Charles Shallcross, historian, Elizabeth, New Jersey, 30 November 1997.

17. Arvidson, p. 141.

18. Henry Stephen Gordon, "The Story of David Wark Griffith," Part IV, *Photoplay*, September 1916, p. 86.

19 "The Girl of a Thousand Faces," *St. Louis Post-Dispatch Sunday Magazine*, 20 March 1910, p. 3.

20. Lawrence, Part 3, p. 103.

21. Roberta Pearson, *Eloquent Gestures: The Transformation of Performance Style in the Griffith Biograph Films* (Berkeley: University of California Press, 1992), p. 51. Pearson also carefully points out the awareness scholars and viewers must have in classifying performances in the two types. Using the word "melodramatic," for histrionic, stereotypes the performance, just as "realism" does for verisimilar. Histrionic is not bad acting, as many viewers would like to believe; it is a style.

22. Gauntier, p. 16.

23. Annette D'Agostino, *An Index to Short and Feature Film Reviews in the Moving Picture World, The Early Years, 1907–1915* (Westport, Connecticut: Greenwood, 1995), p. x (preface). This invaluable resource covers the editorial changes in *MPW*'s reviews from the beginning, as well as indexing all of the reviews.

24. Griffith, not paginated; also Arvidson, p. 63.

25. *"Taming of the Shrew"* [review], *Moving Picture World*, 21 November 1908, p. 398; and *"Taming of the Shrew"* [review], *Moving Picture World*, 28 November 1908, p. 423.

26. *Ibid.*, 28 November 1908.

27. Scott Simmon, notes on *Taming of the Shrew* in "Pordenone Silent Film Programme," 1997, p. 46.

28. Robert Hamilton Ball, *Shakespeare on Silent Film: A Strange Eventful History*. (New York: Theatre Arts, 1968), p.65.
29. Lawrence, Part 3, p. 105.
30. Personal correspondence with Carlos Bustamante, 22 January 1998.
31. Florence Lawrence, "Growing Up with the Movies," Part 2, *Photoplay*, December 1914, p. 105.
32. Gish, p. 67.
33. Mary Pickford, *Sunshine and Shadow* (Garden City, New York: Doubleday, 1955), p. 71.
34. Lawrence, Part 3, p. 105.
35. *Ibid.*, pp. 105–106.
36. "*The Resurrection*" [review], *Moving Picture World*, 29 May 1909, p. 712.
37. "Voices from the Past," *Moving Picture World*, 3 November 1917, p. 686.
38. "The Biograph *Lady Helen's Escapade*," *Moving Picture World*, 24 April 1909, p. 515.
39. Tom Gunning, *D.W. Griffith and the Origins of American Narrative Film: The Early Years at Biograph* (Urbana: University of Illinois Press, 1991; Illini Books edition, 1994), p. 113.
40. Henry Stephen Gordon, "The Story of David Wark Griffith," Part IV, *Photoplay*, September 1916, p. 84.
41. *Ibid.*, p. 86.
42. Gunning, pp. 114–115.
43. Kay Sloan, *The Loud Silents: Origins of the Social Problem Film* (Urbana: University of Illinois Press, 1988), pp. 45–46.
44. Thomas Hood, *Poems of Thomas Hood*, William Cole, Editor (New York: Thomas Crowell Company, 1968), p. 88.
45. "*The Song of the Shirt*" [review], *Moving Picture World*, 28 November 1908, p. 423.
46. Henry Stephen Gordon, "The Story of David Wark Griffith," Part III, *Photoplay*, August 1916, p. 86.
47. Lawrence, Part 3, p. 106.
48. Louis Reeves Harrison, "David W. Griffith: The Art Director and His Work," *Moving Picture World*, 22 November 1913, pp. 847–848.
49. Lawrence, Part 3, p.106.
50. "*The Way of Man*" [review], *Moving Picture World*, 3 July 1909, p. 12.
51. Pearson, p. 47.
52. Lux Graphicus, "On the Screen," *Moving Picture World*, 3 July 1909, p. 11.
53. Lawrence, Part 3, p. 107.
54. Harrison, pp. 847–848.

Chapter Four

1. Alexander Walker, *Stardom: The Hollywood Phenomenon* (New York: Stein and Day, 1970), p. 34.
2. Diana Carey, "Old Niles: Cradle of Western Films," *Classic Images*, No. 251, p. 26. Essanay moved to Old Niles, California, in 1912.
3. George C. Pratt, "The Posse Is Ridin' Like Mad," *Image* VII, 5 April 1958, p. 59. Reprinted in *IMAGE on the Art and Evolution of the Film: Photographs and Articles from the Magazine of the International Museum of Photography*, edited by Marshall Deutelbaum (New York: Dover, and International Museum of Photography, 1979).

4. *Ibid.*, pp. 60–61.
5. "The 'Girl of a Thousand Faces,'" *St. Louis Post-Dispatch Sunday Magazine*, 20 March 1910, p. 5.
6. Florence Lawrence, "Growing Up with the Movies," Part 3, *Photoplay*, January 1915, p. 99.
7. Herb Gordon, "The Girls of the Vitagraph and Biograph," *Classic Images*, No. 77, September 1981, p. 27.
8. Linda Arvidson, *When the Movies Were Young* (New York: Benjamin Blom, 1925, reprinted 1988), photo before p. 71.
9. Frederick James Smith, "Unwept, Unhonored, and Unfilmed," *Photoplay*, July 1924, p. 103.
10. *Ibid.*
11. Florence Lawrence, "Growing Up with the Movies," Part 4, *Photoplay*, February 1915, p. 142.
12. "Has Star Actress," *Variety*, 16 October 1909, p. 13.
13. Terry Ramsaye, *A Million and One Nights* (New York: Simon and Schuster/Touchstone, 1986, reprint of 1926 edition), p. 496.
14. *Moving Picture World*, 26 March 1909.
15. Ramsaye, pp. 446–451.
16. Robert Cochran, "Laemmle," *Moving Picture World*, 9 January 1909, p. 35.
17. "Laemmle Becomes Manufacturer," *Moving Picture World*, 5 June 1909, p. 750.
18. [IMP Advertisement] *Moving Picture World*, 3 July 1909, p. 22.
19. "Carl Laemmle," *Moving Picture World*, 3 July 1909, p. 11.
20. John Drinkwater, *The Life and Adventures of Carl Laemmle* (New York: G.P. Putnam's Sons, 1931), pp. 139–140.
21. Selwyn Standhope, "The Jekyll and Hyde of the Photoplay," *Motion Picture Supplement*, October 1915, p. 54. Thanks to Sally Dumaux.
22. *Ibid.*
23. Lawrence, Part 4, *Photoplay*, p. 142.
24. *Ibid.*
25. Standhope, p. 54.
26. Lawrence, Part 4, *Photoplay*, p. 143.
27. Mary Pickford, "Her Own Story," *Ladies' Home Journal*, Part 2, August 1923, p. 118.
28. "The 'Imp' Films," *Moving Picture World*, 20 November 1909, p. 718.
29. "*The Tide of Fortune*," *Moving Picture World*, 8 January 1910, p. 18.
30. "*The Tide of Fortune*" [review], *Moving Picture World*, 29 January 1910, p. 128.
31. "'Imp' Films Are Realistic," *Moving Picture World*, 5 March 1910, p. 343.
32. "*The Eternal Triangle*" [review], *Moving Picture World*, 4 June 1910, p. 943.
33. "'Imp' Films Are Realistic," p. 343.
34. "Imp Notes," *Moving Picture World*, 26 March 1910, p. 472.
35. [IMP Advertisement] *Moving Picture World*, 19 February 1910, p. 239.
36. Standhope, p. 54.
37. Mack Sennett, *King of Comedy* (Garden City, New York: Doubleday, 1954), p. 55.
38. Still is at the Los Angeles County Museum of Natural History.

Chapter Five

1. [IMP Advertisement] *Show World*, 22 January 1910, p. 27.
2. "Photographs of Moving Picture Actors, A New Method of Lobby Advertising," *Moving Picture World*, 15 January 1910, p. 50.
3. *Moving Picture World*, 19 February 1910, p. 262.
4. "Photographs of Moving Picture Players," p. 50.
5. Tom Gunning, *D.W. Griffith and the Origins of American Narrative Film* (Urbana: University of Illinois Press, 1994), p. 224.
6. Florence Lawrence, "Growing Up with the Movies," Part 4, *Photoplay*, February 1914, p. 144.
7. John Drinkwater, *The Life and Adventures of Carl Laemmle* (New York: G.P. Putnam's Sons, 1931), p. 140.
8. *Moving Picture World*, 9 April 1910, p. 549.
9. [IMP Advertisement] *Moving Picture World*, 5 March 1910, p. 323.
10. Lewis Jacobs, *The Rise of the American Film: A Critical History* (New York: Harcourt, Brace, 1939), p. 87.
11. [IMP Advertisement] *Moving Picture World*, 12 March 1910, p. 365.
12. "Famous Picture Actress Is Still in Posing Land," *Louisville Courier-Journal*, 6 March 1910, page unknown, Natural History Museum of Los Angeles County, Seaver Center for Western History Research, The Florence Lawrence Collection, Box 3, Folder 40. Newspaper name and date are written in Florence's handwriting at the bottom of the clipping.
13. "Heroes and Heroines of the Moving Picture Shows," *St. Louis Post-Dispatch Sunday Magazine*, 6 March 1910, p. 4.
14. "The 'Girl of a Thousand Faces,'" *St. Louis Post-Dispatch Sunday Magazine*, 20 March 1910, p. 1. Thanks to Sally Dumaux for all the St. Louis articles.
15. Alexander Walker, *Stardom: The Hollywood Phenomenon* (New York: Stein and Day, 1970), p. 372.
16. Mary Pickford, "My Own Story," *Ladies' Home Journal*, Part 1, July 1923, p. 102, and Part 2, August 1923, p. 121.
17. Anthony Slide, *The Vaudevillians* (Westport, Connecticut: Arlington, 1981), pp. 70–71 (Held) and pp. 146–47 (Tanguay).
18. "The 'Girl of a Thousand Faces,'" pp. 1–3.
19. Linda Arvidson, *When the Movies Were Young* (New York: Benjamin Blom, 1925, reprint 1968), p. 59.
20. "The 'Girl of a Thousand Faces,'" p. 3.
21. *Ibid.*
22. "Heroes and Heroines of the Moving Picture Shows," p. 4.
23. [Advertisement] *St. Louis Times*, 25 March 1910, p. unknown.
24. "Film Star Will Arrive on Time," *St. Louis Times*, 25 March 1910, p. 1.
25. Drinkwater, p. 141.
26. *Ibid.*
27. "Ovation for Film Star at Union Station," *St. Louis Times*, 26 March 1910, p. 3.
28. *Ibid.*
29. *Ibid.*
30. *Ibid.*
31. Drinkwater, p. 141.
32. "Ovation for Film Star at Union Station," p. 3.
33. *Ibid.*

34. *Ibid.*
35. Drinkwater, p. 142.
36. [Advertisement] *St. Louis Star*, 27 March 1910, p. 6.
37. "Across the Footlights," *St. Louis Post-Dispatch Sunday Magazine*, 27 March 1910, p. 10.
38. *Ibid.*
39. Anita Moore, "Posing for Pictures Preserves Her Youth," *St. Louis Star*, 28 March 1910, p. unknown.
40. *Ibid.*

Chapter Six

1. Florence Lawrence, "Growing Up with the Movies," *Photoplay*, Part 4, February 1915, p. 146.
2. "Vitagraph Girl Feted," *Moving Picture World*, 23 April 1910, p. 644.
3. "*The Eternal Triangle*" [review], *Moving Picture World*, 13 August 1910, p. 352.
4. "*The Taming of Jane*" [review], *Moving Picture World*, 3 September 1910, p. 521.
5. "Notes of the Trade," *Moving Picture World*, 7 May 1910, p. 741.
6. Personal correspondence with Lubin biographer Joe (Joseph) Eckhardt, 31 January 1997.
7. Harry Solter, letter to Florence Lawrence, 1 August 1910, Natural History Museum of Los Angeles County, Seaver Center for Western History Research, The Florence Lawrence Collection, Box 1, Folder 3.
8. Harry Solter, letter to Florence Lawrence, undated, Natural History Museum of Los Angeles County, Seaver Center for Western History Research, The Florence Lawrence Collection, Box 1, Folder 3.
9. Florence Lawrence, letter to Lotta Lawrence, 10 September 1911, Wisconsin Center for Film and Theater Research, Madison, Wisconsin.
10. Florence Lawrence, letter to Lotta Lawrence, 18 September 1910, Wisconsin Center for Film and Theater Research, Madison, Wisconsin.
11. Siegmund Lubin, letter to Harry and Florence Solter, 19 October 1910, Natural History Museum of Los Angeles County, Seaver Center for Western Historical Research, The Florence Lawrence Collection, Box 1, Folder 9.
12. Florence Lawrence, "Growing Up with the Movies," *Photoplay*, Part 4, February 1915, p. 146.
13. Lubin Manufacturing Company, letter, 25 November 1910; Edison National Historical Site, West Orange, New Jersey. Thanks to Joe Eckhardt for bringing this letter to my attention.
14. Norman Bridgwood, letter to Florence Lawrence, 12 January 1911, Natural History Museum of Los Angeles County, Seaver Center for Western Historical Research, The Florence Lawrence Collection, Box 1, Folder 2.
15. Norman Bridgwood, letter to Florence Lawrence, 25 December 1910, Natural History Museum of Los Angeles County, Seaver Center for Western Historical Research, The Florence Lawrence Collection, Box 1, Folder 2.
16. Norman Bridgwood, letter to Florence Lawrence, 31 December 1910, Natural History Museum of Los Angeles County, Seaver Center for Western History Research, The Florence Lawrence Collection, Box 1, Folder 2.

17. Florence Lawrence, letter to Norman Bridgwood, 14 January 1911, Natural History Museum of Los Angeles County, Seaver Center for Western History Research, The Florence Lawrence Collection, Box 1, Folder 2.
18. John Drinkwater, *The Life and Adventures of Carl Laemmle* (New York: G.P. Putnam's Sons, 1931), p. 141.
19. *Ibid.*, p. 144.
20. "*His Bogus Uncle*" [review], *Moving Picture World*, 11 February 1911, p. 316.
21. Edward Wagenknecht, *Movies in the Age of Innocence* (Norman: University of Oklahoma Press, 1962), p. 52.
22. "Picture Personalities, Arthur Johnson," *Moving Picture World*, 18 February 1911, p. 341.
23. Florence Lawrence, "Growing Up with the Movies," Part 1, *Photoplay*, November 1914, pp. 33–34.
24. Notes of Joe Eckhardt, "The Two Fathers."
25. "*The Hoyden*" [review], *New York Dramatic Mirror*, 3 May 1911.
26. Florence Lawrence, letter to Lotta Lawrence, 1 May 1911, Wisconsin Center for Film and Theater Research, Madison, Wisconsin.
27. "*The Professor's Ward*" [review], *New York Dramatic Mirror*, June 14, 1911.
28. Vachel Lindsay, *The Art of the Moving Picture* (New York: Macmillan, 1915) p. 43. Although Lindsay is pointedly dealing with a Biograph film, *The Battle*, in his discussion of Crowd Splendor, his comments about the era are general.
29. Eileen Bowser, *The Transformation of Cinema, 1907–1915*, Volume 2 of the History of the American Cinema series, (New York: Charles Scribner's Sons, 1990), p. 117.
30. Peter Wade, "*Art Versus Music*," *Motion Picture Story*, January 1912, p. 103.
31. Anthony Slide, *Aspects of American Film History Prior to 1920* (Metuchen, New Jersey: Scarecrow, 1978), p. 102. This excellent chapter, "Early Film Magazines," reveals much about what periodicals came when.
32. Alice Burt, letter to Florence Lawrence, 1 June 1911, Natural History Museum of Los Angeles County, Seaver Center for Western History Research, The Florence Lawrence Collection, Box 1, Folder 10. Miss Burt had evidently corresponded with Florence before; the envelope is addressed to Miss Florence A. Lawrence and the P.S. says, "Hope I don't bother you. Don't be afraid to say so if I do."
33. George A. DeCottes, letter to Florence Lawrence, 28 June 1911; Natural History Museum of Los Angeles County, Seaver Center for Western History Research, The Florence Lawrence Collection, Box 1, Folder 10. This letter is address to "Miss Amy Lawrence."
34. Daniel Blum, *A Pictorial History of the American Theatre, 1900–1951* (New York: Greenberg, 1951), p. 114–129.
35. Anthony Slide, *The Vaudevillians: A Dictionary of Vaudeville Performers* (Westport, Connecticut: Arlington, 1981).
36. "The Dearth of Comedy," *Moving Picture World*, 10 June 1911, p. 1293.
37. Louis Reeves Harrison, "Punk Plays," *Moving Picture World*, 12 August 1911, p. 356.
38. [Lubin advertisement] *Moving Picture World*, 24 June 1911, p. 1453.

Chapter Seven

1. Harry Webb, "My Days as an Old-Time Movie Cowboy," *Westerner*, Fall 1975, p. 48. Thanks to Joe Eckhardt for a copy of this article.

Notes: Chapter Seven

2. Florence Lawrence, letter to Lotta Lawrence, 1 May 1911, Wisconsin Center for Film and Theater Research, Madison, Wisconsin, Florence Lawrence file.

3. Lotta Lawrence, letter to Florence Lawrence, 13 October 1910, Natural History Museum of Los Angeles County, Seaver Center for Western History Research, The Florence Lawrence Collection, Box 1, Folder 1.

4. Lotta Lawrence, letter to Florence Lawrence, 25 August 1911, Natural History Museum of Los Angeles County, Seaver Center for Western History Research, The Florence Lawrence Collection, Box 1, Folder 1.

5. Lotta Lawrence, letter to Florence Lawrence, 27 October 1911, Natural History Museum of Los Angeles County, Seaver Center for Western History Research, The Florence Lawrence Collection, Box 1, Folder 1.

6. Lotta Lawrence, letter, 25 August 1911.

7. Florence Lawrence, letter, 1 May 1911.

8. "'Flo' Lawrence Satisfies Our Curiosity at Last," *Chicago Record Herald*, hand dated 12 April 1914, page unknown.

9. Lotta Lawrence, letter to Florence Lawrence, 1 December 1911, Natural History Museum of Los Angeles County, Seaver Center for Western History Research, The Florence Lawrence Collection, Box 1, Folder 1.

10. Florence Lawrence, letter to Lotta Lawrence, 4 April 1912, Wisconsin Center for Film and Theater Research, Madison, Wisconsin, Florence Lawrence file.

11. *Ibid.*

12. "Inquiries," *Moving Picture World*, 1 June 1912, p. 832.

13. "Inquiries," *Moving Picture World*, 15 June 1912, p. 1028.

14. "Florence Lawrence: Who and What She Is," *New York Star*, 4 April 1914, p. 21.

15. [Victor Advertisement] *The Universal Weekly*, 22 June 1912, p. 30. Florence Lawrence was trumpeted in this ad as the one "Who plays upon the heart strings of an audience like a master musician on a harp." Thanks to Sally Dumaux for providing a copy of this ad.

16. [Victor Advertisement] *Moving Picture World*, 29 June 1912, p. 1190.

17. [California Film Exchange Advertisement], *Moving Picture World*, 27 July 1912, p. 394.

18. Thomas Bedding, "Florence Lawrence: An Appreciation," *The Universal Weekly*, 20 July 1912, p. 3. Thanks to Sally Dumaux.

19. Thomas Bedding, "The Art of Florence Lawrence," *The Universal Weekly* 10 August 1912, p. 7. Thanks to Sally Dumaux.

20. "Florence Lawrence's Company," *New York Dramatic Mirror*, 5 June 1912, p. 26. Additional information about Pat Powers can be found in Anthony Slide, *The American Film Industry* (Westport, Connecticut: Greenwood, 1986; reprint, Lake Geneva, Wisconsin: Limelight, 1990) and Terry Ramsaye, *A Million and One Nights* (New York: Simon and Schuster/Touchstone, 1986; reprint of 1926 edition).

21. Information on Miss Gardner can be found in "Helen Gardner to Have Her a Company of Her Own," *Moving Picture World*, 8 June 1912, p. 917; and Edward Wagenknecht, *The Movies in the Age of Innocence* (Norman: University of Oklahoma Press, 1962), pp. 46–47.

22. C.B. Claff, "Florence Lawrence, Famous Picture Star," *New York Dramatic Mirror*, 31 July 1912. Thanks to William Drew and Bill Mann for copies of this article.

23. *"The Chance Shot"* [review], *Moving Picture World*, 24 August 1912, p. 772.

24. *"The Mill Buyers"* [review], *Moving Picture World*, 17 August 1912, p. 676.

25. *"The Advent of Jane"* [review], *Moving Picture World*, 5 October 1912, p. 42.

26. *"Flo's Discipline"* [review], *Moving Picture World*, 28 September 1912, p. 1277.

27. Harry's letters and notes to Florence are undated, except for the day of the week, but numbered in sequence because he could not mail them at sea. All are located at the Natural History Museum of Los Angeles County, Seaver Center for Western History Research, The Florence Lawrence Collection, Box 1, Folder 5. His will is in Folder 27.
28. Harry Solter, letter to Lotta Lawrence, 27 September [1912], Natural History Museum of Los Angeles County, Seaver Center for Western History Research, The Florence Lawrence Collection, Box 1, Folder 5.
29. Florence Lawrence, letter to Lotta Lawrence, 25 October 1912, Natural History Museum of Los Angeles County, Seaver Center for Western History Research, The Florence Lawrence Collection, Box 1, Folder 2.
30. Scenario writer Giles Warren was the senior Victor officer on the August 6 trip, signing the register for everyone at the Caudebec Inn. Others with Florence were Victory Bateman, Frederic Malcolm, Owen Moore, Gladden James, Edmund Norris, J.B. Smith, and J.T. Van Buskirk. Thanks to Donna Steffens at the Neversink Valley Area Museum, Cuddebackville, New York.
31. "Harry Solter on Vacation," *Moving Picture World*, 28 September 1912, p. 1265.

Chapter Eight

1. Florence Lawrence, "Just About Myself," *Pictures and the Picturegoer*, 18 April 1912, p. 199.
2. Correspondence with River Vale historian, Edmund Moderacki, 22 August 1997.
3. Rita Ecke Altomara, *Hollywood on the Palisades: A Filmography of Silent Features Made in Fort Lee, New Jersey, 1903–1927* (New York: Garland, 1983), p. xiv.
4. Norman Bridgwood, letter to Florence Lawrence, 27 October 1911, Natural History Museum of Los Angeles County, Seaver Center for Western History Research, The Florence Lawrence Collection, Box 1, Folder 4.
5. "The Return of Miss Lawrence," *Moving Picture World*, 9 August 1913, p. 620.
6. Henrietta Eisenburg, poem, *Motion Picture Story*, September 1913.
7. Letters section, *Photoplay*, November 1912, p. 136.
8. *Ibid.*, p. 138.
9. William K. Everson, *American Silent Film* (New York: Oxford University Press, 1978), p. 54.
10. Everson, pp. 57–58. Edward Wagenknecht agreed with Everson's assessment of *Cleopatra*, saying Miss Gardner's performance in it was "inexplicably bad." Wagenknecht, *The Movies in the Age of Innocence* (Norman: University of Oklahoma Press), p. 26.
11. "*The Closed Door*" [review], *Moving Picture World*, 4 October 1913, p. 28.
12. Gladys Roosevelt, "Miss Florence Lawrence, of the Victor Company," *Moving Picture Story Magazine*, October 1913, p. 124.
13. Florence Lawrence, "Just About Myself," *Pictures and the Picturegoer*, 18 April 1914, p. 200.
14. "Florence Lawrence—The Star Who Came Back," *Photoplay*, January 1914, p. 72.
15. The popular players in that issue were Mabel Norman (Keystone), Harry Benham (Thanhouser), King Baggot (IMP), Jack Kerrigan (Universal), Vivian Rich (American), Marguerite Snow (Thanhouser), Rosemary Theby (Reliance), James

Cruz (Thanhouser), J.W. Johnstone (Eclair), Marie Eline (Thanhouser Kid), Will Sheerer (Eclair), Pearl White (Crystal), Florence, Wallace Reid (101 Bison), and Margarita Fischer (Rex).

16. "A Recruit from the Legitimate," *Moving Picture World*, 1 November 1913, p. 499.

17. "Florence Lawrence: Who and What She Is," *New York Star*, 4 April 1914, p. 21.

18. "*Girl O' the Woods*" [review], *Moving Picture World*, 11 October 1913, p. 158.

19. "*The Coryphee*" [review], *Moving Picture World*, 10 January 1914, p. 174.

20. "*The Spender*" [review], *Moving Picture World*, 1 November 1913, p. 498.

21. "*Unto the Third Generation*" [review], *Moving Picture World*, 29 November 1913, p. 1008; "*Influence of Sympathy*" [review], *Moving Picture World*, 6 December 1913, p. 1153; "*The Stepmother*" [review], *Moving Picture World*, 28 February 1914, p. 1090.

22. "*Diplomatic Flo*" [review], *Moving Picture World*, 28 March 1914, p. 1682; "*The Man Who Was Never Kissed*" [review], *Moving Picture World*, 10 October 1914, p. 189.

23. "*His Wife's Child*" [review], *Moving Picture World*, 22 November 1913, p. 870.

24. "*A Disenchantment*" [review], *Moving Picture World*, 6 June 1914, p. 1040.

25. "*A Mysterious Mystery*" [review], *Moving Picture World*, 19 September 1914, p. 1646.

26. "*The Honor of the Humble*" [review], *Moving Picture World*, 22 August 1914, p. 1101.

27. Edwin Bryant, "The Hero Brothers," *Photoplay*, August 1915, p. 80.

28. Anthony Slide, *The American Film Industry* (Westport, Connecticut: Greenwood, 1986; reprint, Lake Geneva, Wisconsin: Limelight, 1990), p. 330.

29. Creighton Hamilton, "Girls Who Play with Death," *Picture-Play Magazine*, May 1916, pp. 177–186.

30. Gladys Jones, "A Breakfast Chat with Florence Lawrence," *Feature Movie*, March 1916, p. 14.

31. "Florence Lawrence: Who and What She Is," p. 21.

32. Larry Lee Holland, "Florence Lawrence," *Films in Review*, August/September 1980, Volume XXXI, Number 7, p. 391.

33. "Growing Up with the Movies," *Moving Picture World*, 26 September 1914, p. 1754.

34. "Editorial Announcement," *Photoplay*, November 1914, p. 3.

35. Florence Lawrence, "Growing Up with the Movies," Part 4, *Photoplay*, February 1915, p. 146.

Chapter Nine

1. "Miss Florence Lawrence, Premier, Prominent Picture Play Actress," Unico News Service, 44 East 23rd Street, New York, March 1915; Natural History Museum of Los Angeles County, Seaver Center for Western History Research, The Florence Lawrence Collection, Box 3, Folder 36.

2. *Photoplay*, August 1915, p. 169.

3. "Florence Laurence [sic] Seriously Ill," *Moving Picture World*, 7 August 1915, p. 972.

4. "Florence Lawrence in Auto Accident," *Moving Picture World*, 4 September 1915, p. 1654.

5. Gladys Jones, "A Breakfast Chat with Florence Lawrence," *Feature Movie*, March 1916, p. 15. Thanks to Annette D'Agostino.

6. *Ibid,* p. 14.
7. "Florence Lawrence to Return to the Screen," *Moving Picture World,* 11 December 1915, p. 1998.
8. "Universal Gets Florence Lawrence," *Moving Picture World,* 1 January 1916, p. 86.
9. "Plays and Players," *Photoplay,* March 1916, p. 121.
10. Undated clipping, "Florence Lawrence to Universal," Natural History Museum of Los Angeles County, Seaver Center for Western History Research, The Florence Lawrence Collection, Box 3, Folder 35.
11. "Universal Gets Florence Lawrence," p. 86.
12. Jones, p. 14.
13. Untitled clipping, 15 January 1916, unknown New York newspaper, New York Public Library for the Performing Arts, Florence Lawrence file. Thanks to Bill Mann.
14. "Wrappers Change to Negligees," *Salem (Oregon) Statesman,* 27 February 1916, Natural History Museum of Los Angeles County, Seaver Center for Western History Research, The Florence Lawrence Collection, Box 3, Folder 37.
15. Jones, p. 15.
16. Carol Neuls-Bates, "Emma Roberto Steiner," Julie Anne Sadie and Rhian Samuel, editors, *The Norton/Grove Dictionary of Women Composers* (New York: W.W. Norton, 1995), p. 439.
17. "Florence Lawrence Has Paris Gowns," *Moving Picture World,* 8 April 1916, p. 264.
18. "*Elusive Isabel*" [review], *Moving Picture World,* 20 May 1916, p. 1404.
19. "*Elusive Isabel*" [review], *Variety,* 5 May 1916, p. 26.
20. "*Florence Lawrence Out of Universal's Employ,*" *The Billboard,* 1 April 1916, p. 52.
21. *Photoplay,* July 1916, p. 100.
22. "Florence Lawrence Resigns," *Moving Picture World,* 22 April 1916, p. 631.
23. "Bluebird Productions," *The Billboard,* 17 June 1916, p. 58.
24. Gene Brown, *Movie Time: A Chronology of Hollywood and the Movie Industry from Its Beginnings to the Present* (New York: Macmillan, 1995), p. 34.
25. Ethan Mordden, *Movie Star: A Look at the Women Who Made Hollywood* (New York: St. Martin's, 1983), p. 8.
26. Daniel Blum, *A Pictorial History of the Silent Screen* (New York: Grosset and Dunlap, 1953), pp. 66–83.
27. Jones, p. 15.
28. "Universal Plans for Miss Lawrence," *Moving Picture World,* 8 January 1916, p. 232.
29. "*A Girlish Impulse*" [film preview], *Moving Picture World,* 2 December 1911, p. 729.
30. Jones, p. 15.
31. Undated, handwritten sheet entitled "From a Moving Picture Actress," Natural History Museum of Los Angeles County, Seaver Center for Western History Research, The Florence Lawrence Collection, Box 1, Folder 2.
32. Jones, p. 15.
33. A handwritten copy of "Broken Hearted" is at the Wisconsin Center for Film and Theater Research, Madison, Wisconsin, Florence Lawrence file; a typed copy is at the Natural History Museum of Los Angeles County, Seaver Center for Western History Research, The Florence Lawrence Collection, Box 3, Folder 26.
34. "Right from the Heart," *The Billboard,* 20 May 1916, p. 61.
35. Herbert Howe, "Why Many Movie Marriages Fail!" *Photoplay,* October 1926, p. 31.

36. Florence Lawrence, "Growing Up with the Movies," Part 1, *Photoplay*, November 1914, p. 36.

37. George Lawrence, letter to Lotta Lawrence, 12 July 1916, History Museum of Los Angeles County, Seaver Center for Western History Research, The Florence Lawrence Collection, Box 1, Folder 3. Letter was written on a blank report form from the San Francisco Police Department.

38. "Florence Lawrence Out of Universal's Employ," p. 52.

39. "Cure for Blues," Natural History Museum of Los Angeles County, Seaver Center for Western History Research, The Florence Lawrence Collection, Box 3, Folder 26.

40. Florence Lawrence, letter to Carl Laemmle [draft], 15 October 1916, Natural History Museum of Los Angles County, Seaver Center for Western History Research, The Florence Lawrence Collection, Box 1, Folder 2.

41. Florence Lawrence, contract with attorney Max D. Josephson, 1 November 1916, Natural History Museum of Los Angeles County, Seaver Center for Western History Research, The Florence Lawrence Collection, Box 3, Folder 27.

42. *Photoplay*, March 1916, p. 121. Also reported in *Moving Picture World*, "Damages for Moving Picture Actress," 1 January 1916, p. 86.

43. "Picture Players' Insurance," *Moving Picture World*, 11 December 1915, p. 1998.

44. Creighton Hamilton, "Girls Who Play with Death," *Picture-Play Magazine*, May 1916, pp. 178–179.

Chapter Ten

1. "Actors Fund Fair Nets $80,000," *Moving Picture World*, 9 June 1917, p. 1620.

2. "Florence Lawrence Entertains," *Moving Picture World*, 13 January 1917, p. 212.

3. "A Film Favorite Who Is an Inventor," *Green Book Magazine*, May 1916, p. 844.

4. "Men Are Stupid in the Care of Autos, Little Revue Whistler Declares," unknown newspaper, 27 August 1920, page unknown. Clipping at Natural History Museum of Los Angeles County, Seaver Center for Western History Research, The Florence Lawrence Collection, Box 3, Folder 38.

5. William Drew, "Speeding Sweethearts of the Silent Screen, 1908–1921," Internet-published article located at http://www.mindspring.com/~kallym/sweethearts.htm, 1997.

6. "Voices from the Past," *Moving Picture World*, 3 November 1917, p. 686.

7. "Harry L. Solter Dies Suddenly," *Moving Picture World*, 3 April 1920, p. 54. Other information about the death of Harry Solter was culled from his death certificate (Texas, E551518) and records from Kastor, Maxon and Futrell Funeral Home, El Paso, Texas.

8. "Men Are Stupid in the Care of Autos, Little Revue Whistler Declares," 27 August 1920.

9. "Producers Pictures Corporation Formed for Florence Lawrence, First Film Star," *Moving Picture World*, 27 November 1920, p. 462.

10. "Florence Lawrence," *Photoplay*, February 1921, p. 75.

11. Press release in Florence Lawrence file in the Jimmy Starr Film History Collection, Arizona State University, Tempe, Arizona.

12. "It's a Strange Business But True," newspaper unknown [probably *Los Angeles Examiner*], date unknown [mid-1921], page unknown. Clipping at Natural History Museum of Los Angeles County, Seaver Center for Western History Research, The Florence Lawrence Collection, Box 3, Folder 40.

13. Adela Rogers St. Johns, "The Return of Florence Lawrence," *Photoplay*, May 1921, pp. 33, 34, 91.
14. *Ibid.*, p. 34.
15. Information about the Woodring marriage comes from their marriage certificate (California 21-034484); "Florence Lawrence, Film Star, San Francisco Bride," *San Francisco Examiner*, 27 June 1921; and "Florence Lawrence, Actress, Secretly Wed," *San Francisco Examiner*, 28 June 1921.
16. Roger Ferri, "In the Independent Field" [column], *Moving Picture World*, 7 January 1922, p. 83.
17. "*The Unfoldment*" [Associated Exhibitors Incorporated Advertisement], *Moving Picture World*, 28 January 1922, p. 359.
18. "Florence Lawrence Comes Back in *The Unfoldment*," *Moving Picture World*, 28 January 1922, p. 391.

Chapter Eleven

1. Arthur James, "The Lessons of Adversity," *Moving Picture World*, 18 February 1922, p. 707.
2. "It's a Strange Business But True," unknown newspaper [probably *Los Angeles Examiner*], unknown date [mid-1921], page unknown. Clipping at Natural History Museum of Los Angeles County, Seaver Center for Western History Research, The Florence Lawrence Collection, Box 3, Folder 40.
3. Terry Ramsaye, *A Million and One Nights: A Modern Classic* (New York: Simon and Schuster/Touchstone, 1986; reprint of 1926 edition), pp. 819–821.
4. For a modern and current updating and discussion of the murder of William Desmond Taylor, see Bruce Long's *Taylorology* newsletters at http://www.public.asu.edu/~ialong/Taylor, or http://www.angelfire.com/az/Taylorology.
5. Richard de Cordova, *Picture Personality: The Emergence of the Star System in America* (Urbana, IL: University of Illinois Press, 1990), p.136.
6. "Dell Henderson," *Moving Picture World*, 27 October 1917, p. 516.
7. "Veteran Screen Girl Is Interesting," 3 March 1926, unknown San Jose newspaper, p. 4. Clipping at the Natural History Museum of Los Angeles County, Seaver Center for Western History Research, The Florence Lawrence Collection, Box 3 Folder 39.
8. "Nose 'Bobbed,'" *Los Angeles Examiner*, 12 June 1924, page unknown. Clipping courtesy of Arizona State University, Jimmy Starr Film History Collection, Tempe, Arizona.
9. "Florence Lawrence," *Photoplay*, September 1924, pp. 52–53.
10. Frederick James Smith, "Unwept, Unhonored and Unfilmed," *Photoplay*, July 1924, p. 64.
11. Wil Rex, "Where Are the Stars of Yesterday?" *Picture Play*, September 1916, pp. 39–46. Rex did not attempt to contact any of the fallen stars, but rather just report on who was still in and who was out of the industry. Thanks to William Drew.
12. Smith, "Unwept, Unhonored and Unfilmed," pp. 64–67, 101–105.
13. "The Romantic History of the Motion Picture," Chapter 21, *Photoplay*, December 1923, pp. 118–119. In some cases, romantic means imaginary.
14. Smith, "Unwept, Unhonored and Unfilmed," pp. 64–66.
15. The signed contract is at the Natural History Museum of Los Angeles County, Seaver Center for Western History Research, The Florence Lawrence Collection, Box 3, Folder 27. Other clippings indicating shows and dates are scattered throughout Box 3, Folders 27 through 40.

16. "Veteran Screen Girl Is Interesting," p. 4.
17. Note is in Florence Lawrence photo file, Wisconsin Center for Film and Theater Research, Madison, Wisconsin.
18. Margaret Allen, *Selling Dreams: Inside the Beauty Business* (New York: Simon and Schuster, 1981), pp. 21–46.
19. Lina Basquette, *Lina: DeMille's Godless Girl* (Fairfax, Virginia: Denlinger's, 1990), p. 147.
20. Gerald D. McDonald, "Origin of the Star System," *Films in Review*, Vol. 4, Number 9, November 1953, pp. 449–458. Article is subtitled, "Out of Man's Need for Myths Came the Stars in the Movie Firmament."
21. Thanks to Bill Mann for sending copies of *Woodring vs. Woodring*, Superior Court, Los Angeles County, case D91671. The papers, signed by Florence, said that the marriage took place on 12 May 1921 and separation took place on or around 12 December 1929. Oddly, in two places she agreed that the "time elapsing from said date of marriage to said date of separation is 1 year and 5 months." Florence's attorney was Joseph M. Wapner.
22. "Invention May Bring Millions to Ex-Actress," unknown paper [possibly *Los Angeles Express*], 1 December 1930, page unknown. Clipping courtesy of Arizona State University, Jimmy Starr Film History Collection, Tempe, Arizona.
23. United States Patent Office, Patent No. 1,274,983, issued to Charlotte A. Bridgwood of Westwood, New Jersey, applied for 16 October 1917, issued 6 August 1918.
24. Thanks to Bill Mann for fiinding *Bolton vs. Bolton*, Superior Court, Los Angeles County, case D119403. Florence's attorney was Edwin F. Franke.

Chapter Twelve

1. Gene Brown, *Movie Time* (New York: Macmillan, 1995), p. 99. A million other wonderful facts hide in this book.
2. Lina Basquette, *Lina: DeMille's Godless Girl* (Fairfax, Virginia: Denlinger's, 1990), p. 161.
3. Michael R. Pitts, *Poverty Row Studios, 1929–1940* (Jefferson, North Carolina: McFarland, 1997), p. viii.
4. Pitts, pp. 19–20.
5. Chester B. Bahn, "Florence's Lawrence and Turner," *Cinema Digest* (originally printed in *Syracuse Herald*), 13 June 1932, p. 7.
6. Mary Pickford, *Sunshine and Shadow* (Garden City, New York: Doubleday, 1955), p.187.
7. "The 'Biograph Girl' Returns," photo with cutline, *Detroit News*, 17 June 1934, page unknown. Clipping in Florence Lawrence file, Detroit Public Library, Detroit, Michigan.
8. Gary Carey, *All the Stars in Heaven: Louis B. Mayer's M-G-M* (New York: E.P. Dutton, 1981), pp. 111, 303.
9. "Blackton Founds Organization of Screen Pioneers," *Motion Picture Herald*, 5 September 1936, p. 36.
10. Philip K. Scheuer, "Town Called Hollywood" [column], *Los Angeles Times*, 27 December 1937, p. 11.
11. "Hamilton-Born Film Star Ends Life in Hollywood," *Toronto Star*, 29 December 1938.
12. "Despair," Natural History Museum of Los Angeles County, Seaver Center for Western History Research, The Florence Lawrence Collection, Box 3, Folder 26.

13. Thanks to Pierce Brothers Cunningham and O'Connor Mortuary, Los Angeles, for providing copies of their records of Florence's service.

14. "'Biograph Girl' Suicide Ends Tragic Career," (*Hollywood*) *Citizen-News*, 29 December 1938, p. 1.

15. *Ibid.*

16. Edward Wagenknecht, *The Movies in the Age of Innocence* (Norman: University of Oklahoma Press, 1962), pp. 52–53. Mr. Wagenknecht, unfortunately, does not give a source for this anecdote, leaving for speculation just who one of Florence's last fans was.

Chapter Thirteen

1. This chapter uses much personal correspondence between the author and various film historians. Questionnaires were sent and answered during the last part of 1997. Among the questions asked:

   What do you consider Florence's role in movie history to be?
   What do you think made Florence Lawrence special to early movie audiences?
   Which film of Florence's do you particularly remember?
   Why do you think Florence's story has been lost to contemporary film viewers and many film historians?
   What part of early film history do you want people to know, to remember?

Those listed in the text and notes are only a sampling of those who responded to the questionnaire. Several film historians declined, saying that they simply did not know the subject (Florence Lawrence) well enough to make a qualified opinion.

2. Tom Gunning, response to questionnaire, 26 November 1997.
3. Annette D'Agostino, response to questionnaire, 23 September 1997.
4. Charles Musser, response to questionnaire, 20 October 1997.
5. *Entertainment Weekly, the 100 Greatest Movie Stars of All Time*, Time, Inc. Special Collector's Issue, Fall 1996.
6. Ken Wlaschin, *The Illustrated Encyclopedia of the World's Greatest Movie Stars and Their Films* (New York: Bonanza/Crown, 1979), p. 32.
7. Ty Burr, "The 100 Greatest Movie Stars" [introduction], *Entertainment Weekly, the 100 Greatest Movie Stars of All Time*, p. 12.
8. Wlaschin, p. 25.
9. John Cocchi, response to questionnaire, 26 October 1997.
10. Anthony Slide, response to questionnaire, 23 October 1997.
11. Richard de Cordova, *Picture Personalities: The Emergence of the Star System in America* (Urbana: University of Illinois Press, 1990), p. 64.
12. D'Agostino, 23 September 1997.
13. Gunning, 26 November 1997.
14. Cocchi, 26 October 1997.
15. Correspondence with Joseph Eckhardt, 13 January 1998.
16. Musser, 20 October 1997.
17. Correspondence with Carlos Bustamante, 22 January 1998.
18. Gene Vazzana, response to questionnaire, 9 October 1997.
19. Slide, 23 October 1997.
20. D'Agostino, 23 September 1997.
21. Gunning, 26 November 1997.
22. Musser, 20 October 1997, and Musser, "Pre-Classical American Cinema: Its

Changing Modes of Film Production," in *Silent Film*, Richard Abel, ed. (New Brunswick, New Jersey: Rutgers University Press, 1996), p. 86. This essay first appeared in *Persistence of Vision* 9 (1991).

23. Cocchi, 26 October 1997.
24. Philip Leibfried, response to questionnaire, 9 October 1997.
25. Slide, 23 October 1997.
26. Cocchi, 26 October 1997.
27. Gunning, 26 November 1997.
28. Ethan Mordden, *Movie Star: A Look at the Women Who Made Hollywood* (New York: St. Martin's, 1983), p. 3.
29. Linda Arvidson, *When the Movies Were Young* (New York: Benjamin Blom 1968, reprint of 1925 edition), p. 137.
30. Gene Gauntier, "Blazing the Trail," *Woman's Home Companion*, November 1928, p. 134.
31. William M. Drew, "Damsels in Distress: Strong Women Held Hostage in Film Archives," Internet-published article located at http://www.mdle.com/ClassicFilms/Guest/drew1.htm, 1996.
32. Mary Pickford, "My Own Story," *Ladies' Home Journal*, July 1923, p. 102.
33. Arvidson, pp. 59, 77.
34. Mack Sennett, *King of Comedy* (Garden City, New York: Doubleday, 1954; reprinted San Francisco: Mercury, 1990), p. 55.

BIBLIOGRAPHY

Books

Abel, Richard, editor. *Silent Film*. New Brunswick, NJ: Rutgers University Press, 1996.
Allen, Frederick Lewis. *Only Yesterday*. New York: Harper and Row, 1931. Reprinted 1964.
Allen, Margaret. *Selling Dreams: Inside the Beauty Business*. New York: Simon and Schuster, 1981.
Altomara, Rita Ecke. *Hollywood on the Palisades: A Filmography of Silent Features Made in Fort Lee, New Jersey, 1903–1927*. New York: Garland, 1983.
Archbold, Rick, and Dana McCauley. *Last Dinner on the Titanic*. New York: Hyperion/Madison, 1997.
Arvidson, Linda (Mrs. D.W. Griffith). *When the Movies Were Young*. New York: Benjamin Blom, 1925. Reprinted 1968.
Ball, Robert Hamilton. *Shakespeare on Silent Film: A Strange Eventful History*. New York: Theatre Arts, 1968.
Balshofer, Fred J., and Arthur C. Miller. *One Reel a Week*. Berkeley: University of California Press, 1967.
Basquette, Lina. *Lina: DeMille's Godless Girl*. Fairfax, VA: Denlinger's, 1990.
Belton, John, editor. *Movies and Mass Culture*. New Brunswick, NJ: Rutgers University Press, 1996.
Bitzer, G.W. *Billy Bitzer: His Story*. New York: Farrar, Straus and Giroux, 1973.
Blum, Daniel. *A Pictorial History of the American Theatre, 1900–1951*. New York: Greenberg, 1951.
_____. *A Pictorial History of the Silent Screen*. New York: Grosset and Dunlap, 1953.
Bowser, Eileen. *The Transformation of Cinema, 1907–1915*. Volume 2 of the History of American Cinema series. New York: Charles Scribner's Sons, 1990.
_____, editor. *Biograph Bulletins, 1908–1912*. New York: Octagon Books/Farrar, Straus and Giroux, 1973.
Brown, Gene. *Movie Time: A Chronology of Hollywood and the Movie Industry from Its Beginnings to the Present*. New York: Macmillan, 1995.
Brownlow, Kevin. *The Parade's Gone By...* New York: Alfred A. Knopf, 1968. Reprinted Berkeley: University of California Press, 1976.

Carey, Gary. *All the Stars in Heaven: Louis B. Mayer's M-G-M*. New York: E.P. Dutton, 1981.
D'Agostino, Annette. *An Index to Short and Feature Film Reviews in Moving Picture World: The Early Years, 1907–1915*. Westport, CT: Greenwood, 1995.
———. *Filmmakers in The Moving Picture World: An Index of Articles, 1907–1927*. Jefferson, NC: McFarland, 1997.
de Cordova, Richard. *Picture Personalities: The Emergence of the Star System in America*. Urbana: University of Illinois Press, 1990.
Drew, William M. *Speaking of Silents: First Ladies of the Screen*. Vestal, NY: Vestal, 1989.
Drinkwater, John. *The Life and Adventures of Carl Laemmle*. New York: G.P. Putnam's Sons, 1931.
Eckhardt, Joseph P. *The King of the Movies: Film Pioneer, Siegmund Lubin*. Madison, NJ: Fairleigh Dickinson University Press, 1997.
Everson, William K. *American Silent Film*. New York: Oxford University Press, 1978.
Eyman, Scott. *The Speed of Sound: Hollywood and the Talkie Revolution*. New York: Simon and Schuster, 1997.
Fell, John L., editor. *Film Before Griffith*. Berkeley: University of California Press, 1983.
Gish, Lillian. *The Movies, Mr. Griffith, and Me*. Englewood Cliffs, NJ: Prentice Hall, 1969.
Griffith, D.W., with editing by James Hart. *The Man Who Invented Hollywood: The Autobiography of D.W. Griffith*. Louisville, KY: Touchstone, 1972.
Griffith, Linda Arvidson (Mrs. D.W. Griffith). *Film Flashes, the Wit and Humor of a Nation in Pictures*. New York: Leslie-Judge, 1916.
Grun, Bernard. *The Timetables of History*. New York: Simon and Schuster, 1991.
Gunning, Tom. *D.W. Griffith and the Origins of American Narrative Film, The Early Years at Biograph*. Urbana: University of Illinois Press, 1991.
Hughes, Laurence A., editor. *The Truth About the Movies by the Stars*. Hollywood, CA: Hollywood, 1924.
Jacobs, Lewis. *The Rise of the American Film: A Critical History*. New York: Harcourt, Brace, 1939.
James, Edward T., editor. *Notable American Women, 1607–1950: A Biographical Dictionary*. Cambridge, MA: Harvard University Press, 1971.
Knight, Arthur. *The Liveliest Art: A Panoramic History of the Movies*. New York: Macmillan, 1957. Reprinted 1978.
Lauritzen, Einar, and Gunnar Lundquist. *American Film Index. Volume 1: 1908–1915*, and *Volume 2: 1916–1920*. Stockholm: Film Index, 1976.
Leish, Kenneth. *Cinema*. New York: Newsweek Books, 1974.
Leyda, Charles, and Charles Musser. *Before Hollywood: Turn of the Century American Film*. New York: Hudson Hills (in association with the American Federation of Arts), 1987.
Liebman, Roy. *Silent Film Performers: An Annotated Bibliography of Published, Unpublished and Archival Sources for Over 350 Actors and Actresses*. Jefferson, NC: McFarland, 1996.
Lindsay, Vachel. *The Art of the Moving Picture*. New York: Macmillan, 1915.
Magliozzi, Ronald S. *Treasures from the Film Archives: A Catalogue of Short Silent Fiction Films Held by FIAF Archives*. Metuchen, NJ: Scarecrow, 1988.
Manchel, Frank. *Women on the Hollywood Screen*. New York: Franklin Watts, 1977.
Mast, Gerald, revised by Bruce F. Kawin. *A Short History of the Movies* (5th edition). New York: Macmillan, 1992.
Mordden, Ethan. *Movie Star: A Look at the Women Who Made Hollywood*. New York: St. Martin's, 1983.
Musser, Charles. *The Emergence of Cinema: The American Screen to 1907*. Volume 1 of

the History of the American Cinema series. New York: Charles Scribner's Sons, 1991.
Niver, Kemp R. *The First Twenty Years: A Segment of Film History.* Los Angeles: Locare Research Group, 1968.
Parish, James Robert. *The Hollywood Celebrity Death Book.* Las Vegas: Pioneer, 1993.
Pearson, Roberta E. *Eloquent Gestures: The Transformation of Performance Style in the Griffith Biograph Films.* Berkeley: University of California Press, 1992.
_____, and William Uricchio. *Reframing Culture: The Case of Vitagraph Quality Films.* Princeton, NJ: Princeton University Press, 1993.
Pickford, Mary. *Sunshine and Shadow.* Garden City, NY: Doubleday, 1955.
Pitts, Michael R. *Poverty Row Studios, 1929–1940: An Illustrated History of 53 Independent Film Companies, with a Filmography for Each.* Jefferson, NC: McFarland, 1997.
Pratt, George C. *Spellbound in Darkness: A History of the Silent Film.* Rochester, NY: University of Rochester, 1966. Revised Greenwich, CT: New York Graphic Society, 1973.
Ramsaye, Terry. *A Million and One Nights: A Modern Classic, a History of the Motion Picture Through 1925.* New York: Simon and Schuster, 1926. Reprinted New York: Simon and Schuster/Touchstone, 1986.
St. James, Adela Rogers. *Love, Laughter and Tears: My Hollywood Story.* Garden City, NY: Doubleday, 1978.
Schickel, Richard. *The Stars.* New York: Bonanza/Crown/Dial, 1962.
Sennett, Mack. *King of Comedy.* Garden City, NY: Doubleday, 1954. Reprinted San Francisco: Mercury House, 1990.
Slide, Anthony. *The American Film Industry: A Historical Dictionary.* Westport, CT: Greenwood, 1986. Reprinted Lake Geneva, WI: Tiare/Limelight, 1990.
_____. *Aspects of American Film History Prior to 1920.* Metuchen, NJ: Scarecrow, 1978.
_____. *The Big V: A History of the Vitagraph Company.* Metuchen, NJ: Scarecrow, 1987.
_____. *The Griffith Actresses.* Cranbury, NJ: Barnes, 1973.
_____. *The Idols of Silence.* Cranbury, NJ: Barnes, 1976.
_____. *The Vaudevillians: A Dictionary of Vaudeville Performers.* Westport, CT: Arlington, 1981.
Sloan, Kay. *The Loud Silents: Origins of the Social Problem Film.* Urbana: University of Illinois Press, 1988.
Spehr, Paul C. *American Film Personnel and Company Credits, 1908–1920: Filmographies Reordered by Authoritative Organizational and Personal Names from Lauritzen and Lundquist's* American Film Index. Jefferson, NC: McFarland, 1996.
Thomas, Nicholas, editor. *International Dictionary of Films and Filmmakers. Volume 3: Actors and Actresses.* Detroit: St. James, 1993.
Trager, James. *The Women's Chronology: A Year-by-Year Record from Prehistory to the Present.* New York: Holt, 1994.
Vazzana, Eugene M. *Silent Film Necrology.* Jefferson, NC: McFarland, 1995.
Wagenknecht, Edward. *The Movies in the Age of Innocence.* Norman: University of Oklahoma Press, 1962.
Walker, Alexander. *Stardom: The Hollywood Phenomenon.* New York: Stein and Day, 1970.
Windeler, Robert. *Sweetheart: The Story of Mary Pickford.* New York: Praeger, 1974.
Wlaschin, Ken. *The Illustrated Encyclopedia of the World's Greatest Movie Stars and Their Films.* New York: Bonanza/Crown, 1979.

Periodicals and Newspapers

The Billboard
(Hollywood) Citizen-News
Classic Images
Detroit News
Entertainment Weekly
Film Flashes
Films in Review
Ladies' Home Journal
Los Angeles Examiner
Moving Picture Stories
Moving Picture Story Magazine
Moving Picture World
New York Dramatic Mirror
New York Star

New York Times
Photoplay
Picture-Play Magazine
Pictures and the Picturegoer
St. Louis Post-Dispatch Sunday Magazine
St. Louis Star
St. Louis Times
San Francisco Examiner
Saturday Evening Post
Silent Film Newsletter
Toronto Star
The Universal Weekly
Variety
Woman's Home Companion

Other Resources

Internet Sites

http.//www.HaroldLloyd.com (Best links to all of silent filmdom on the Internet)
http.//www.mdle.com (The Silents Majority)
http.//www.mindspring.com/~kallym/ (Kally Mavromatis's silent film appreciation page)
http.//www.imdb.com (Internet Movie Database)
http.//www.nhm.com (Natural History Museum of Los Angeles County)
http.//www.cs.monash.edu.au/~pringle/silent/ (Glen Pringle's silent film page)
http.//www.afionline.org (American Film Institute Online)
http.//www.angelfire.com/az/Taylorology or http://www.public.ase.edu/~ialong/Taylor (Bruce Long's *Taylorology* Newsletter)

Silent Film Sources

Grapevine Video, PO Box 46161, Phoenix, AZ 85063 (602-973-3661)
Kino on Video, 333 West 39th Street, Suite 503, New York, NY 10018 (800-562-3330)
Movies Unlimited, 3015 Darnell Road, Philadelphia, PA 19154 (800-466-8437)
Video Yesteryear, Box C, Sandy Hook, CT 06482-0847 (800-243-0987)
Critics' Choice, PO Box 749, Itasca, IL 60143-0749 (800-367-7765)
Smithsonian Video, PO Box 23345, Washington, DC 20077-5365 (800-669-1559)
Thanhouser Company Film Preservation, 705 NW Albemarle Terrace, Portland, OR 97210 (fax 503-233-3733)

Newsletters/Communications

Classic Images Magazine, PO Box 809, Muscatine, IA 52761
Silent Film Monthly, 700 5th Street #12, Oakmont, PA 15139

INDEX

Page references in *italics* refer to the filmography. Page references in **bold** refer to photographs. Florence Lawrence is abbreviated as FL, Harry Solter as HS, and Lotta Lawrence as LL.

A.G. Whyte Stock Company 52
Academy of Motion Picture Arts and Sciences 133
Acker, Jean 129
Acord, Art 148
Across the Border 112
Actors Fund *see* Motion Picture Relief Fund
The Actress and the Singer 66, *172*
Adams, Maude 52, 70
The Advent of Jane 80, *176*
The Adventures of Dollie 18
After All 176
After Many Years 26, 32, 154, *162*
Age Versus Youth 172
Aiken, Spottiswoode *173*
Alexander, Ross 147
"Alexander's Rag Time Band" 70
All for Love 176
All the World's a Stage 172
Allen, Judith *180*
Allen, Robert 19
Allied Pictures 140, *179*
Allison, May *179*
Always a Way 174
American Film Institute 15
American Mutoscope and Biograph Company [Biograph]: atmosphere 27; Bernard 131; Edison lawsuit 9; fan mail 26–27; film in St. Louis 57; and FL 18, 24–25, 27–28, 29, 31–32, 37–40, 51, 69, 78, 89, 95, 104, 122, 154–158; Gish 87; Griffith at 17 32–33; Griffith's techniques 32–33; Harron 120; HS at 118–119; hasty endings 35–36; Henderson 130; in Motion Picture Patents Company 36–37, 64–65, 68; magical brownstone 23–24; Mutoscopes 7; old reels rereleased 97; on location 33; Pickford at 34–35, 66; production company *160–169*; projector 2; Ramsaye 132, 151; reels well preserved 151–152; *Resurrection* 30–31, 117; secret relationships 25–26; Sweet 144; system 59; Williams 21
American Theatre 8
Ames, Adrienne *180*
Among the Roses 62, *172*
And a Little Child Shall Lead Them 166
Anderson, Gilbert M. "Broncho Billy" 39
Anderson, John 8
The Angel of the Studio 176
Anglin, Margaret 52
Antony and Cleopatra 16, *160*
Apfel, Oscar 147
Arbuckle, Roscoe "Fatty" 124, 128, 129
Arden, Elizabeth 133
Arliss, George 70

203

Index

Arnat, Thomas 2
Arrow Productions *179*
Art Versus Music 69, *175*
Artclass Pictures 141
Arthur, Julia 3–4
Arvidson, Linda [Mrs. D.W. Griffith]: at Biograph 32, 117; Biograph films *161–169*; and FL 18; with Griffith 17, 18; nickelodeons 20; on stage 5; Sennett 157; women working 155
Associated Cinema Stars 143
Associated Exhibitors Inc. 125, 126, *179*
Astor, Gertrude 115
Astor, Mary 137
At the Altar 165
The Athletic Girls of America 15
Auer, Florence *160, 168*
August, Edwin 69, 144
Aunt Jane's Legacy 175
automobiles 98, 115–116, 120, 136
Avery, Stephen Morehouse *180*
The Awakening of Bess 43, *170*
An Awful Moment 163
Ayers, Agnes 143, 144

A Baby's Shoe 167
Baggot, King: *Great Universal Mystery* 93; at IMP 42–43, *43*, 60, 66; IMP films *170–172*; Metro contract 142; remembers FL 149; St. Louis 51–52, 56–57
Bahn, Chester 141
Bainbridge, Rolinda 52
Baird, Leah 41
Balked at the Altar 25, *161*
Ball, Robert 15, 16, 28
Baltimore, MD 17, 118
Baltimore Sun 119
The Bandit's Waterloo 25, *160*
Bara, Theda 103–104, 155
The Barbarian, Ingomar 32, *162*
Barker, Florence 116, *163, 164, 166*
Barrymore, Ethel 52
Barrymore, John 137
Basquette, Lina 134, 140, 141, *186*
Bateman, Victory *176*
Beachcomber 180
Bear Ye One Another's Burdens 171
Beaudine, William *180*
Bedding, Thomas 78
Bedford, Barbara 121, 144, *179*
Beery, Noah *180*
Behind the Scenes: Where All Is Not Gold That Glitters 25, *161*
Belasco, David 5, 53

Belmont, Alva 89
Benham, Harry 117, *179*
Ben Hur [1908] 70
Ben Hur [1925] 114
Ben Wilson Productions *179*
Bennett, Constance 137
Bennett, Frank *177*
Berlin, Irving 70
Berlin 63
Bernard, Dorothy 131, *163, 167*
Bernhardt, Sarah 57, 87, 99, 122
Besserer, Eugenia 110
Betrayed by a Handprint 25, *161*
Betty's Nightmare 176
Beverly 57
Beverly Hills Emergency Hospital 146
The Billboard 19, 50, 101, 103
Biograph *see* American Mutoscope and Biograph Company
"Biograph Girl" 31, 34, 40, 46, 48–49, 50, 51, 78, 132, 141, 148, 153, 157
The Birth of a Nation 87, 103–104, 114, 154
Bison [New York Motion Picture Company] 79, 82
Bitzer, Billy 18, 20, 28, 157; cameraman *161–169*
Blackton, J. Stuart 10, 13, 14, 15, 25, 71, 92, 95, 143, *159, 160*
Blanche, Alice Guy 155
A Blind Deception 175
The Blind Man's Tact 170
Bluebird Productions 103, 114, 115, 117, 140, *179*
The Blue Flame 133
Blum, Daniel 15, 54, 70, 104, 137
Blyston, John 147
Blythe, Betty 144
Bolton, Henry 137–138, 146
Booker, Wilma 146
Borzage, Frank *180*
Bosworth, Hobart 21
Boteler, Wade *179*
Boucicault, Dion 10, *159*
Bow, Clara 152
Bowser, Eileen 19, 28, 69
The Boy, the Bust and the Bath 159
Bracey, Clara T. 30, *161, 163–168*
Bracy, Sydney 99, *179*
Brady, Alice 70
The Brahma Diamond 164
Brenon, Herbert 110
Brian, Mary *180*
The Bribe 91, *178*

Index

Bridgwood, Charlotte Dunn *see* Lawrence, Lotta
Bridgwood, Charlotte Louise [FL half-sister] 2
Bridgwood, Florence *see* Lawrence, Florence
Bridgwood, George, Jr. *see* Lawrence, George
Bridgwood, George, Sr. [FL father]: marriage to Lotta Lawrence 2; death 5, 124, 146
Bridgwood, James [FL half-brother] 2
Bridgwood, John [FL half-brother] 2
Bridgwood, Walter Norman [FL brother]: birth 2; fixes Buffalo house 65–66; letter 86; lives in Buffalo 6–7; starts school 5
Bridgwood, William [FL half brother] 2
Bridgwood Manufacturing Company 115
Briscoe, Lottie 131
Brock, Dorothy *179*
"Broken-Hearted" 105–106, 107
The Broken Oath 170
Bronson, Betty 131
Brooks, Louise 144
Brower, Otto 141, *179*, *180*
Brown, Gene 19, 103
Brown, Melville 147
Brownell, John 42, *178*
Bruce, Kate *161*, 163–169
Bruckman, Clyde *180*
Brunette, Fritzi 89
Buchanan, Don *178*
Buffalo, NY: Blasdell subdivision 65; FL moves to 5; Powers 78; school system 6–7; Victor Film Company 79, 124
Bunny, John 116, 142
Burke, Billie 70, 130
Burr, Ty 152
"The Burra Pundit" 101
Burton, Clarence *179*
Bustamante, Carlos 29, 153
Butler, William J. 169

Cairo 75
The Calamitous Elopement 161
Calder, Stirling 23
California Film Exchange 77
California Motion Picture Company 110, 112
California Perfume Company 134
The Call of the Circus 171
The Call of the Wild 162
Cannon, Raymond 121

The Cardinal's Conspiracy 169
Carlton 79
Carter, Jane *177*
Carter, Owen 110
Carver, Mr. and Mrs. William 9
Cecelia of the Pink Roses 117
Chadwick, Helene 142
Champion Film Company 82
The Chance Shot 80, *176*
Chaplin, Charlie 104, 124, 129, 137, 152
Chaplin, Mildred Harris 129, 130
Chicago, IL 41, 42, 43, 50
Childers, Naomi 142
Christie Company 121
The Christmas Burglars 163
Cinematograph 1, 9
Clark, Margarite 43
Clarke, Wallace 99, *179*
Clayton, Ethel 143, *180*
Cleaver, James 8
Clifford, Ruth 144
Cliffside, NJ 162
The Closed Door 89, 90, *177*
Cleopatra 88
The Clubman and the Tramp 163
Coast-to-Coast Vaudeville 133
Cocchi, John 152, 153, 154, 155
Cochran, Robert 41–42, 57, 62
Colbert, Claudette 137
"Come Help Me Tie My Shoe String" 4
Comont, Mathilda 140, *180*
Concealing the Burglar 162
Confidence 167
Conklin, William 121, 143, *179*
Continental Hotel [Cairo] 75
Coos Bay, OR 48
Corelli, Marie 99
The Coryphee 91, *177*
Cos Cob, CT *162*, *163*
Cosgrove, Luke *180*
Costello, Helene 144
Costello, Maurice 69, 143, 144, 148
The Count of Montebello 172
The Count of Monte Cristo 88
Counterfeiters 178
The Country Doctor 169
Courtleigh, William, Jr. 116
Cowes, Jules 142
Coyle, Helen 100
Coytesville, NJ *162*, *163*, 169
Craig, Charles *168*, *177*, *178*
Crampton, Howard 115
Crane, Ward 130, *179*
Craven, Mr. and Mrs. William *159*

Cricks and Martin 79
The Criminal Hypnotist 91, *164, 178*
"Crossing the Bar" 147
Crystal Film Company 110
Cuba 66
Cuddebackville, NY 33, 40–41, 77, 81, 90, *169, 175*
Cummings, Dwight *163*
Cummings, Richard 147
Cumpson, John 29, 42, 60, 143, 149, *161–169, 171*
Cunningham, Jack *180*
"Curfew Shall Not Ring Tonight" 6
Curley, Pauline *176*
The Curtain Pole *165*

Daeheel, Frank 55
D'Agostino, Annette 148, 152, 153, 154
Daily Coast Mail 48
Dalton, Ellen 2
Daly, William 60, *172*
Dampfer Prinz Friedrich Wilhelm 81
"Damsels in Distress: Strong Silent Women Held Hostage in Film Archives" 156
The Dancer and the King, a Romantic Story of Spain 160
Dane, Karl 147
Daniel Boone 9–10, 132, 154, *159*
Davenport, Dorothy [Mrs. Wallace Reid] 143
Davidson, Max *179*
Davies, Marion 117, 132, 137, 147
Davis, Bette 137
Davis, Miss *178*
Daw, Marjorie 130, *179*
Dean, Julia 70
Deasy, Frank 124
De Brulier, Nigel *179*
Debt *172*
The Deception *166*
de Cordova, Richard 130, 153
DeGarde, Adele *163–166, 168, 169*
de Maupassant, Guy 31, *168*
Dempster, William 43
Denver, CO 124
Der Rosenkavalier 70
"Despair" 145
The Despatch Bearer 13, 15, 16, 18, *159*
The Devil 161
"Diamond Cut Diamond" 133
Dillon, Eddie *163, 164, 166*
Dion, Hector *178*

Diplomatic Flo 91, *178*
The Disenchantment 91, *178*
divorce: Bolton 138; 1920s Hollywood 128–129; Solter 106–107, 117–118; Woodring 135
Dix, Richard 137
The Doctor's Perfidy *171*
The Doctor's Testimony *178*
Dodd, Rev. Neal 147
"Dora Thorne" 4
Dougherty, Joe 18, *165*
Dove, Billie 137
"Down in the Shady Dell" 4
Drew, Rankin Sidney 116
Drew, William 116, 156
Drinkwater, John 50, 55, 56
The Drive for a Life *167*
A Drunkard's Reformation *166*
Duke de Ribbon Counter *174*
The Dummy 117
Dunn, Ann [FL's grandmother] 5, 75
Durfee, Minta 129
During Cherry Time *174*
Dustin, E.W. 121
D.W. Griffith and the Origins of the American Narrative Film 151

Earle, Edward 130
"East Lynne" 4
Eastman, George 1
Eastman House 14
The Eavesdropper *167*
Eckhardt, Joseph 61, 67, 153
Eclair 86
Edgewater, NJ *168*
Edginton, May *180*
Edison, Thomas 1, 2, 9, 64–65, 87
Edison Film Manufacturing Company 8, 9, 17, 37, 52, 95, 130, *159*
Edwards, Earle *179*
Edwards, Sam *178*
Egan, Gladys *161–166, 168, 169*
Egypt 75, 100
Elder, Ethel *173*
Elizabeth, NJ 25
Ellis, Celie 110
Eloping with Auntie *168*
Eloquent Gestures 27
El Paso, TX 118
Eltinge, Julien 70
Elusive Isabel 99, 101, 103, 109, 114, 156, *179*
The Elusive Isabel (novel) 99
Emerson, Betty *178*

Emory, Richard 114
Engel, Joseph 78
"Enoch Arden" 32, *162*
Entertainment Weekly, the 100 Greatest Movie Stars of All Time 152
Entwistle, Peg 147
Eradicating Aunty 168
Essanay Film Manufacturing Company 37, 39–40, 86, 104
The Eternal Triangle 45, 46, 60, *171*
Ethan Frome 70
Evans, Frank *162*
Everson, William 87
The Exploits of Elaine 104

The Face on the Screen, 114, *179*
Factor, Max 133
Fairbanks, Douglas 70, 104, 116, 128, 147
Falconetti, Renée 139
The False Bride 90, *177*
Famous Players-Lasky 86, 93, 104, 144
fan mail 26–27, 153
Farnum, William 144
Farrar, Geraldine 130
A Fascinating Bachelor 173
The Fascinating Mrs. Francis 164
The Fatal Ring 90
Father Gets in the Game 162
Feature Movie Magazine 99
Ferguson, Helen 131
The Feud and the Turkey 163
Fields, W.C. 104, 142, *180*
Film D'Art 79
Films in Review 15, 93, 135
Finch, Flora 33, 116, 142, *163–168*
First National *179*
Fischer, Margarita 117, 153
"The Flag—Forever May it Wave" 101
Fleming, Will 17
Florence Lawrence Super Productions 125
Flo's Discipline 80–81, 84, *176*
Flynn, Errol 137
A Fool There Was 104
Foolish Wives 126, 127–128
A Fool's Revenge 31, *165*
Forde, Victoria 131
The Forest Ranger's Daughter 48, *169*
Forman, Tom 147
Forrest, Mabel *179*
Fort Lee, NJ 25, 33, 77, 86, 101, 103, *161, 162, 164, 166, 167, 168*
The Four Horsemen of the Apocalypse 124
Fox *179*

Foxe, Earle 90, *177*
Francesca da Rimini, or The Two Brothers 14, 15, *160*
Francisco, Betty 130, *179*
Frank, Alexander 88, 89, *177*
Frederick, Pauline 147
French, Charles 121, *179*
Fuller, Mary 131, 153
Futrelle, Jacques 99, *179*

Gable, Clark 145
Gaines, Eleanor 52
Gambling Wives 130, *179*
A Game for Two 171
A Game of Deception 173
Gardner, Helen 79, 88, 153
Garland, Judy 145
Garson, Greer 145
Gaudio, Eugene *179*
Gauntier, Gene 18; the Kalem Girl 24, 27, 75, 131, 156, 157, *168*
Gaynor, Janet 134, 137, 152, *179*
Gebhardt, Frank *161*
Gebhardt, George *161, 164, 165*
General Film Company *see* Motion Picture Patents Company
Gerstad, Merritt *180*
Gibbs, Alfred *180*
Gibson, Helen 92, 112, *179*
Gibson, Hoot 140, *179*
"The Gift of the Magi" *164*
Gilbert, Florence *179*
Gillingwater, Claude 148
Girard, Joe *179*
A Girl and Her Money 91, *177*
The Girl and the Outlaw 25, *161*
"Girl of a Thousand Faces" 53, 99
Girl O' the Woods 90, *177*
A Girlish Impulse 175
The Girls and Daddy 164
Gish, Dorothy 24, 33, 152
Gish, Lillian 2, 4, 23, 24, 30, 33, 35–36, 87, 152
Golden, CO 39
The Golden Louis 165
Gonzalez, Myrtle 116
A Good Turn 173
Gordon, Julia Swayne *160*
Gore, Rosa *180*
Gorman, Charles *162, 164, 165*
The Governor's Pardon 170
Graham, Grace 52
Grand-Asher Distribution Corporation *179*

Grant, Cary 141, *180*
The Great Train Robbery 7, 40
The Great Universal Mystery 93, *178*
The Greater Glory 134, *179*
Greenwich, CT *169*
Grey, Virginia *180*
Griffith, David Wark [D.W.]: actress appeal 2, 155–156; autobiography 157; becoming dated 141, 143; at Biograph 18, 24–25, 25–26, **26**, 27–28; *The Birth of a Nation* 87, 103, 114; as director *160–169*; early recognition 36, 70–71; Gunning 151; and HS 17, 25, 41, 118–119; Henderson 130; *Judith of Bethulia* 88; *Resurrection* 30–31, 32–33, 33–34, 35–36, 40–41, 45–46, 64; *Taming of the Shrew* 28–29
Growing Up with the World's Newest Art 93
Guinan, Texas 70
Gunn, Charles 116
Gunning, Tom 32, 50, 64, 71, 151, 153, 154, 155
The Gypsy 174

Hall, Alexander *180*
Hall, Ella 114
Hall, Ellen 114
Hamilton, Creighton 92
Hamilton, Mahlon 142
Hamilton, Ontario, Canada 2–3, 124, 148
The Hard Hombre 140, 154, *179*
Harlan, Kenneth 114–115
Harlow, Jean 137
Harris, Caroline *168*
Harrison, Louis Reeves 36, 70
Harron, Charles 120
Harron, Mary 120
Harron, Robert 120, *161*, *163–165*, *167*, *168*
Harstn and Company 41
Hayes, Helen 70
Hays, Will 128
Hazards of Helen 112
A Head for Business 175
The Heart of O Yama 161
Hedlund, Guy *161–163*, *168*
Held, Anna 53, 70
The Helping Hand 163
Henderson, Dell 130, 142, *166*, *179*
Hendrie, Anita 26, 117, *166*, *168*
Henry, O. *164*, *166*
Hepwix 79
Herbert, Hugh *180*

Her Artistic Temperament 173
Her Child's Honor 67, *173*
Her Cousin Fred 176
Her First Biscuits 168
Her Generous Way 169
Her Humble Ministry 67, *173*
Her Ragged Knight 91, *178*
Her Two Sons 174
Hersholt, Jean 134, *179*
Hiawatha 41
Higgenses Versus Judsons 174
His Bogus Uncle 66, *172*
His Chorus Girl Wife **61**, *175*
His Friend, the Burglar 66, *172*
His Second Wife 171
His Sick Friend 170
His Ward's Love 165
His Wife's Child 91, *177*
His Wife's Mother 165
A History of Women in America 156
histrionic acting 27
Hoadley, Charles 88, *177*
Hoboken, NJ *163*
Hollywood, CA 103; Argyle Street 128; Cahuenga Boulevard 137, 157–158
Hollywood Boulevard 144
Hollywood Chamber of Commerce 141
(*Hollywood*) *Citizen-News* 147, 148
Hollywood Cosmetics 133–134, **136**
Hollywood Memorial Cemetery [Hollywood Forever Cemetery] 135, 147
Holmes, Helen 92
Homicide Squad 180
The Honeymooners 178
The Honor of the Humble 92, *178*
The Honor of Thieves 164
Hood, Thomas 33, *162*
Hopkins, Frank 79
Hopper, Hedda 130, *179*
horses 9, 13, 140
Horsley, David 117
Hotaling, Arthur 147
Howard, Kathleen *180*
Howard, Leslie *180*
The Hoyden 67, 80, *173*
Hoyt, Ruth 110
Hugo, Victor 165
Hulette, Gladys 41, 42

I Did It, Mamma 166
The Illustrated History of the World's Greatest Movie Stars 152
"Imp Girl" 40, 46, 50, 51, 148
In Swift Water 77, *175*

Index 209

Ince, Thomas 34, 42, *160, 169*
Independent Motion Picture Company [IMP]: and Baggot 42–43, *43*, 149; first films 41–42; in Fort Lee 86; with FL 41, 45, 48–49, 50, 59, 60, 63–64, 66, 78, 95, 156, 158; with HS 45–46, 63–64; Isabel Rea 83; Katterjohn 93–95; in Louisville 51–52; Mace 116; Motion Picture Distributing and Sales Company 82; problems 44, 62, 64–65; production company *169–172;* Ramsaye 132; reviews 44–45; in St. Louis 51, 52–58; success 46, 60–62
An Index to Short and Feature Film Reviews in Moving Picture World 154
Influence of Sympathy 91, *177*
Ingraham, Lloyd *178*
The Ingrate *163*
Inslee, Charles 32, 117, *161, 162, 164, 165, 167, 178*
Internet Movie Database 41, 46
The Irony of Fate 60, *171*
Irwin, May 70
Itala Film Company 41, 79

James, Arthur 127
James, Gladden *175*
Jane and the Stranger *170*
Janice Meredith 132
Janis, Elsie 142
Jealousy and the Man *169*
Jeanne Doré 99
Jefferson, Joseph 7
Jefferson, Mrs. Thomas 144
Jenkins, Francis 1
The Jilt *168*
Joan the Woman 121
Johnson, Arthur V.: alcohol 30, 116, 128; at Biograph 28–29, 30–31, 34–35, 117; and Briscoe 131; death 116, 143; Dimitri 30–31, *30;* films *160–169, 172–174;* and FL 29–30, 66–67, 149; at Lubin 66–67, 68, 73; Petruchio 28–29; postcards 69; *The Way of Man* 34–35
The Johnstown Flood 134, *179*
Joliet, IL 12
Jones, Gladys 99
Jones and His New Neighbors *166*
Jones and the Lady Book Agent *167*
Jones' Burglar *169*
Jones Comedies 28, 29, 154, 157, *161*
The Joneses Have Amateur Theatricals 29, *165*
Jordan, Sid *179*

Josephson, Max 110
Jowett, Garth 19
Joyce, Alice 129
Judith of Bethulia 88
Julius Caesar 15, *160*
June, Ray *180*
Just Nuts 104
Justice in the Far North *170*

Kalem Film Manufacturing Company 17, 37, 47, 49, 70, 75, 112, 131, 134
Katterjohn, Monte 4, 6, 93–94
Katz, Ephraim 15
Keaton, Buster 152
Keefe, William 121–122
Keith, Ian *179*
Kelley, J. Winthrop 117, *179*
Kendall, Ezra 41, 43
Kent, Betty 16
Kent, Charles 16
Kern, George 121, *179*
Kerry, Norman 117, 130, *179*
Keystone Kops 87
The Kid 124
Kinemacolor 89, *177*
Kinetophone 87
Kinetoscope 1, 2, 7, 9
King, Rose *168*
Kirkwood, James 26, 89, 123, *165, 166, 168, 169*
Kleine Optical Company 37
Knott, Lydia *179*

LaBadie, Florence 33–34, 116, *165, 166*
LaCossit, Henry *180*
Ladies' Home Journal 44, 157
Lady Helen's Escapade 31–32, 69, 91, 104, *167*
Lady Jane's Flight, a 17th Century Romance 16, *160*
The Lady Leone 85, *176*
Lamarr, Hedy 145
Langdon, Lillian *176*
Laemmle, Carl: and Baggot 42–43, 66; and FL 41, 43–44, 47, 49–50, 63–64, 72, 77–78, 80, 88–89, 97, 99, 109–110, 121, 158; and IMP 40, 41–42, 45, 46, 49, 50–51, 53, 55, 57; Universal 82–83, 93, 100, 140; and Victor 78–79
The Lash of Power 114
Lauder, Harry 70
Laurian, Dr. Lester 144
Lauritzen and Lundquist 15
Lawrence, D.H. 70
Lawrence, Florence [drama critic] 122

Lawrence, Florence Annie [FL]: and Allied Pictures 140–141; and Ben Wilson 130; at Biograph 3, 18, 21, 23–33, 30, 35–36, 36–37, 152, 154; birth 2; and Bolton 137–138; clothes 104–105, **119, 123, 129, 136**; death 146–147, **148**; at Edison 8–10; and film 7–8, 20–21, 141–142; films *159–180;* and George 6, 124, 146; and HS 16–18, 25, 36–37, 45–46, 60, 62–63, 75, 81–82, 83–84, 85–86, 95, 98, 106–108, 114, 117–120; at IMP 44–46, 50–58, 59–60; and Laemmle 46, 49–50, 63–64, 66, 72, 77, 88–89, 93, 109–110; and LL 6, 8–9, 10, 12, 41, 67, 73–74, 75–77, 83–84, 115–116, 134–135, 136; at Lubin **11, 61,** 62–74, **68, 71**; and Metro 142–143, **143**; and Norman 6, 7, 65–66; on stage 4–5, 12, 41, 107, 120, 121, 153; and Pickford 34–35, 120, 152, 157; and Producers Pictures 121–122, **125**, 125–126; remembered 148–149, 157, 158; in St. Louis 50–58, 59; schooling 5, 6; at Universal 99–103, 109–110, **111**; at Victor 77–81, 88–95, **94, 102, 108**; at Vitagraph 10–12, 13–14, 15–16; whistling 4, 63, 120; and Woodring 124–128, 133, 134, 135

Lawrence, George [FL brother]: birth 2; letter 107, 124; moves to San Francisco 6; received suicide note 146; works in Buffalo 5

Lawrence, Lotta [LL; FL mother]: actress 4, 7, 8–9, 10, 12; death 135; and Dunn 5; and FL 6, 8–9, 10, 12, 41, 62, 67, 73–74, 75–76, 115; and George 107; and HS 17, 81, 82–83, 83–84; inventor 115–116, 134–135, 136–137; marriage 2

Lawrence Dramatic Company 2, 7

The Law's Decree 177

Layton, Lowder and Sarah 63, 81

Lederer, Francis *180*

Lederer, Gretchen 114

Lee, Rowland V. *180*

Leibfried, Philip 155

Leonard, Marion 18, 25, 28, 29, 33, 62, 69, 88, 117, 157, *160–168*

LeRoy, Baby 142, *180*

Lest We Forget 169

Lester, Kate *179*

Levar, P.C. 48–49, 58

Lewis, Ida *see* Arthur, Julia

Library of Congress [Washington, DC] 14, 152

Life of An American Firefighter 7

The Life Saver 174

Lincoln 86

Linder, Max 147

Lindsay, Vachel 69

Little Falls, NJ *162, 163*

"Little Lord Fauntleroy" [stage] 4

Little Lord Fauntleroy [1921] 124

The Little Mail Carrier 178

The Little Rebel 67, *174*

Lloyd, Doris *180*

Lloyd, Harold 104, 124, 125, 144

Lockwood, Harold 116

Lombard, Carole 141, *180*

London, Jack *162*

London 63, 67

Lonesome Luke 104

Longfellow, Stephanie *168, 169*

Loretto Academy 6, 56

Los Angeles, CA 103, 118; Biltmore Hotel 143, 157–158; Mason Opera House 121, 122

Los Angeles Examiner 122, 131

Los Angeles County Museum of National History *see* National History Museum of Los Angeles County

Louisville, KY 12

Louisville Courier-Journal 51, 54

The Love Craze 117, *179*

Love Laughs at Locksmiths, an Eighteenth Century Romance 15

Love's Strategem 41; no interiors 44, *169*

Lubin, Siegmund: film pioneer 9; and FL 62, 63, 65, 72; and HS 62, 63–64, 83

Lubin Film Manufacturing Company: early work 52; expansion 71; and FL 65, 66, 67–68, 69, 74, 78, 80, 83, 95, 98, 104, 156; *His Chorus Girl Wife* **61**; and Johnson 66–67, 131; on location 74

Lucas, Wilfred 26, *161, 162, 164, 165*

Lumière Brothers 1

Lupino, Ida *180*

The Lure of the Gown 166

Luxor 75

Macbeth, Shakespeare's Sublime Tragedy 14, 16, *160*

McCullough, John *175*

McCutcheon, George Barr 57

McCutcheon, Wallace 9, 18, 129, *159*

MacDermont, Marc *179*

McDonald, Gerald 135

MacDonald, J. Farrell 42

MacDonald, Jeannette 145

MacDonald, Joseph *177*

MacDonald and Steiner Company **108**
Mace, Fred 116, *165*
McGovern, Albert 65, 66, *174*
McHugh, Grace 110
MacPherson, Jeanie *161–167*
MacQuarrie, Murdock 121, *179*
The Mad Man's Ward 91, *178*
Madison, Cleo 92, 131
The Maelstrom 171
Maher, M.B. *176*
Mailes, Charles Hill 115, *165*
Malcolm, Fred *174*
"The Man from Paris" 101
The Man on the Flying Trapeze 142, 180
The Man Who Was Never Kissed 91, *178*
The Maniac 175
Marcel, Sonia *179*
Marcus Revue 120, 121
Marey, Etienne 1
Marion, Francis *180*
Marley, J. Peverell *180*
Marlowe, Julia 52
marriages: Biographers 25–26; Bolton 137; George and Lotta Lawrence 2; Harry and Florence Solter 26; Woodring 124; Yuma, AZ 137
Marsh, Mae 33, 121, 152
Marvin, Arthur 18; cameraman *160–168*
Marx Brothers 145
The Matchmaker 174
Mathis, June *179*
Mayer, Louis B. 142–143
The Medicine Bottle 166
Melford, George *180*
Méliès Company 37, 41
Melvin B. Raymond Musical Travesty Company 10, 11
The Mended Lute 169
Menzer, Marian 145, 146
Merion [ship] 62
Mersereau, Violet 100, *163*
Metro-Goldwyn-Mayer [Metro] 142, 144, 145, *180*
Metropolis 139
Metropolitan 93
Miles, David 26, 117, *163*, *166*, *167*, *168*
Miles, Herbert *163*
Miles, Herbert Mrs. *165*, *168*
Milford, MA 98
The Mill Buyers 176
Millarde, Harry 99, *179*
Miller, W. Chrystie *167*
A Million and One Nights 132, 151
Minter, Mary Miles 70, 128

The Miser's Daughter 170
The Mistake 60, *171*
Mr. Jones at the Ball 163
Mr. Jones Has a Card Party 164
Mix, Tom 116
Money Mad 163
Moonshiners 7
Moore, Anita 57–58
Moore, Colleen 134
Moore, Mary 116
Moore, Matt 88, 92, 93, 143–144, *176–179*
Moore, Owen: at IMP 42; with Mary Pickford 33; with Victor 77, 78, 80, 87, 89, 92, 117, 128, 143–144, *163–169*, *171*, *172*, *175*, *176*
Moore, Tom 92, 129
Moran, Lee 130, *179*
Mordden, Ethan 104, 155
Morgan, Rev. Brockholst 25
Morris, Chester *180*
Morris, Edwin *176*, *177*
Morrison, Joe *180*
Mother Love 44–45, 60, 80, *170*
Mothers of France 116
Motiograph 20
Motion Picture Distributing and Sales Company 78; split 82–83
Motion Picture Herald 143
Motion Picture Patents Company 36–37, 63–65, 70, 88, 155, 157
Motion Picture Relief Fund and Home 113, 134, 144, 146, 147
Motofilm 79
Movie Costume and Civic Ball 100
movies: actor's disdain of 7–8; 1930 attendance 140; birth of 1–2; early actors 20; growing up 87–88; mechanics 54; number of theaters 19; quality 70; studio system 142; talking 138–139; unnamed actors 39; Westerns 40
The Movies in the Age of Innocence 149
Moving Picture Men's Association 55
Moving Picture Story Magazine 69; poem 86, 89
Moving Picture Weekly 99, **111**
Moving Picture World: acknowledges press stunt 51, 59, 60, 61, 66; Actors' Fund 113, 114; *Antony and Cleopatra* 16; costuming credit 104, 105, 110; covers return 89, 90, 91, 92, 98, 99; *Boone* 10; first reviews 28; FL leaves Universal 101–102; FL memories 117; Gardner Company 79, 84, 86, 88; HS death 119, 120, 126; reviews initial IMP product

44; "Inquiries" 77; *Lady Helen's Escapade* 31; interviews Laemmle 42; names players 67, 70–71; nickelodeon recipe 20; player advertising 47–49; praises Griffith 36; *Resurrection* 31; *Song of the Shirt* 32–33, 35; *Taming of the Shrew* 28–29; Taylor murder 127, 130; Universal Ball 100, 101; Vitagraph 14
Mrs. Jones Entertains 164
Mrs. Jones' Lover, or I Want My Hat 169
Mulvey, Ben 12
Murray, Charles 33, 110
Murray, Mae 144
Museum of Modern Art 28
Musser, Charles 152, 153, 154
Mutoscope 7
Muybridge, Eadweard 1
myelofibrosis 144
Myers, Carmel 114–115, 141
Myers, Harry C. 66, 67, 144, 147, *172, 173, 174*
A Mysterious Mystery 90, *178*

Nan's Diplomacy 172
Natteford, Jack *179*
Natural History Museum of Los Angeles County 137, 145
The Necklace 31, *168*
Neilan, Marshall 144, *180*
Nelson, Jack 115
Nestor Company 79, 82
New Machiavelli 70
The New Shawl 171
Newsweek 148
Newton, Jack 99, *177–179*
New York City: Bleeker St. *165*; Bronx Park *159*; Central Park *159, 168*; 8th Ave. *163, 165*; filmmaking in 9; Grand Central Palace 100, 113; HS 118; Hippodrome 9; Hotel Marie Antoinette 82, 85; Hudson St. *164*; Lawrences move to 7; location of theaters 19, 75; Metropolitan Opera House 101; Perry St. *166*; Proctor Theater 99; Regent Theatre 103; Riverside Dr. *168*; Vitagraph Company 14; Victor Company 77, 82; West 12th St. *163*
New York Dramatic Mirror: first reviews 28; interviews FL 79–80; praises Griffith 36, 66; names players 67, 78
New York Exhibitors Association 100
New York Times: first reviews 28
The Nichols on a Vacation 60, *171*
Nicholls, George 34, *161, 168*

Nicholson, Paul *179*
nickelodeons 19, 20
Niemeyer, Bernadt *178*
Nilsson, Anna Q. 134, *179*
Normand, Mabel 23, 24, 33, 128, 144
Not Like Other Girls 78, 80, *176*
The Note in the Shoe 167

Oakley, Laura *178*
O'Brien, George 134, *179*
Oland, Warner 147
Olcott, Sidney 75, *167*
The Old-Fashioned Way 142, *180*
Old Heads and Young Hearts 60, *171*
Oliver Twist 14
O'Neill, William J. *178*
Once Upon a Time 171
One on Reno **68**, *175*
One Rainy Afternoon 180
One Touch of Nature 27, *164*
Opportunity and the Man 173
Orphans of the Storm 124
O'Shaughnessy, Edith *179*
Oshkosh, WI 41
O'Sullivan, Tony *161, 162, 167–169*
'Ostler Joe 18
Ott, Fred 1
The Outlaw and the Girl 25
Owl 79

Paget, Alfred *161, 162, 165*
Panzer, Paul 15, 21, 142, *160, 179*
Paralta 93
Paramount 93, 130, 141, *180*
Paris 82; Maison Maurice 105
La Passion de Jeanne d'Arc 139
Pathé Frères 10, 37, 68, 104, 125
Paton, Stuart 99, 101, *179*
The Pawns of Destiny 92, 93, *178*
Payne, Edna *174*
The Peachbasket Hat 168
Peacock, Leslie 88, *177, 179*
Pearson, Roberta 27
Peerless 86
The Perils of Pauline 21
Perry, Walter *179*
Peter Pan 130–131
Phantascope 9
Philadelphia, PA 63, 72, 82
Photoplay 4, 15, 41, 59, 66, 69; autobiography 93–94, 97–98, 101, 106–107, 110, 121; 1913 contest 89–90; nose bobbed 131; poems 86–87; St. Johns interview 122, 124; "Unsung" article 131–132

Pickford, Jack 117, 120
Pickford, Lottie *168*
Pickford, Mary: at Biograph 23–24, 30, 33, 34–35, 50, 117; at Famous Players 87; films *166–169*, *180*; and FL 34–35, 120, 121, 122, 132, 142, 148; at IMP 44, 66; with Moore 26, 66, 128; on stage 2, 4, 5; "super star" 88, 104, 124, 135, 141, 152, 157; World War I 116
A Pictorial History of the American Theatre 1900–1951 70, 137
A Pictorial History of the Silent Screen 54, 137, *160*
A Pictorial History of the Talkies 137
Picture Personalities 130, 153
Picture-Play Magazine 92
Pictures and the Picturegoer 89
Pierce Brothers Mortuary 146, 147
Pilar-Morin, Mlle. 52
The Pirate's Gold 162
Pitts, Michael 140
The Planter's Wife 162
The Players 175
Pleasure 141
poetry: "Broken-Hearted" 105–106; "Despair" 145; "Feel Blue" 109; "Her Eyes Were Blue" 118
The Politician's Love Story 165
Polly of the Storm Country 130
Pordonone Silent Film Festival [1997] 29
Porter, Edwin 9, 71, 88, *159*
Portland, ME 74
Poverty Row 140
Poverty Row Studios, 1929–1940 140
Powell, Constance 52
Powell, Frank 3, 34, *164*, *165*, *169*
Powers, Patrick 78, 81, 83
Powers Players 77, 79, 82
Prescott, Vivien *165–167*
Pressed Roses 60
Prior, Herbert 117, *162*, *167*
Prisco, Albert 121, *179*
Producers Pictures Corporation 121, 126, *179*
The Professor's Ward 67, *173*
The Prussian Spy 165

Queen Elizabeth 87
Quirk, Billy 34, 114, *168*, *169*
Quo Vadis? 87

Ramsaye, Terry 8, 41–42, 128, 132, 151, 152, 155
Randolf, Anders *179*

Ranous, Inez 99, *178*
Ranous, William R. 16, 18, 42, 43, 45, 99, *160*, *170*
Rappe, Virginia 124
Rea, Isabel 83
A Rebellious Blossom 174
The Reckoning 69, *163*
Red Cross 31, 114, 117
The Red Girl 161
The Redemption of Riverton 176
Rehfeld, Curt *179*
Reid, Dorothy Davenport 143
Reid, Hazel *177*
Reid, Wallace 128
Reisse, Mrs. Bernadine 52
A Reno Romance 60, *171*
Republic Film Company 82
Rescued from an Eagle's Nest 17
The Resurrection 30, *30*, 117, *168*
reviews: *The Advent of Jane* 80; *Antony and Cleopatra* 16; *The Chance Shot* 80; *The Closed Door* 89; *The Coryphee* 91; *The Disenchantment* 91; early 28; *Elusive Isabel* 101; *Girl O' the Woods* 90; *His Bogus Uncle* 66; *His Wife's Child* 91; *The Honor of the Humble* 92; *The Irony of Fate* 60; *Lady Helen's Escapade* 31–32; *The Man Who Was Never Kissed* 91; *Mother Love* 44–45; *Resurrection* 31; *The Stepmother* 91; *Song of the Shirt* 33; *The Taming of Jane* 60; *Tide of Fortune* 44; *The Way of a Man* 34–35
Reynolds, Ben *180*
Rex Company 78, 82
Richard III, a Shakespearean Tragedy 160
The Right Girl 172
The Right of Love 170
Rigoletto 165
Rip Van Winkle 7
River Vale, NJ 76, 77, 85, 86, 88, 98
RMS *Arabic* 75
RMS *Carpathia* 75
RMS *Titanic* 75, 99
Roach, Hal 125
The Road to the Heart 166
Robinson, Gertrude 26, 34, 69, 89
Rock, William 14
"Le Roi s'amuse" 165
Romance of a Jewess 162
Romance of Pond Cove 174
The Romance of the Photograph 177
Rome 75
Romeo and Juliet 14, 15, *160*
Rooney, Mickey 145

Roosevelt, Gladys 8, 89
The Rosary 171
roses 66, 85, 86; American Rose Society 114
Rosey 9
Rosson, Arthur 130, *179*
Rothapfel, Samuel 103
Rottman, Victor 114
The Roue's Heart 166
Rubenstein, Helena 133
A Rural Conquerer 175
Russell, Lillian 57, 70

The Sacrifice 164
A Sailor-Made Man 124
St. Johns, Adela Rogers 122–123
St. Louis, MO 4, 50, 51, 55, 56, 57, 59, 62, 66, 121, 155
St. Louis Post-Dispatch 40, 52, 53, 57
St. Louis Star 57–58
St. Louis Times 55, 56
Salome, or The Dance of the Seven Veils 16, 160
The Salvation Army Lass 154, 166
San Francisco, CA 6, 98, 118, 120, 124
San Jose, CA 133
San Rafael, CA 39
Sandford, Tiny 140, *179*
The Satin Girl 130, *179*
Scardon, Paul 26
Schaper, H.C. 121
Schickel, Richard 25
Schmidt, Arthur 79
Schneider's Anti-Noise Crusade 167
The School for Scandal 91, *177*
Schrock, Raymond *179*
Screen Club 100, 109, 114
Sears and Roebuck 20
Secrets 142, *180*
A Self-Made Hero 171
Selig Film Manufacturing Company 37, 52, 86
The Seminary Girl 10, 11, 12, 13
The Senator's Double 172
Sennett, Mack 2, 34, 46, 87, 117, 121, 157, *161–169*
The Senorita 52
Seton, Ernest Thompson *162*
Sex 121
Shadyside, NJ *163*
Shakespeare 14, 15, 16, 28, *162*
Shalot, Edward *178*
The Shaughraun 10, *159*
Shea, William 12, 143, *159, 160*

The Sheik 128
Shepheard's Hotel [Cairo] 75
The Sheriff and the Man 173
A Show Girl's Strategem 172
Show World 47
Silent Film Monthly 154
Singleton, Joseph *177*
A Singular Cynic 178
Sinners in the Sun 141, *180*
Sisters 176
Skipworth, Alison *180*
The Slave 169
The Slavey 80
The Slavey's Affinity 175
Slide, Anthony 14, 16, 92, 152, 155
Sloan, Kay 32–33
Smith, Albert 10, 13, 14, 15, 16, *159*
Smith, C. Aubrey *180*
Smith, Charlotte 135
Smith, Frederick James 131–132
Smith, Gladys *see* Pickford, Mary
The Smoked Husband 161
The Snare of Society 71, *174*
Solax Company 86
Solter, Harry Lewis [HS]: actor *160–169*; at Biograph 18, 26, 34, 36–37, 41, 132; director *169–179*; early work 16, 17; and FL 17–18, 21, 24–25, 25–26, 39, 40, 62–63, 73, 74, 75, 81–84, 85–86, 88, 90, 93, 95, 97, 98, 99, 105–109, 114–115, 117–119, 122, 132, 146, 156; at IMP 43, 44, 45–46, 60; and LL 17, 81, 82–83; at Lubin 63–64, 71, 74; at Victor 77–79, 82–83, 88, 89, 92
The Song of the Shirt 32–33, 154, *162*
Sparks, Ned *180*
Speaking of Silents: First Ladies of the Screen 156
The Spender 91, *177*
Spoor, George K. 39
The Spotted Lily 114
Spratt, George 40
Spring Time and Tillie Todd 101
The Stage Note 170
Standhope, Selwyn 43
Standing, Jack **71**, *173*
Standing, Percy D. *177, 178*
Stardom 53
The State Line 173
Stebbins, Jack *177*
Stedman, Myrtle 147
Steiner, Emma 100–101
The Stepmother 91, *177*
Stevens, Walter *179*

Stewart, Anita 153
The Stolen Jewels 173
The Story of Rosie's Rose 174
Stoughton, Mabel *161, 163*
Strange, Glenn *180*
Strauss, Richard 70
Stuart, Julia *174*
Suburban Stock Company 52
Suffragettes Parade in Washington 177
suicide : FL 146; Harry's threats 81–82; Hollywood 147–148, 149; *The Way of Man* 34–35
Sully, Daniel 4
Sunshine, Marion *161, 168, 169*
Sunshine and Shadow 157
The Surgeon's Heroism 74, *175*
Sweet, Blanche 33, 121, 144
Sweet and Twenty 169
Syracuse Herald 141

Taking a Chance 176
Talbot, Frank 55, 56
The Taming of Jane 60, *172*
The Taming of the Shrew 28, 69, *162*
Tangled Relations 176
Tanguay, Eva 53, 70
Tansey, Johnny *166*
Taurog, Norman *180*
Taylor, E. V. Stanner 26, 34, 88, *161, 162, 164, 167, 169*
Taylor, Laurette 70
Taylor, William Desmond 126, 127, 128, 144
Tearle, Conway 141, 147, *179*
Tellegen, Lou 147
Tennyson, Alfred 32, *162*
The Test 69, 90, *172*
The Test of Friendship 163
Thanhouser Film Corporation 79, 104
That Awful Brother 173
theater: American 1900–1915 8; losing actors to screen 70
Theby, Rosemary 144
Thelma 99
Thomas, Olive 120
Thornton, Marjorie 52
Those Awful Hats 164
Those Boys! 164
The Three Musketeers 124
Through Jealous Eyes 174
Through the Breakers 48
Tide of Fortune 44, 60, *170*
'Tis an Ill Wind That Blows No Good 167
To Hell with the Kaiser 116

Tol'able David 124
Tolstoy, Leo 30, *168*
Toncray, Kate *161, 167*
Tracy, Spencer 145
Traffic in Souls 115
Trafton, Leigh B. 97
"The Tramp" 104
The Transformation of Cinema 19
Transfusion 45, *170*
A Troublesome Satchel 167
Trust *see* Motion Picture Patents Company
Trying to Get Arrested 166
Tucker, George Loane 42
Turner, Celie *see* Ellis, Celie
Turner, Florence 15, 18, 24, 59, 69, 131, 132, 137, 142, 143, 153, *160*
Turner, William *179*
20,000 Leagues Under the Sea 101
Twinkletoes 134
The Two Fathers 67, *173*
Two Memories 171
Two Men 171

Uncle Sam 79
The Unfoldment 121, 125, 126, 128, 156, *179*
Unico News Service 97
United Artists *180*
Universal Ball 100–101
Universal City, CA 103, 137
Universal Film Manufacturing 77, 82–83, 97, 99, 100, 110, 114, 126, 140, *180*
Universal Weekly 77, 78
Unto the Third Generation 91, 177

Vale, Myrtle 116
Valentino, Rudolph 129, 147
The Valet's Wife 163
Vanity and Its Cure 172
The Vaquero's Vow 162
Variety 41, 126, 135, 148
vaudeville 2, 107, 118, 133, 154
Vazzana, Gene 154
Verdi, Giuseppe *165*
verisimilar acting 27
Verne, Jules 101
Victor Company 51, 77, 78–79, 80, 82–83, 83–84, 89, 90, 95, 98, 110, 156
Victor Film Company 79
The Viennese Melody see *The Greater Glory*
Views and Film Index 14
The Viking's Daughter, the Story of the Ancient Norseman 15, *160*

A Village Romance 175
Vitagraph Company 2, 10, 13, 14, 21, 37, 59, 64, 92, 95, *159*, *160*
"Vitagraph Girl" 59, 131, 132, 141
Vitascope 1
Von Ottinger, Lenora 90, *177*

Wagenknecht, Edward 66, 149
Walcamp, Marie 147
Walker, Alexander 53
Wallace, Irene *177*
Walthall, Henry 33, 121, *169*
Ward, Fanny 70
Warren, Giles 78, 88
The Warrens of Virginia 5
Warwick 41
Washington, DC 101, 128, *179*
The Way of Man 34, *168*
Webb, Harry [George] 73
Weber, Lois 155
Wehrengerg, Fred 55
Wells, H.G. 70
Welsh, William 99, *179*
"We Nail a Lie" 51, 54
West, Charles *164*, *168*
West, Dorothy *161*, *163*, *165*–*167*
West Hollywood, CA: Fairfax Avenue 133–135
Western film genre 18, 25, 39–40, 140, 154
Westwood, NJ 31, 117
Wharton, Edith 70
What Drink Did 168
When Knights Were Bold 18
"When Our Heads Are Bowed with Woe" 147
Where the Breakers Roar 161
White, Pearl 69, 90, 104, 116, 129, 147
White Peacock 70
Who Pays? 104
The Widow 172
Wid's Year Book 119

The Wife He Bought 114
Wife of Marcius 52
The Wife's Awakening 173
Williams, Earle *160*
Williams, Kathlyn 21, *165*
Willis, Susanna 9, *159*
Wilson, Ben 130
Wing, Red *169*
Wings 139
The Winning Coat 167
The Winning Punch (1910) 170
The Winning Punch (1912) 176
Wisconsin Center for Film and Theater Research 137
Wlaschin, Ken 152
Woman Voter 156
The Woman Who Won see *The Man Who Was Never Kissed*
Woman's Almanac 156
A Woman's Way 163
Women's Chronology 156
Won Ton Ton, the Dog Who Saved Hollywood 115
The Wooden Leg 31, *166*
Woodring, Charles 124, 128, 133, 134, 146
Woods, Frank 28, 32, *162*, *163*, *168*
World War I 113, 115, 116, 124, 132, 139
A Wreath in Time 165
Wright, Helen 115

Yost, Herbert *163*, *165*, *166*
Young, Clara Kimball 116, 143, 144, 148
Young, Loretta 137
Young, Roland *180*
Youngdeer, James *169*
Yuma, AZ 137

Zola, Emile *166*
Zudora 104
Zukor, Adolph 87
The Zulu's Heart *161*

www.ingramcontent.com/pod-product-compliance
Ingram Content Group UK Ltd.
Pitfield, Milton Keynes, MK11 3LW, UK
UKHW041951140426
5217IPUK00014B/741

9 780786 430895